Guided Teachings from Spirit

The Journey Continues

Mike Ellis

Guided Teachings from Spirit
Copyright © 2022 by Mike Ellis

All rights reserved. No part of this publication may be reproduced, distributed, or transmitted in any form or by any means, including photocopying, recording, or other electronic or mechanical methods, without the prior written permission of the author, except in the case of brief quotations embodied in critical reviews and certain other non-commercial uses permitted by copyright law.

Tellwell Talent
www.tellwell.ca

ISBN
978-0-22887-747-9 (Hardcover)
978-0-22887-746-2 (Paperback)
978-0-22887-748-6 (eBook)

To Sasha,

Continued Success for all that you do. The world is waiting for you.

love
Pampa

*To Stacey.
You have made me so much more.
Love you.*

There are several people I need to thank for helping me get to this point.

First, I want to thank my family, and I mean all my family, including my extended family, whether through marriage or newly discovered family members. All of you are important to me and make me who I am. I am better for having all of you in my life. Sue, Peter, and Mark, I am blessed to have you as siblings.

I will always say thank you to Stephanie and Tyler. You make me so proud all the time. I have so much love for you both. I look forward to your future endeavors and all that they hold for you. To Sophie and Sasha, you have accomplished so much already, and I expect nothing less from you. I know your futures are bright.

To Trish and family, you are part of the extended family I mentioned above. You are all so gifted. I can't wait to see what is in store for the kids in the years ahead. I'm determined to be around to see that. Lol. Trish, you are amazing. With such joy and dedication, the work you do is truly inspiring and a godsend to so many. Thank you for your kind words.

Now, to a very important person that the spiritual family lost way too soon – Claudette. I think of you often. We had such wonderful talks, and I learned so much about spiritual matters from all your experiences and episodes, the many consequential people you came across in your journey, and you told it all with tremendous joy. You saw something in me and were determined to remove that doubt that plagued me. You never gave up on me but pushed me to do better. I will always hold a place in my heart for you.

Thank you to all the mediums who bring the important messages from spirit to those who long to hear them. Your work makes a difference.

Finally, to my biggest fan and supporter— and, as you are reading this, my wife, Stacey. Your proofreading and editing were invaluable to the finished manuscript. I do not have the words to express just how important you are to me. The two of us found each other in the most marvelous way, as though it was something out of a fairy tale or romance novel. It was serendipitous at a place called Serendipity's. Go figure. We found each other again. You truly do add everything to me that I am lacking and make me complete. I did not expect to find a love like this, especially after being on my own for some time and establishing where I was. We have so much in common that it's scary. You are my joy, my passion, and I thank the Universe every day for you. This is LOVE.

Stacey, Stephanie, Tyler, Peter, Kathy, Susie, Patrick, Mark, Candise, Jordan and Jett, Tim and Naomi, Matt, Amanda, Valerie and Owen, Richard and Aurea, Stacey Jr., Connor and Char, Michael, Maureen, Sophie, Sasha, Monique and Sam, Kay, Roger, Gregg, Bugsy and the rest of our English family. Thank you. I love you all.

Table of Contents

Introduction xi

2016 1

2017 75

2018 181

2019 255

2020 313

Psychic art 357

Wind up 369

Multi-talented. Creative. Highly intuitive. Passionate. One of a kind.

These are only a few of the many ways to describe Mike.

Mike has been on a lifelong quest for answers, and he has not been one to shy away from deep inner exploration. His dedicated daily spiritual practice allows him to be anchored in awareness and completely embodied by unparalleled levels of inner peace. His peaceful presence is infused in everything he does and is required for connection beyond what most of us can normally conceive.

Mike's strong other-world connections might feel confusing or even intimidating to some; however, through his thoughtful expression, quick wit, and down-home nature, he is sure to put anyone at ease. In and of itself, that is one of his many gifts—the gift of connection.

Armed with an unwavering presence and a complete surrender to "what is," Mike not only inspires us, but leaves us feeling uplifted, curiously fascinated, and light in spirit. His grounded approach and warm personality make for the perfect combination when receiving his wisdom and opening our minds to all that is possible and all that exists just beyond our "usual view." Whether you are lucky to know Mike in person or as a reader—or both—one thing is for sure, your life will be further blessed by that connection.

—Trish Prevost, *healingwithtrish.com*

It's hard to know what to write when you've started as the audience and ended up being cast in the main story. But then again, that's how the Universe works—if you let it. And I have never known anyone more willing to seek the universal plan than Mike Ellis.

We met serendipitously at an establishment by the same name—Serendipity's. Mike was giving a talk about his first book, the events that had brought him to write it, and what he had learned from those difficult experiences. The audience was riveted, and so was I. Here was a man that anyone could identify with, living his life like anyone else, until the Universe hit him on the head—hard—repeatedly. What he had managed to journey through—the humbling, the listening, the surrendering, and the lifelong commitment to continuing to seek and learn— left the audience speechless that night. Before us was a man at peace with the storms he had been through and, more importantly, wanted others to know they could experience the same.

Long story short, I bought the book and, fast-forward two years, I am marrying the author this month!

But, as I like to remind Mike, I still count myself as an unbiased reviewer, no doubt largely fed by the realization that the Universe had been knocking on my own door for many years, but I always wanted to maintain control. I couldn't seek because I was too busy leading the charge, and it wasn't working. I wasn't my true self, wasn't tapping into my gifts, and there was so much more on the other side that held wonderful things. My own personal journey had been waiting all along.

Mike has journeyed all of that and, in the true spirit of universality, knows it has to be shared. This, his second offering, takes us all deeper into what could be our own journey if only we would let it.

—Stacey Gilkinson

Introduction

In 2016, I published *Guided Messages from the Other Side – A Spiritual Journey*. It describes five sessions I had with Claudette Godin, a gifted medium, over eleven years. It begins with me in a very dark place, how I got out of it, the circumstances leading up to my meeting Claudette, and all the energies that came through in those meetings. The book reveals my thoughts on each get-together and what the future held for me.

Little did I know then what an amazing quest it would turn into. My spiritual journey led me to buy a notebook at a dollar store and write whatever came to me; this after meditating and asking spirit to come forth and communicate with me. The suggestion for doing this was given to me by Claudette in one of our sessions. She told me she saw me writing and that this was a good way to get started. What transpired was quite astonishing. It was like I was on auto-pilot, putting pen to paper and writing. I later had the feeling that spirit had been trying to get my attention for some time, and this was the way it was going to be. I never asked Claudette whether she saw this happening for me in this way when she gave me the suggestion, and I did not realize what a big part it would play in my life, and still does.

The spirits that came through at the start were my guides, and they brought with them a vast body of information to help me move forward physically, mentally, and spiritually.

After my first sessions with Claudette, my interest in spiritual matters grew. I wanted to know more about what was out there regarding the afterlife. I had seen mediums connecting to spirit and receiving valuable information, and I wondered whether it was something I could do. In my younger years, I had read a few metaphysical books that piqued my interest, but life stepped in, other events took precedence, and those pursuits fell away. I am a lot older now, with time to rediscover and take up the material again.

I filled up my first notebook and ten others over a few years. The information I received during that time was extraordinary. Spirit, mainly in the form of my guides, was there to move me forward, or maybe I should say upward, to raise my vibration.

These guides worked with me on a daily basis, helping me to improve my sensitivity to spirit, reinforcing me when my doubts crept in (which was often), reminding me to watch my diet (which wasn't always the healthiest), and showing me where my mediumship abilities lay, and so much more. They became a part of my life. It was like communicating with a best friend.

I usually started in the morning after meditating with my notebook and pen and would ask the question from whichever guide I was working with at the time, "Is there anything you would like to say today?" They would greet me, and the response was almost always "Yes," and they would go on from there with whatever they thought I needed to either work on or hear at the time.

I wrote the responses from spirit verbatim, the way they came from my pen, and how I believe they gave them to me. The sentence structure or wording might not always be correct, but I wanted to get the feel of their messages and how they spoke to me.

There were times when their advice was overly repetitive, so I cut back on some of that in this book but left some in because I wanted the reader to see how determined my guides were to get the information to me that they thought I needed to hear.

Along with engaging these guides, I was also taking development classes on improving my abilities. Through these classes, a whole new world, or I should say worlds, opened up to me in ways I never would or could have imagined.

Here's the story of how I met my guides and so many more along the way.

2016

It had been several months since I wrote and published *Guided Messages from the Other Side – A Spiritual Journey*. That book starts in 2004, with my life going to hell in a handbasket—nothing is going right for me, and I have reached the point where I no longer want to deal with the troubles plaguing me. In the book, I document my lowest point and the serendipitous events that slowly started taking place thereafter, my gradual understanding of what was happening, the incredible circumstances that led me to a psychic medium, and the five sessions I had with that medium over eleven years. Those sessions are transcribed in the book and detail all the family members, friends, and even pets that came through. The transcriptions also include the angels and spirit guides that came through and the future possibilities they foresaw for me.

The medium's name is Claudette Godin. She is an incredible person with astounding abilities and is known both here and overseas. She has met many well-known names in the spiritualist community and is now the representative for Canada of the ISF (International Spiritualist Federation). The International Spiritualist Federation is a group of people interested in global spiritualism. They meet to support, share, and learn from each other. It includes healers, mediums, and anyone interested in furthering their education, communicating their knowledge, or demonstrating that death is not the end. That is the definition of spiritualism—the belief that there is more after we die and that spirit lives on. I have been most blessed to have experienced Claudette's talents.

In one of our sessions, Claudette told me that she foresaw me writing books and that the first book would be a precursor for more to come and was mainly to get me into the habit of writing. She also mentioned that I had abilities, which surprised me. I had some experiences in the past that pointed in that direction, but she told me that I needed to develop these abilities. Some months later, after my five sessions with Claudette, I started taking classes with her.

Claudette told me to buy a notebook and start writing. One day, not long after, I saw some notebooks in a store, and her words popped into my head, so I bought one. The next day, I sat down after my meditation, grabbed the notebook, and this is what came out with no thought whatsoever on my part:

July 06, 2016

A spirit guide.

Love is the answer.

Love is the be-all.

Don't be afraid.

I am here to help you.

It is all good.

Never let it be said that we don't hear you.

Finally, we are getting somewhere.

This is a good start.

This is something that we need to get into the habit of doing.

It is important for your development.

Once done, I read the words and asked myself, "Where did that come from? Was this really *a spirit guide* or just me subconsciously writing what I might be hoping for?" At that moment, I decided to do this every day and see what occurred.

The following transcriptions are what followed.

July 7, 2016

I feel a connection to my dog Buster, who has long passed. He's happy to connect with me. (This is what I wrote that day in the notebook after having that sense come to me.)

Later, I sensed the presence of my kids, and this is the message I received:

We're here, Dad. We love you. We're proud of you. We like the book. Yes, there will be many. There will be lots who get something out of it.

I have two children in spirit, as Claudette told me in separate sessions, and I mentioned them in my first book. Their names are John and Katie.

They are children that never drew breath, either through miscarriage or abortion, and they were never meant to be born. I was told at the time that they wanted to be recognized and given a name. John came through first at around ten to twelve years old. I named him John Michael. Katie came through in a later session at around six years old. I named her Kaitlin Alexia but have always called her Katie. Katie loves wildflowers. She would have been older if they both lived; however, this was how they chose to be seen by me. In the spiritual realm, there is no age; it is all energy. I will speak more on this later. Occasionally, as my sensitivities have become a bit better, I get the suggestion that one or both are present. When I ask if they are around, I feel a tingling throughout my body. To me, that is confirmation that spirit is present and acknowledging me.

The next bit of writing is what I sensed to be the "guide" from the day before:

We have the power, the energy to do all manner of things. There isn't anything we can't do. It's matching our desires and vibrations to make it happen.

Life is the ultimate testing ground. Have fun with it.

Look at the obstacles as something to be overcome and learn from.

There will always be roadblocks. What is to be learned from an easy sail-through except pure enjoyment and paying attention to all that is around us? Loving all that is around us, and staying in the Now.

The "being" is important. Be happy and grateful for everything.

Well, that certainly doesn't sound like something I would say.

During the first few days of doing this, I eventually realized that this was a guide—my guide—communicating with me, with both of us getting a feel for each other. My guide was getting me comfortable with the process. Did I have doubts? Yes, tons. And I must say that after doing this for more than three years now, I no longer have doubts about this particular facet, but I still doubt myself when it comes to other aspects of spiritual occurrences that I sense occasionally.

I didn't write down the questions in the first few days. Instead, I asked my questions out loud and wrote the answers. Later, I started writing my questions down.

July 8, 2016

I feel a good connection with my brow chakra and my solar plexus chakra.

Keep working on the root chakra.

Health is still important. It's never too late to start.

July 10, 2016

When should we get together?

Connecting in the morning may be better.

Yes. I agree.

Open up and let go. Open up and let go. Open up and let go. Open up and let go. Trust. Open up and let go.

We have all been given free will and thereby live with the choices we make. We can always change those choices. There are no wrong choices. Choices that may seem "wrong" may actually be more beneficial to us, as experiencing something we weren't expecting. And no matter what, we will never get it all done. We will always be looking at new desires. When we stop looking for new desires, when we stop creating, then our time is done, and it's time to go.

Happiness is one of the most important emotions we can have. That old saying, "Always try to look on the bright side," is very apt.

When it looks darkest, know that it will pass. Worry serves no purpose. Give your problems over to the angels. Let them handle them.

The Yin and Yang—there is up and down, hot and cold. There's always another point of view, and because we are all different, with free *choice, there will always be those who don't agree or don't want to understand your point of view, and that's okay.*

Right. Well, that was a lot. And I'm sure that wasn't me coming through with all those words of wisdom. I believe I'm fairly intelligent, but that seemed more than what I could see myself coming up with on my own.

July 18, 2016

Is there something you would like to say?

I am from a place of Love. Love is inside me. Let the Love in and out. Feel the Love. Open up to the Love. Let your heart fill with Love. There is nothing greater than Love. There is so much Love sent your way. Embrace it. Let it flow. Surround yourself with its glow and know that it is always there for you.

July 19, 2016

What would you like to say?

Live your life. Be you! Love is forever.

I hadn't yet started doing this regularly, as I would come to do and would learn that it was important.

Your spirit guides want to work with you; they want to see you succeed and are there to help you. They are only waiting for you to initiate the communication. They have probably been dropping subtle hints that you haven't picked up on, like things being misplaced only to turn up in places we had already looked. We scratch our heads and think, *What?* Objects that moved from where they were or something falling from what should have been a solid base. This is their way of trying to get your attention. They are waiting for that introduction, and if we continue to ignore them, the Universe may step in and take matters to a whole new level.

This happened to me, where my world suddenly turned upside down to such an extreme that I was ready to pack it all in and say, "Beam me up, Scotty. I'm ready to go." Then little things started happening to get me back on track. Emails came in with inspirational words, websites, or books that had meaning for me in a relevant way. From there, it steamrolled. It was my "awakening." I was becoming aware. I was starting to fulfill my destiny. I'm sure my guides breathed a sigh of relief, knowing I was finally back on my path. They had been trying to get my attention for some time, and I wasn't catching on, so greater influences were brought to bear. A more comprehensive explanation of my distressful time can be found in my first book.

Another part of my awakening was due to meditation. I am a firm believer in meditation because it centers you. When you go into that quiet place, you find your true self and the Divine. It's where you come to understand that there is so much more to us. I believe that if all of us meditated for fifteen or twenty minutes each day, the world would be a better place. I have had some amazing revelations while in that solitude. The revelations don't happen all the time, but you always feel better after those few minutes of quietude. I know I do.

I can't prove it, but I believe it is a great health benefit. Complete body relaxation, inside and out, must be good for you. The body wants to be well, and when that tenseness disappears, healing takes place.

Start your meditation by being with the "Love" vibration. Feel that unconditional love for all things. This is not always easy to do, but you must let go of your hang-ups for the things you feel are wronging you. You need to forgive, especially yourself. You need to love yourself and let go of any judgments from the past, which can be very hard to do. Whatever has happened is over. It's a new day, a new start. I know we've all heard this before, but it is true. It is never too late.

Meditation is not always easy when starting. The mind has a hard time letting go. It seems to be constantly focusing on something else. When these thoughts creep in, you acknowledge them and let them go. Focus on your breathing. In and out. If you persist, it will get easier. I have been meditating for many years, and I still have the odd day when my mind is cluttered. I can pull through it most of the time, and occasionally, I just say, "You know what? Today's not the day." No regrets.

There will be more information on this subject from my guides in the days ahead.

July 23, 2016

Note: Each day, I asked, "Is there something you wish to say?" This was my way of opening my discussion with spirit. I will forego writing this so that it doesn't become monotonous to the reader.

I want to work with you.

Good.

Let's get started.

Life is all about choices.

There are no good or bad choices.

Each choice moves us along our way.

We are defined by the choices we make.

It should be exhilarating, not a chore.

This was a good start. Not too long, but a sign that you are willing to get on with the process. We need to set a time and get into the habit of performing this routine every day, preferably right after your meditation. Namaste. With Love and Joy.

So, again, this was my guide. I know there is no way I would be issuing this information myself. As I said, I asked the question, put my pen to paper, and started writing, and this is what appeared. There was no stopping and starting. It was a continuous flow of words. I was not thinking of words until they appeared on the page.

I believe anyone can do this with a bit of preparation. Again, I think meditation is important before asking your guides for help.* Maybe nothing will happen the first few times, but keep at it. I was interested in the paranormal when I was in my early twenties, like Out of Body Experiences (OBEs) and the Third Eye. But I am just like the rest of you, life gets in the way, and I got away from all of that until I reached that point where my life had spiraled downward, and I was ready to say, "The hell with it all, I'm done."

If this is something you are interested in, give it a try. You may be surprised by what comes through.

*There's more on this process in the July 26th entry.

July 24, 2016

Today, let's talk about healthier choices for the body. It's just as important to look after oneself physically as it is spiritually.

It's not helping the growth of the soul if the body breaks down. Eating properly and exercising are very important if you want to continue to move forward. You maintain your vehicles for peak performance to maintain their efficiency. So do the same for your bodies.

Everyone's journey is their own, and the paths they choose.

We cannot take their journey for them, nor should they want us to. It's the whole point. It belongs to them.

Okay, good for today. More tomorrow.

July 25, 2016

Money is good. There isn't anything wrong with having or wanting to be wealthy. It is there for us. You are not depriving anyone else of having it. It is just a matter of being in vibrational harmony with the money energy, and it is through the proper emotion that harmonizes with the vibration that manifestation will occur. Wish wealth on others to get wealth yourself. Wish health on others to be healthy, and do it joyfully. We can be all that we want.

Being is important. Being in the moment. Being who we are. Being that what was meant when we incarnated and staying true to that preamble. Life is good.

A little bit each day will get it done.

We will do more and more as the connection gets stronger, but that is good for now.

July 26, 2016

Listen. Listen with your heart. Open up. Let the words flow. Let the pen write. Don't overthink it. Clear the mind. Feel the energy. Relax. It is a joining of the two. It is a melding of the minds. Block out the outside disturbances. Love the process and be thankful. You must be willing to work with spirit and be part of the process. It will get easier and easier as we progress. It is all about accepting. We will do great things that will benefit others as well as yourself.

See you tomorrow.

July 27, 2016

Is there anything you would like to say today?

Let us continue. Creativity. It is all about Creativity in everything we do. It is the main reason that we incarnate to this physical world. We are creating all the time. We are constantly thinking of new things. The day we stop is the day it's over. It's our sole (soul) purpose. We need to create, whether it be art, music, inventions, business ideas, or any other variety of things. Everyone creates, including their own circumstances. Where you are, what's going on in your life, your health, your wealth, or lack of. All of it is about creating. The channel between us is creating. Everything around you has been created by everyone around you.

There isn't anything that hasn't been created. Thoughts create. Good or bad. You are creating a book. You are in the process of creating a website for that book. Your thoughts are on creating other books. You are creating art. You are re-creating yourself, the way you look, the way you feel, where you want to live, how you want to live, and who you want to live it with. They have been created; they just haven't been realized yet. It is all in the works. Creating is the major part of our makeup. So love the process.

We are taking tiny steps, but it is good, and it will get better.

July 28, 2016

Your art is important to you. It is a part of who you are. It fulfills that creativity we spoke of yesterday. It is important to continue with this. Set aside some time every day, if possible, to pursue this. You will begin to notice a difference.

(Here, I asked whether I would audibly hear my guide at any point in time.)

In time, this will happen. You will hear a voice. I am here for your writing, but your spirit guide will make themselves known to you, and you will hear a voice. That voice you heard years ago* was your spirit guide. It's taken a long time to get that connection again. Keep doing what you are doing. Meditating. Making this connection with your writing. Keep the lines open, and it will happen. There is also the possibility of channeling energy, but that will come when the time is right. In the meantime, stay the course. There will be workshops that will help.

It will be successful. There are good days ahead. Your health will hold you in good stead. Everything is rolling out as it should.

*When I was in my mid-twenties, I was doing some reading on parapsychology subjects. One book I remember was by an author named Lobsang Rampa. There were some incredible declarations, one of which was Out of Body or Astral Travelling. I found this amazing and decided this was something I had to try. I would try to experience this phenomenon by slow breathing and seeing it occur as I lay in bed at night. This went on for quite a while, but nothing happened, and I eventually left it all behind.

Some years later, I worked nights as a part-time bartender near where I lived while going to school for a diploma in Public Administration. (I spent most of my working life in the stock brokerage business but left for a period when the market went soft in the seventies.) One night, I got home late and went to bed, but I couldn't fall asleep. I was restless all night. As the sun was about to rise, I was not quite asleep and not quite awake. At this moment, I felt a tremendous vibration right around my navel. It was like a whirlpool effect. I could feel myself pulling out of my body. As this was happening, I heard a voice, clear as a bell, say, "Hi, Michael. I am here." I immediately felt afraid because I had read, way back when, that there could be nasty things waiting for you on the *Other Side,* wanting to take you over. Anyway, as soon as that fear hit me, I pulled right back, and that was it. I got up immediately. No one will ever convince me that this was anything but spirit communication. I believe it with all my heart and soul. Unfortunately, that was the last time I had that experience. Since then, I have learned so much and have nothing but regret for blowing that huge opportunity. That was my spirit guide greeting me, and I missed it. That was clairaudience, which I will discuss further later. I have tried to get back to that place, that feeling, but it hasn't happened yet. I look forward to another chance.

July 29, 2016

(Here, I ask spirit if they are ready.)

I am good. I am ready.

We would like to speak on meditation today. The importance of quieting the mind cannot be overstated. There are unlimited benefits to the body and soul. This can be a vast subject. Just thirty minutes a day will reap immense rewards.

This connection is possible because of your meditations. It opens up the lines of communication. It makes it easier when you relax. Let the mind go, and write what comes through.

These sessions don't have to be lengthy, though that will come. It is more the connecting.

Have a good day. Peace.

Okay. I am a big fan of meditation. As I said earlier, I believe that if we could get the world to meditate, it would be a much better place. I have been meditating now for several years. I have had some amazing experiences during meditation. They don't happen as much as I wish they would, but that half-hour of quietude regenerates me. The mind is at rest and open to whatever may present itself.

In most cases, it is the body at complete relaxation, and I believe that the body needs that. When the body is entirely at rest, it can heal itself in many ways. The body doesn't want to be ill, and there is no better way to reduce stress, which can be debilitating if you are already suffering from an illness, than by meditation—putting the body at ease and being relaxed lets that healing begin. When I'm about to start meditating, I say: "My body rests and rejuvenates itself whenever I consciously relax. I am relaxed now."

A good way to begin is to feel yourself relax, starting at the top of your head and working your way down bit by bit. Feel your face relax, then your neck, shoulders, especially the shoulders, which can hold a lot of tension, chest, and so forth, even your organs. You won't feel the organs relax, but picture them in that state, relaxed and healthy. As you get more proficient, you won't need to do these steps; it will be a complete looseness of the body. Feel your body sinking into your chair or seat. I recommend sitting, as lying down will make you more susceptible to falling asleep.

Another suitable method is to focus on your breathing. Feel the breath in and out. Put your focus on that.

When you begin this practice, you might find that you fall asleep. That's okay. Stick with it. Like everything, it requires practice, practice, practice. Also, you may find that you are having a difficult time quieting your mind. This is probably the main reason most people give up, and I understand that. Focus on the thought and release it. You may have to do this a few times when starting, but it will get easier. I believe that it will get better if you hang in there and persist.

I imagine a band around my forehead, just above my eyes. This is the brow chakra or third eye area, and I concentrate on that. I can do that now quite readily with little concentration. However, many recordings are available now to help you get into that state. Check YouTube for a long list and pick something that resonates with you.

It could be the sound of waves or water, or Tibetan singing bowls, whatever will get you to that quiet, relaxed state.

There is a lot of information on meditation, techniques, and benefits on the internet. This is merely a quick conversation on the subject.

Meditation may offer many benefits, such as helping with concentration, relaxation, inner peace, stress reduction, and fatigue.

> Research has found that meditation may help reduce symptoms of anxiety and depression. When combined with conventional medicine, meditation may improve physical health. For example, some research suggests meditation can help manage symptoms of conditions such as insomnia, heart disease, pain, cancer, and digestive problems.
>
> —taken from the Mayo Clinic website

July 30, 2016

I am here.

Again, I would like to speak on the importance of feeding the physical body as well as the spiritual. It is important to keep the physical body in working order through proper nutrition and exercise.

You will know and pay attention to that voice when you hear it when it comes to eating properly. It is all right to have a free day but stick with what is right for you. Digestion matters. You do not need as much food as you think you do. Your body will adjust, especially as you get older. You can get all the vitamins and nutrients you need through your food, but supplements can't hurt as long as you don't overdo it.

Keeping the body fit is also important. You are getting there. Slow and steady wins the race. Keep strong. Stay with it. Don't falter. It will benefit you immensely in the long run.

August 01, 2016

Hello. It is a good day. We are proud of you and how far you have come. But there is much to be done.

Have you any questions?

Are you one spirit or energies of many?

We are more than a few of like energies but speak as one. We are here to help you with this process.

A quick word about spirit guides.

Most of our guides incarnated onto the earth plane at some point in time, differentiating them from, say, angels. However, you may have guides that have never incarnated but are there for you because of the wisdom they have accumulated from their work on the other side. We have several guides there for us. We have a main guide who is with us from the beginning of our incarnation through to our passing. We can call on special guides, like "doctor" guides for health issues. The guide that I am conversing with daily is a few guides coming through as one. My son and daughter in spirit are my Joy guides. We may have a totem animal that acts as a guide for us. You can see this with many indigenous people. We have guides who are always with us to help with our major life lessons, which were established before we incarnated. And we have other guides who step in temporarily to help us with specific issues. For example, I will ask my guides and angels to watch over me when I travel.

As the name implies, guides are there for guidance. They will help you, but you must ask. They will make recommendations to you, but it is up to you whether you want to follow their advice or not. They will not interfere with your free will. That is sacrosanct.

At some point in my journey, my guide at the time was getting on me about watching my diet. This was coming up quite regularly, and I finally told him, "I appreciate you looking out for me, and I know you are doing it for my welfare, but could you cut back a little? I will try to do better, but I don't want to hear this all the time. You can remind me occasionally, and I am grateful." So, this was on me. And he did just that. He still reminds me sometimes, and that is fine. As I said, I appreciate him looking out for me, and I do need to be reminded that it is in my own best interest.

Above, I referred to "my guide at the time." I have found that the guide I converse with daily changes every couple of years. A new guide will come in as you progress to help you with a new set of coaching or enlightenment. This can be hard when it happens, as you get used to the guide you have been working with. It's almost like losing a close friend. There will be more about this later.

Can we start now? Am I ready to progress with it at this time?

Yes.

We will start by saying how happy we are to be doing this with you and really welcome the opportunity to get our views out to you.

I am also happy to be involved with this.

Good. Let's begin.

Okay.

Much has been said about the "Other Side." Let us clarify some of that. Everything is energy and can be whatever it wants. It can look like it wants and can be perceived as it wants to be perceived. There are no disappointments. There is only Love and Happiness. Everything is as it is according to each, and these feelings can and should be used in the physical. It can happen even though it may seem just a pipedream. Again, it is all energy. If enough energies have a common goal or synchronicity, it will manifest as such. Don't be dissuaded by what is thought as improbable or impossible. There is no such thing.

This is a good start. We will continue and look forward to our next communication. Peace.

Thank you.

August 2, 2016

Yes, I am here.

(Here, I explain to my guide the dream I had the night before.)

I had a dream last night that I was a British soldier who died at Rorke's Drift. The year was 1879. I saw myself in a hospital wearing a uniform with a red jacket and bandages around my head. The Zulu attempted to get to those defending the hospital and came in through the straw roof. I was killed by a Zulu spear while fighting, even though I was a patient in the hospital. I saw the spear go into my chest. Thankfully, there was no pain, and then the dream was over. Was this a review of a past life?

Yes. It was. You did live that life as a British soldier, and you did die at Rorke's Drift. It was from a spear wound to the chest. You were 28. Your name was Henkins James.

There is a lot to be said about my dream. First, it was very vivid. I've never had such a vivid dream before. I saw everything clearly.

Years before, I had seen a movie called ZULU that was made in 1964 and remembered it. I looked up the battle and the casualties and found a man named James Jenkins who was killed by an assegai spear, a throwing or thrusting spear. He was a private who had been sick and was in the hospital. Three soldiers died in the hospital when they refused to leave, one of which was James Jenkins. Sometimes, there are slight discrepancies when communicating with spirit, especially with names, in this case, James Henkins / James Jenkins. However, James Jenkins wasn't mentioned in the movie, and I couldn't find the age James Jenkins died.

The Battle of Rorke's Drift was an amazing story. Just over one hundred British soldiers masterfully defended a mission post against 3000 – 4000 Zulu warriors. The British army had suffered a terrible defeat just days before against the Zulu at Isandlwana. More Victoria Crosses were awarded for the Rorke's Drift battle than any other battle in English history. If you get a chance, see the movie. It was very well done.

Now, I dream every night and try to remember at least little pieces of what I dreamed, but I typically can't unless I write it down right after waking up. However, with this dream, I remembered every part of it vividly. It was like watching a movie, except I was the actor. It stayed with me.

August 3, 2016

I am here.

(I asked whether this was the way we would continue to communicate.)

You are right. That is the way it is working now. Start slowly and build up. We don't want you to suddenly hear a voice and pull back. We want you to be comfortable with the process. That's correct.

Yes. There isn't anything that can't happen. It will all be there for you.

Good.

(Here, I mentioned feeling the vibration in my brow, the brow chakra. It has always been the strongest of my chakras. I get a tingling sensation easily, without concentrating.)

Can you feel the vibration?

Yes.

The throat chakra will be important and will need strengthening for the purposes of communications. So this is something that you need to start working on. Uniting all your chakras is important, but spending some time on individual ones for specific purposes is also a must.

Keep doing what you are doing in your meditation, but vary between them. Work on Root, Throat, and Heart chakras. Your Brow chakra is already strong. The others will come along.

Don't worry about finances. It is going to be taken care of. It is putting your concentration towards these other areas now.

This is a good time then to talk about the chakras.

There are seven main chakras. There are many chakras, but to keep it simple, I will write about the seven main chakras, which are the major spiritual energy centers.*

The Root Chakra – First chakra. At the base of the spine. Associated with the color red. Grounding.

The Sacral Chakra – Second chakra. About three inches below the navel. Orange. Sensuality, pleasure, creativity.

The Solar Plexus Chakra – Third chakra. Between the navel and the lower part of the chest. Yellow. The seat of power, mastering emotions, willpower, perception.

The Heart Chakra – Fourth chakra. Center of the chest. Green. Love, balance.

The Throat Chakra – Fifth chakra. Center of the neck. Blue. Expression and communication. Sound vibration is important.

The Brow Chakra (Third Eye) – Sixth chakra. Between the eyebrows. Indigo. The gateway to enlightenment, the seat of understanding, intuition.

The Crown Chakra – Seventh Chakra. Center of the top of the head. Violet and white. The spiritual connection to the Universe.

The major chakras are like energy wheels, where energies flow around and through energy points. There are hundreds of smaller chakras or energy points that can affect both the body and mind. We can clear these chakras through meditation, breathing, yoga, and other exercises.

Keeping these chakras in balance is important for our health and well-being. If they become blocked, they can significantly affect the way we feel.

Many books have been written on the chakras. The information I have provided is very preliminary and is meant as a brief introduction.

*Lately, I have been working with twelve chakras. The Stellar Gate Chakra is positioned about three feet above the Crown Chakra. The Soul Star Chakra is about eighteen inches above the crown. The Causal or Past Life Chakra is approximately one hand above the crown. The Navel Chakra, at the navel, and the Earth Star Chakra, about twelve inches below the feet. These chakras have become common for many as we move from 3D to 5D consciousness.

August 4, 2016

Is there something you would like to say?

What about vibration again. Vibration is the energy moving. Everything gives off energy. Everything is moving. Your vibration changes all the time according to what you are thinking, what you are feeling. Other vibrations that match yours will manifest or come into your physical being. This doesn't happen immediately. There is a time lag, unless the vibration is extremely profound, then it materializes very quickly. So, it is important to watch your thoughts, or better still, keep vigilant with your emotions which wield more power.

Keep happy. When negative thoughts occur, try to find the positive and flip them. What can I learn from the negative? Are there benefits to be gained? All will turn in your favor. It is a wondrous existence when you become aware of how it all works and fits together. Peace.

August 6, 2016

You have a lot of support on this side that is available for help in many ways. You have your health guides. You have guides for your spiritual development. You know of your Joy guides, especially John and Katie and Buster. You have your totem guides or animal guides. You have guides for your creative side like your art, your writing, and your music. You also have all your family and friends who are there to support you with their love and in other small ways to make your physical journey easier.

Yes. Your animal guide is the Bear that has come to you several times in your dreams. (I had asked about this.)

You can speak to God just as you can speak to anyone here. You know you asked to speak to Archangel Michael and he quickly replied. You were a little overwhelmed, and might be all the more so if you heard from God, but HE/SHE would not let you down.

Does my Guardian Angel have a name?

Of course. Ezekiel.

Thank you. Thank you, Ezekiel, for watching over me all these years, especially in my younger years when I did so many stupid and risky things that could have easily gone wrong for me.*

Thank you, Michael, for being you.

*The same way I write for my guide, I write when contacting other spirit energies. I know someone must have been watching over me in my late teens and twenties, as some incidents could have gone badly for me.

August 7, 2016

Am I starting to feel your presence more and more?

Yes. Again, the more we do this, the stronger the reaction will be.

Okay.

Always ground yourself.* Keep working on clearing your chakras. Keep up with your painting. There will be some travel happening.

Will I be able to help my family?

Yes. That will happen.

I always get a "yes" answer whenever I ask a question. Is that me hoping that's the answer? Or will you give me a "no" answer when appropriate?

I will give you a "no" answer if appropriate.

Is there a way of speeding up the process? I'm not getting any younger.

No. You must go through the process as required. Don't worry about age.

(Hah. There's my "no" answer.) **Can we continue this later?**

Of course.

*Grounding, simply put, is readjusting one's energy by connecting to the earth. It's centering yourself. This can be accomplished by touching the earth with your feet, going for a nature walk, meditating, eating healthy, practicing yoga, and using crystals while putting your intention out there.

During my morning meditation, I asked my guide's name. The name that popped into my head was Phillip. Therefore, I will use this name when referring to my guide going forward. Since the guides are a collective of "like" energies, it doesn't matter what I call them.

August 8, 2016

Phillip, is there something you would like to expound on today?

Yes. I would like to talk about "time," which is strictly a physical measurement. The dimension we are in, of course, there is no such thing as time or space.

I have a lot of trouble with the concept of everything happening simultaneously, as in all my "selves" in other dimensions and all my "past lives."

It is all about the "Now" moment. It is always the "Now" moment. If you look at it that way, it may help you. It is not an easy subject for the physical mind to digest.

Time is irrelevant except to the physical being. You are only a part of your true self – your Higher Self, which is made up of all your past endeavors. So it is your Higher Self that is experiencing all of that at the same moment—the "Now" moment.

The more you can stay in the "Now" moment, and stay there with a happy, loving emotion, the better, then your life seems easy and filled with joy, and everything good flows to you.

August 9, 2016

Will I be able to see "pictures" in my connection to spirit, or will it only be auditory?

Yes, you will be able to see pictures eventually. These will help you in confirming what you are getting.

Is the connection stronger here at Birch Bay?*

Yes, it is stronger. There is a vortex or energy boost here, which helps in the receiving of thoughts.

Everything has an opposite, but they work in conjunction with each other. So you have a Mother God and Father God. Male and female angels. You yourself have had lives as male and female, though your predominant self is male.

Just as there is up and down, light and dark, in and out, etc.

When they say "get in touch with your feminine side," that is viewed as an asset that is helping round you out as a person.

*Birch Bay is a small resort area just south of the Canada/U.S. border in Washington State on the water. My wife and I had a weekend place there for several years until we separated. Later, I used my dear friends' place, who also had property there. I always felt a sense of peace there. It was close to nature, quiet, and an area where I could easily meditate.

August 11, 2016

Here, I asked about writing a new book.

Yes, there will be more. We look forward to that process and getting our own thoughts put into the written word.

It will be different from the first one, but it will be relevant and of interest to many in the physical.

You will learn much from this endeavor and continue to move forward with your own progression.

Is there anything else you would like to discuss?

Not right now, but let's continue to keep this going every day, if possible, for this is how you will progress, move forward, get stronger, and become more capable.

August 12, 2016

While sleeping, do I interact with those in spirit?

Yes. And some of that interaction may come through in the way of dreams, though what you dream may not seem like it makes any sense.

What about the dreams I have of those who have not yet passed?

There is interaction there as well, and some of that may be due to circumstances from past lives.

I am gathering that there is so much more to do with dreaming?

Yes, it can be a vast subject, taking in many aspects.

Is this something that we will discuss again, possibly for the book?

Most definitely. For now, we are keeping it short and simple.

Okay, I'm off to bed.

Sweet dreams.

Hah.

August 13, 2016

Yes, I would like to discuss the topic of money.

Money has its own vibration and can be looked at as a tool to help you obtain and get to where you wish to be.

You can have as much as you deem necessary to assist you in your endeavors, which could include helping others.

There is no limit. It can come to you in many ways. Always be open to receiving it, and never concern yourself with how it is going to get to you. Be open to receiving it and allowing it to flow to you. Be grateful for the wealth and abundance that comes your way.

Feeling gratitude and happiness increases the flow. Be in a state of already being wealthy and abundant. The Universe provides according to your feelings. It is Law.

Wishing good fortune to others shows the Universe that you yourself are in a place of abundance.

August 14, 2016

Here I ask about the place in Birch Bay once again. *You will be in a position to carry on down there. It is a good spot for you. It is important for you to get out. Maybe consider starting your walks again. There is a peace there for you. Nature is important. You need the trees. You are in a good place mindset-wise.*

Everything will work as it is meant to. Don't worry, leave it in our hands. Keep busy. Keep at it. Enjoy. Enjoyment is where good things occur and keep on occurring. Life is meant to be easy. Let it be so.

August 15, 2016

I hope you will now be there for me when the workshops continue?

(I had started development workshops with Claudette, the medium. She told me they would be good for me.)

You know I will.

It will be great to be able to add more to the group than I have in the past.

Don't beat yourself up. You have added more than you know.

That's good to hear.

You will get stronger and better as we move forward.

Positive reinforcement is good for me.

You have to learn to feel that "Love" that flows to you. You have to open up to it. There is so much Love here for you. Relax and let it in.

You have family and friends, angels and guides, all here for you, wishing you well and wanting the best for you.

Thank you. I am grateful.

Remember to be there for others as well. Be the smile. Transfer that goodness to others. Be the energy, the force that can change those around you. It's a powerful force that can change the world.

There are going to be many sessions ahead, with much to be written and said. We will lead you. We will guide you. We are a team and can make a difference.

The world is changing. A new day is coming, and you are a part of it. It is why you are here. You are a participant in the new age of enlightenment. So grab the reins and hold on; it's going to be quite the ride.

August 16, 2016

I have been having some detailed but weird dreams lately, where there seems to be discord between me and loved ones who have passed. There were no problems before their passing. Can you explain such dreams? Thank you.

There is a whole different aspect to dreams. What you are remembering in your dream isn't what is taking place. There is that connection there, but it is of a different nature. It may be a "cleansing" of some hurt feelings that may have taken place many, many years ago. Think of it as washing out a spot and bringing it back to purity. There is no anguish.

Many small incidents can leave a mark that can stay with you for decades, and you aren't even aware of them. This is getting rid of those marks. It is all good.

Is my changing the dream affecting it in any way?

No. The basic premise of the dream still works. All you are doing is making it more comfortable for you. There is no negativity flowing to anyone.

Any disputes from the past from members who have passed are completely let go of upon passing. Those who have passed will quickly apologize and ask for forgiveness for even the littlest slight, even those you don't remember.

Remember, it is all about "Love," and they are totally about sending that "Love" your way.

The cleansing is for your benefit. So, again, be grateful for this and do not worry or fret about what seems like a dream that doesn't correspond to someone that you love.

Thank you, Phillip.

August 17, 2016

Relax. Let go.

Can I hear from John and Katie?

Yes. Definitely.

John and Katie, are you there?

Yes. We are here. So nice to hear from you, Dad. How are you doing?

I am doing well. Thank you for joining me.

We are thrilled to be with you.

How are things with the both of you? Are you doing other things there?

Phillip is here with us, and we are glad that you are finally making this connection.

I hope to get better at this—stronger and more adept.

It will come, and we will have good talks and connections ahead.

I love you both. I am happy to have you in my life.

We love you very much and are very proud of you and what you are accomplishing.

We will have some good walks sometime. I look forward to that with both of you as well as Buster and Toby. (Toby was my last dog that passed. I sometimes feel they are both with me on my walks.)

We look forward to that also.

Give Buster and Toby a pat on the head for me.

We will. They are happy also to know you are connecting with them.

Great. I love you all.

August 18, 2016

So, Phillip, I have been thinking that these communications with you could be the start of another book.

Are you giving me these thoughts? Is this something you see happening?

Yes, to both of those questions. We will continue with these writings, and it will eventually evolve into another book.

Your last book was a good starter. This one will be longer, and we will get into many areas. Watch it evolve.

Good. I can already see some thoughts coming in for the writing of this.

Yes. You have to keep up with these sessions, and it will turn into something you can be proud of.

I like the sound of that.

Good. As it slowly transforms, we will get to a place where the writing becomes easier, and the sessions will be longer as we progress into the many topics we will be discussing.

I need to find a better way of writing. Maybe it would be better to do this sitting at a desk instead of having the pad on my knees.

That would be better.

Thank you, Phillip.

Absolutely.

August 21, 2016

Hi, Phillip. Is there something you would like to talk about?

Yes. Well-being. It is a state of mind. Don't let past experiences affect who you are now or who you are meant to be.

Don't let the words of others set you apart from who you are meant to be.

All those phrases said to you when you were little shaped many of your thoughts. And, as we know, thoughts become things. Those thoughts had an impact on what transpired in your life.

Now it is time to let go of those past thoughts that are or were hurting you and changing to new thoughts that will benefit you and enhance who you are and who you are meant to be; a better image of your old self with better things coming your way. You were meant to survive. You were meant to thrive. You were meant to enjoy this existence. So let it be so.

You can overcome anything if you allow the positive thinking; if you allow the existential you to become. Give it room to thrive and overcome.

All that you are meant to be is there. Give it its chance to burst forth and show itself. As the Beatles said, "Let It Be."* And you don't have to overthink it. Circumstances will arise that will help you in your endeavors. You have many on the other side who are here working for your success.

Look for the signs. Look for new possibilities that may show up, go with the flow.

Nothing you do is wrong; it's just a different way. There will always be new experiences and new ways of dealing with them.

*Let It Be is the twelfth and final studio album by the English rock band the Beatles, released May 08, 1970. —Wikipedia

August 22, 2016

As we get further into this, can I ask questions that interest me, such as Bigfoot (think portals), Atlantis, extraterrestrials (already here), and such? I believe many people are interested in these topics, and it would be interesting to get a perspective from the other side.

Most definitely. There is an immense interest in such topics, and there is a lot that can be said about them.

I intend to fill another book with a broader range and more detail.

We will do that.

Also, I would like to discuss the planet and where we are heading. There is a lot of concern about climate change and what we can do to reverse the damage we have already done.

A very important subject and one we will spend much time on.

Will I be able to keep up once you get going? Or will you take over my hand and do the writing?

No. You will do the writing, but there may come a time later on after these sessions when another energy will channel through you and actually do the writing.

There will be a smooth transition through the different topics, and it will be seamless.

I will do a little typing on the computer to get started. Will you be there to assist me with that?

Yes. Absolutely. As always, just ask when you are having trouble or need assistance. I am always around, ready to lend a hand.

Keep up with your painting. It is important to you and is a part of who you are and your progression.

August 23, 2016

I feel I can connect with you much easier and not just for the writing of my book. I can connect with you whenever; I just need to ask, and you are there.

That is true. Because we have started this rapport, the more that you have been doing it, the stronger and more confident you have become. I am always around, but only when you ask or think of connecting with me will I answer. I am not here to interfere in any way with your daily routines.

I'm not sure why, but I have been feeling tired lately, so I hope you don't mind if we keep this one short.

Sometimes dealing with spirit can be tiring. It can sap your energy at times. Don't worry about it, though. It's only occasional, and you will get stronger. We'll call it a night and talk tomorrow.

Good. Thank you. I'm always grateful that you and all my guides and angels are there for me. I love you all.

We love you.

August 24, 2016

I would like to speak of your commitment. This is your undertaking, and it would be advantageous for you to set aside a certain time every day for this.

The morning would be the best time for me. I have to get my routines straight and decide what I want to do and in what order. My meditations are better in the morning. Maybe I could cut down on my computer time and move my exercises until later.

I will work on being available at 10:00 each morning for our writing.

Good.

Leaving it until the evening is not the best.

I agree.

Okay, shall we leave it then, and I will be ready at 10:00 tomorrow?

Good. I will be ready to go.

August 25, 2016

That was quite the good meditation I just had.*

Yes, it was. There will be many more.

*I had a lengthy and profound meditation that I wrote down immediately when I finished:

I just had a meditation following the "Spirit Guide Connection" on YouTube. During the meditation, I could hear the trickling sound of water over rocks. This put me into a forest with a trickling stream. Then my guides showed up, including John and Katie. After spending a few moments with my kids, I sat down with my guides. They told me that I had completed the physical part of my life, for the most part, and it was now time for me to complete the spiritual side. This is the reason I am here, along with many others who have incarnated at this time to help take the planet into a new age of awareness. I have come to help in this regard. It is time to spread the light to the people and the world, to nudge it along to this next stage. As was told to me, there are many working in this regard, and it is my time to step forward and do my part. It is the main reason I am here. I've done my earlier living and escapades; now it's time to shine.

After hearing this from my guides, I spent a few more moments by the stream with my children. Several animals joined us—deer, a bear, and others.

I told my children I loved them and thanked them for being with me. They said they loved me too.

I then got back into my meditation, quieting my mind.

Sometime later, I saw a grey haze, and while noticing it, I felt my father's presence.

I told him I was grateful for him coming through in my sessions with Claudette, and I loved him.

He said he loved me and was proud of me. He said he has come a long way (with regards to his thinking and understanding).

I continued for several more minutes with my meditation and then ended it. My meditation took approximately fifty minutes.

Writing about your experience was a good start. It was important to hear from your many guides and what they told you.

You know now what you are here for, and you will be shown your way.

Things will start showing up, pointing you along your path, showing you the way.

It is your duty to comply.

It is why you are at this point in your development.

Don't be afraid. We are all here to help you. Be happy with what is coming. Enjoy the process.

Try to keep this as your writing time, but it doesn't have to be rigid. We know that sometimes other things crop up that need to be taken care of. You still need to paint and express your creativity. And, you still need to live your life. It doesn't mean that you are giving yourself completely over to spirit. Like Claudette said, "There has to be a merging of the two." There is lots of time. Just take it bit by bit.

August 26, 2016

Is there anything you would like to talk about today?

Looking after yourself. It is important to keep your body functioning properly, especially with good nutrition and exercise. You have been exercising, but your nutrition could be better. More fruits and vegetables, and less meat and cheese.

I'm having a tough time eating vegetables. They're kind of boring.

You have to get in the habit. Mix them up to make it more interesting. It's a good time of year for lots of vegetables.

They are not cheap, though.

Yes, unfortunately, the foods that are best for you are not the most reasonable price-wise. But, it is worth the investment for your body's well-being.

I understand and will try to do better.

As you can see, I have become more comfortable with the process. It's like having a conversation with someone, but they are not physically there. Eventually, I will get to the point where this becomes a regular part of my morning—talking to my guides through writing.

I am going to skip the next couple of days because the messages are repetitions of previous discussions. For example, there are many instances in the future when I am reminded about my diet. This sometimes happened as my journey progressed, so I will not include those conversations unless there was something new or of interest.

August 30, 2016

(I am in Birch Bay.)

Is this a place I will have access to in the future?

Most definitely. We've spoken of this before. It is a good place for you. You appreciate the quietude and the access to Nature.

Yes, I seem to do better here.

For sure.

(Here, I connect with my good friend Marilyn who had passed. The place in Birch Bay used to be hers, and her son lets me use it. She and her husband Dick were also part of my first book.)

Hi, Mike. It's Marilyn. So wonderful to connect with you and see you at the trailer. You are a good friend to both of us. I'm excited to speak with you.

I miss you both.

Yes, we had a lot of fun together. Dick says hi. We are good. It is wonderful to help others in the transition.

(I ask Marilyn whether she had met Katie.)

She is wonderful. We watch over her.

We must keep in contact.

Absolutely. We love you and will help you strengthen your abilities.

Okay. There is much to talk about here. Before ending my communication with Phillip, I asked him whether my connection with Marilyn actually happened or whether it was just my desire to talk to her that was being brought forward. His reply:

Deep down, you know it is. There is bound to be some doubt, but you have the ability, and it is just you writing the words as the communication comes through. It is true. Don't doubt yourself. Be strong in your conviction, and be thankful for this ability. You will get better and become more confident. Don't resist. Be open. Let it flow through you.

Doubting whether an experience actually occurred to me and by me was a constant struggle for me. Even today, some years later and after several mediumship workshops, I still have moments of doubt.

In one of our sessions (mentioned in my first book), Claudette told me that I had mediumship abilities, and little by little, I had come to see some accomplishment in that regard. I have had enormous help, both here and from the other side. I know they will never give up on me, but they must have had moments when they thought, "Please, please, get this" or "What's he doing now?"

Marilyn and her husband, Dick, were very dear friends of ours. The two of them had health issues, so they were happy to have me go down and look after their place in Birch Bay. This was wonderful for me because I loved it there so much. I always felt at peace there. The ocean was close by, and there were lots of trees and animals. Nature is my tonic. It restores me. It brings me back into balance.

Sadly, this wonderful couple passed within months of each other. Their son, Rich, was fine with me continuing to use their place. So, to sit down and start my conversation with Phillip and ask him about the place at Birch Bay and suddenly Marilyn coming through was awesome.

Marilyn and Dick both came through in sessions with Claudette. They are helping others who are transitioning to the other side. Marilyn is helping those who pass quickly by earthly disasters like earthquakes or tornadoes, who are traumatized and not sure what happened or even where they are. And Dick is working with the youth, especially with suicides. My father is also a healer and greets those who pass quickly from conflicts, as in war.

So, as you can see, we help and nurture others when we pass. Our souls continue to expand and rise even after our earthly experience is finished for the moment. And they do that out of love because they want to. You can have any experience on the other side that you want. Many choose to serve. Others continue bringing joy and love through their creativity, be it music, art, or whatever. And then there are some who put the pieces together for their next incarnation. Keep in mind, no space, no time.

September 1, 2016

Regarding the book, as you stated before, "Let it be." Everything will work out the way it is supposed to. Right?

Exactly. We will help from this side. You will have some work to do promoting it. But it will happen.

I had brief communications with some of my family and friends who have passed. Was I actually getting impressions of them and what they were saying?

Stop doubting yourself. You have these abilities. You just need to keep practicing and believing. You will get better. You can do this. Like everything, it takes time and doing some work on it. Everyone here is rooting for you and helping in any way they can. You have lots of support.

I know I have support, and I am grateful for every one of you.

September 4, 2016

There isn't anything greater than "Love." It is the "Be All," the "End All."

Love does make the world go round. It can cure anything. Health. Wars. Environment.

It is always present. It's just to what degree.

So, feel Love. Give Love. Be Love. And with that, you have it all.

When you pass, you will feel a love like nothing you could imagine. This love is always present. If you felt the power of this love on the earth plane, nothing would get done.

You have felt just a very small sense of this love, and you would give everything to feel it again and again. That small taste was to let you know that it is real, that it is there, and it is there for everyone.

You can and do make the world a better place when you focus on love. With more people doing this, the world will transform and get through these trying times. Never doubt that this will be so. All of you are important. All of you are necessary for the change to take place. All of you matter.

Love. Love. Love.

I've felt that complete "Love" on occasion during meditation. It is overwhelming; it is bliss. You never want it to end. Yet that is a mere snippet of what you will experience when you pass. If that absolute Love were a constant, you wouldn't get anything done. You'd want to bathe nonstop in the magnificence of it.

September 5, 2016

Is there anything you would like to discuss today?

I would like to speak of your determination. You have to commit yourself to this project, as well as other projects like your art. There can be no procrastination, which you are susceptible to. Be determined in your mind to proceed and get on with it. This is important in all that you do. No more flip, flop. Just do it. I don't mean this in a harsh way, but say it out of love and concern. It is all about moving along and getting done those things that are meant to be handled, including daily chores. There is much to be done. Just take it step by step.

(The next couple of days, we talked about plans for my first book.)

September 9, 2016

Hi, Phillip. Is there anything you would like to discuss today?

Yes. I would like to speak about loyalty. It is not only important to be loyal to your family and friends but also to the values that you hold dear.

You must be loyal above all else to yourself—the many traits and beliefs that you have adhered to over the years that you have obtained through your physical experience that have made you who you are right now. Be loyal to those truths, for they mean you well. It is not enough to say the things that you believe but to live them.

You have gone through much to become you, so treasure them and hold them close, and abide by the values that are now yours through your living.

September 11, 2016

Yes. I would like to speak of Love.

We have talked about this before.

Yes. But it is a broad subject. I would like to speak of the Love we have for Nature—the love of the trees, flowers, rivers, rocks, deserts, and oceans. This planet's Nature is suffering, and we need to set it right. We can no longer put off ways of fixing what you, as a species, have done to contaminate the planet. Time is of the essence. There is much that needs to be put right.

The air is getting worse. The oceans are getting bogged up with debris, like plastics. You are killing off species of animals. Ice caps are melting and diminishing. It has to end.

Mother Nature is fighting to survive. Storms will get worse. Hurricanes, tornadoes, flash flooding, earthquakes, and wildfires will occur more frequently.

It is time for the population to sit up and notice. Plans need to be made, not tomorrow but starting now. Again, time is of the essence.

New products taking the place of oil-driven machines have to start being used before the pollution becomes any worse.

Political leaders, leaders of industry must be held accountable by the population. It is time.

Well, I can't argue with any of that.

(There's a one-week gap while I visit with my brother at his summer place near Mt. Baker.)

September 16, 2016

I just had a discussion with the publisher (first book). There was a lot of information. I hope you will help me when it comes to marketing.

Absolutely. Let's make it fun. We will get it done.

Money will not be an object. Don't keep on worrying over this. All will be well. It's arriving and will greatly help you in doing those things that you are interested in. All is well and good. Everything is coming along just as it should. It is all coming to fruition. There are great days ahead.

September 17, 2016

Are you doing your art today?

Yes. I will get back to it as soon as I finish here.

Okay. Again, it is important to keep up with this activity, as I have said before.

You should try and do it every day. The more you do, the better you get, and there is a Zen quality to it when you are involved with this creativity.

You are always creating, whether you know it or not. Your thoughts create, and often this can be by default which is maybe not in your best interests. So watch or be cognizant of what you are thinking. You can catch yourself.

September 23, 2016

Do you speak for all the guides, or are you strictly working with me on your own?

We have a collective energy, so what you perceive as one with the name Phillip can be a group of like energies. You do have specific guides, as you know, for specific areas of interest, i.e., arts, health, music, etc., along with your totem guides and your children, who act as Joy guides.

I didn't realize that I hadn't written for six days, with the move and all.*

I knew you were going to be busy with the move, but try and give a bit of time each day to this connection. It is important to keep this dialogue going. It is important to you to strengthen your ability.

Yes, I understand.

There is a lot happening now—moving, the book, marketing, a lot going on. Just take it step by step. Don't let it overwhelm you.

Thank you.

*I was moving into a new complex. There was more back and forth on this for a couple of days.

September 28, 2016

We are here for you in all of that. Be open to inspiration when it comes to marketing the book. Guidance is being sent your way. Be vigilant and aware that this is occurring, and be mindful of the messages sent to you. As always, everything will play out as it is supposed to. Don't fret. Don't get exasperated. If you get bogged down, then give it over to the angels. They are here for you and just need to be asked.

We are all here to assist you in your journey. It doesn't have to be hard. It's your attitude. You can be happy or fearful. Be happy. You are catching yourself and changing over to happy thoughts, which is good. Excellent.

October 1, 2016

Phillip, is there anything I can do for Verine?*

Just be there for her. Her time is approaching. Keep her in your thoughts and prayers, and help where you can.

This was worrying to hear.

I have a workshop with Claudette coming up. I hope you will help me in the workshop. If I know that you are with me, I hope I can do better.

Yes. I am always with you, and I will be there for you to guide you.

Don't put yourself down. You have been helping the group more than you realize. They know it; now you just need to know it.

I began taking mediumship classes with Claudette because she said I needed to increase my sensitivity to spirit. But my abilities were nowhere near what other students in the class showed. Claudette explained that everybody was at different levels and that the students had varied sensitivities. I often felt this shortcoming in the times ahead. However, there is a definite plus to being in a group where you get to experience that associated energy. Trying to improve my awareness on my own would have been much harder.

*Verine and I married in 1979. We separated in 2003 but remained on very friendly terms. She was dealing with health issues, and I had my own concerns going on at the time.

As of October 1, 2016, Verine had struggled even more with health issues, some of which included diabetes, fibromyalgia, and shortness of breath. She was on several medications.

October 3, 2016

(Again, I asked what I could do to help Verine.)

Prayer and continue the healing meditations. Ask the Infinite Spirit for a healing.

Is there something you would like to talk about today?

You have a workshop coming up. Work on freeing yourself. Work on detaching. Let the force take over. Give yourself to spirit. Let us help you to improve, to get stronger connections. It is time to move forward, but you have to let go. Don't be afraid. We are always here to watch over you, and you have angelic protection. Nothing will interfere or harm you. It is the hardest and greatest thing to do—that letting go. But once done, it will become easier, and you will feel and see a tremendous difference—a vast improvement in the channeling of spirit. So work on that for your upcoming workshop.

Okay, Phillip. I will. Thank you.

October 5, 2016

I am concerned for Verine and the pain she is feeling.

It will get remedied. It is all a part of what she must go through, even though it is painful.

Each of you chooses your path, and it's how you handle the circumstances that you yourself have put before you.

Eventually, all your paths will lead to the Transition to the next level.

October 6, 2016

Maybe you could speak on judgment and being judgmental.

Good subject. The physical presence seems to be quite critical of others. It's a very hard trait to overcome—small tirades or thoughts to greater condemnation, leading to wars or physical altercations.

There is no judgment here except for judging yourself when you first return home. Actually, it is less judgmental and more of a review.

Every one of you is different, and it is easy for some to condemn others for not being of the same mind, race, skin color, or class.

Even the slightest affront can cause a curse or quick judgment of another.

The Universe does not judge. Be like the Universe.

This can be very hard to overcome. It's another thing that you must catch yourself on. The Masters* know this. Something to work on.

*Ascended Masters are those who were once human, like all of us, but paid off their karmic debt and mastered ascension. They are here to help us and see this planet survive. They go beyond time.

They no longer have a physical body, but, unlike other spiritual beings like Angels, they once had one and can relate to the frustration of the karmic cycle.

Ascended Masters have a vast knowledge base that we can consult with. They have lived through the physical limitations of the reincarnation cycle and have experienced the great power of higher dimensions. There are many Ascended Masters.

It is believed that they want to work with each of us to guide us through the initiations of ascension. —Mindvalley.com

Once again, there is a lot of information written on Ascended Masters in books and the internet. This is a very brief description.

October 8, 2016

Is there something you wish to talk about today?

Keep your focus on being positive and, above all, be happy. Being unhappy because others are doesn't help you in any way at all. You can sympathize but maintain your own positive feelings of joy.

There is a gap here because I was in the process of moving, cleaning the old place, and taking care of Verine, who was getting worse. Her back pain had become so severe that the powerful pain medications were no longer working. I talked to the pain specialist who was trying to regulate her medications. He suggested that getting her into the hospital might make it easier to monitor different dosages. He told us that there was a bed available, but it was in Palliative Care, which is usually reserved for those who are seriously ill or dying. Still, it was the only bed available, and she should consider taking it. We both agreed it would be easier for the doctors to help her when she was readily available.

I took her to the hospital on a Wednesday and got her settled. I visited her every day, and other friends often dropped by. However, she didn't seem to be getting any better, going in and out of consciousness. The doctors told me this was due to the high doses of medication. I visited her Friday, and she barely knew I was there. I returned on Saturday, and she was completely out.

At six in the morning that Sunday, my phone rang. I immediately knew it was the hospital and that it wouldn't be good news.

They told me Verine had passed away. I was shocked. How did this happen? She was only supposed to be there for a few days to get her dosage fixed. I needed to phone my daughter-in-law and let the family know. This was heart-breaking news for the grandkids.

I went to the hospital right away, and they let me see her. She looked at peace; she was no longer in pain. I tried to find out what happened and they told me the doctor would call me. I picked up her belongings and left. It was October 12, 2016.

I told the family that I would come by a little later. I knew this was going to be the hardest part. I had been holding it together, but as soon as I rang their doorbell and saw them, I lost it. We all did. We talked for some time, and it helped.

I had many questions. The doctor called and said they were just as shocked as I was. They were not expecting this. They asked if I would consider an autopsy, and I agreed; I definitely wanted to know what happened.

I was the executor of Verine's estate, so there was much to do in the months ahead.

From our October 1st session, Phillip's words came back to me: "Her time is approaching." I reflected on this when he told me, but I never thought it would be that soon. We knew she was not well, but we believed she had some time, possibly another year. This was totally unforeseen by everyone.

Several days later, I received the preliminary autopsy report. The doctors said that almost all her organs were in very bad shape and some had failed, but they were still waiting for the toxicology report, which would take several weeks.

Verine was diabetic, had trouble breathing, and had fibromyalgia. The doctor also said she had cirrhosis of the liver, which was shocking because Verine rarely drank. She didn't like the taste of alcohol, which was great for me when we were married because I always had a designated driver. I was known to take a tot or two.

I eventually received the toxicology report, and it showed a couple of things: toxoplasmosis and staph aureus. Toxoplasmosis symptoms can range from barely noticeable to extreme. People who suffer from immune problems can be at high risk of developing symptoms of toxoplasma infection but can be unaware of them.

Staphylococcus, or "staph," is a class of bacteria that can cause a multitude of diseases. Staph can cause high fevers, chills, and low blood pressure.

If Verine had been conscious, she would have complained of some of these symptoms, and the staff could have looked at possible solutions. Unfortunately, with her being unconscious, there was no way for anyone to know, and with her fragile condition, these infections were a death sentence.

October 13, 2016

Phillip, Verine's passing was a shock. Did she make the transition well?

Yes. Everything went well. She is home, being celebrated by her family, friends, and pets. She is so happy to be free from the pain. She is sad that she has caused this grief among you. But know that she is well and very excited to see Lisa (her daughter) and her family, not to mention Toby and her other pets.

It is not easy when you lose someone who is dear to you and part of your life. Think of the happiness and love she is receiving now, and know how grateful she is for all of you who were close to her. She says "thank you" for the part you played in her life in this go around.

Her family is so thrilled to see her and be together again.

Toby is tearing around here like we haven't seen before.

Thank you, Phillip.

October 14, 2016

Is there something you would like to discuss?

Transition. It seems like a good topic to discuss with Verine having just passed over, transitioning home.

This transition can take different forms, in part according to what your beliefs are. If you believe that you will see a tunnel with a white light, that can very well be your experience. If you believe it is an easy move, like walking through a doorway, then you will experience that. It all takes the form of what you believe.

Others may perceive fear because of what their life experiences were and are expecting bad things to come. If that is their assumption, then they may experience darkness or a holding place that is uncomfortable for them. This does not last forever. At some point, they will be guided home by angels. There is no judgment here except what you may put on yourself when you do your life review.

Michael, you believe you will be greeted by angels and guides, and it is like moving through a doorway. When your time comes, that will be your experience, then get prepared for an onslaught of love and warmth from all there who know you. It is a celebration. (Since these notes were taken, I've come to believe that I will be welcomed home by all my family, friends, and pets and that my mom, dad, and kids will be upfront.)

October 15, 2016

Is there something you would like to say?

Yes. I would like to continue our discussion about transition.

All of you are transitioning in many ways and at many moments. You go through your different ages. You go through your relationships, some of which last and others that do not. You have transitions of well-being, of abundance, and, of course, your spirituality. Your beliefs can transition. So, in your lifetime, there are countless ways and means of transitioning. You can even transition little moments in your day – from here to there.

The world itself is constantly transitioning—seasons, weather, rivers, mountains, deserts, and the geography—the lands themselves are all transitioning. A tree transitions. It is all a part of the Master Plan. It is all a part of the Universal Mind. From egg to chicken, from tadpole to frog. You are merely following along on your path, transitioning as you go, until it is your turn to transition from this dimension to the next.

October 18, 2016

Can you tell me the cause of Verine's passing? Was it her back?

Yes. It was the liver. Her organs shut down. They were failing her badly, and this would have happened regardless of the decomposing vertebrae.* It was her time to leave, and she was subconsciously preparing for this. Down deep, she knew that this would occur.

She is still making the rounds of everyone and is very happy to be here. Toby is still tearing around, making everyone laugh. Crazy dog.

*This came through right before I got the autopsy report.

Thank you, Phillip. Now back to work; I have much to do.

It will get done. Don't fret.

(Over the next couple of days, there are short communications about my move, and I have to start thinking about Verine's belongings.)

October 23, 2016

Is there anything you would like to say?

Yes. Are you starting to feel our connection?

I get a slight vibration in my body, noticeably in my legs, which is different.

Good. That is a sign of our connection. As you raise your vibration, you will notice the change more. Constantly work on raising your vibration. It will help you on many levels.

Okay.

You can do this through your meditations. Your guides and angels will help you.

Thank you. I appreciate that.

Then you will start to notice such an improvement in our connections. It will all open up.

It's time to take responsibility for your eating and physical improvements. Keep with your exercising. Drop the sugar. More veggies, less meat. It is all a part of your training to increase your vibration. You can do it bit by bit. Don't try to change everything all at once. It won't work. Take your time, and you will get there. Everything is working out as it should, always.

October 25, 2016

Hi, Phillip. Should I take this workshop Saturday with all I've got going on with these moves?

I think you should. It will be beneficial to you and your progression. You will be able to get everything done. We will help you. Don't fret. It will all work out.

We had more discussions about how to deal with Verine's belongings. She had a lot of clothes, books, and furniture. It wasn't a big place, but it all needed to be dealt with. Phillip assured me that spirit would help, meaning through inspiration and sending some people my way who could use some of her possessions, be it family or friends.

October 28, 2016

Just a little while ago, while I was meditating, I got tingly all over, which means spirit is present.* Then I thought of Verine and felt it was her. I know she has only been away a short time. Was this her?

Yes. She is still meeting and greeting. But she took a moment from that to connect with you so that you knew she was okay and to thank you for all that you have done and are continuing to do, and to let everyone know that she is fine and couldn't be happier. Not to grieve but be happy for her. She will always be around.

*My way of experiencing the presence of spirit is getting a tingly sensation all over my body. This can happen when I particularly do something for someone who has passed or ask about/for someone who has passed. It also occurs when spirits, such as my guides or angels, make themselves known to me. I will feel that sensitivity, and a name suddenly pops into my mind. When this happens, I will ask whoever comes through whether it is who I discern it to be since I still doubt whether these experiences are real. Did that just happen, or was it my imagination?

It had been sixteen days since Verine had passed, so you might be wondering how she could still be meeting and greeting others. We must remember that there is no time and space on the other side. Sixteen days is mere seconds there. I first learned this in a session with Claudette when a good friend of mine who had passed six months earlier came through and told me that it seemed like mere minutes.

So, tomorrow I've got the workshop on the Merkabah.* I know you will help me to participate as well as possible.

Yes. All your guides are excited for you and will be there to assist you. Enjoy.

*The Merkabah is a specific meditation, and it was brought up in a previous workshop, but not the mediumship workshop. I will go into further detail on this later in the book.

November 02, 2016

Can I start speaking with you at any time? I know you are always there for me.

Of course. We've been doing it through the writing. But we can start to try and see if you can feel my words. It's another step forward that we can work on. Eventually, it will go that way, and it will be completely normal.

Okay. We will stick to writing, but we can start trying the other.

Good.

November 03, 2016

Is there anything you would like to say?

Nothing important or pressing. I know you have things to do. We will get back to your normal routine when you get everything sorted out here. But start trying to communicate with me verbally and listen for my response. We can begin to work on that.

There was another gap here with some minor communications back and forth. I spent a few days at Birch Bay. It was good to get away.

November 11, 2016 (Remembrance Day in Canada/Veteran's Day in the U.S.)

Yes. I would like to talk about Remembrance Day. It is a special day to commemorate all of the souls that left this earthly plane to bring you the safety and standards that you now enjoy because of their sacrifice and the fulfilling of their destiny—their sacrifice so that you would remember.

-The hardship, the sadness, the devastation that these earthly conflicts inflict and affect everyone.

-The importance of standing together to try and put an end to this kind of misery.

-Raise the vibrations and bring the planet to a place of peace.

It is good to see the young people involved and for them to recognize how devastating it is to family and friends of the fallen and for those who come back traumatized and invalid. The cost is great. They can make a difference to work towards seeing that this doesn't continue in the future.

November 13, 2016

Yes, there could be a book from these writings. Lots more needs to be done, and we will have longer written sections.

Things that others are interested in and can benefit from.

Absolutely.

I want to ask you if Verine knew about the dinner we had for her last night and what she thought.

She was totally aware of it and couldn't have been happier with the way it went. She is grateful to you for setting it up and for the kind words. She is very grateful for all that you are doing on her behalf.

I am glad I can do it. How is Verine doing now?

She is still in the process of greeting everyone. Remember, there is no time here. Like your friend Dick said in one of your sessions—six months seems like a couple of minutes here. So though it has been a month on the earth plane, it is only moments here.

When you take into account eternity, then what is time? It is an earthly measurement.

I am sending a copy of my book to a known publishing house. Will that help in any way?

Yes. There will be a benefit to you from that. That was a thought that we sent your way. Always keep an open mind, looking out for even the small thoughts that you get. It will be us assisting you. You are the one that has to take the action, though.

Thank you. I will try to be more mindful of what is going on in my head.

Good.

It is a blessing to me to have you and all my guides looking out for my interests.

We are here for you.

November 16, 2016

I wasn't sure whether to put the next question to my guides in this book. It has to do with Verine's son, who had caused many problems, mostly fueled by his drug addiction, and I had to contact him because he was in Verine's will. I decided to go ahead with it because I wanted to demonstrate the guides' guidance on all matters.

Phillip, I could use your guidance in dealing with C. I know he's lying to me. I'm concerned with his criminal activities, and I'm not comfortable coping with him, especially after all he put his mother through. I could use my guides' wisdom and advice in this matter.

Okay, Michael. Here's the thing. Be open in a nonthreatening manner. Explain the situation and how you feel. Don't be harsh. Be polite but *firm that you are not happy with what is going on and you don't want to be involved with all the negativity. You'd appreciate it if he didn't contact you in the future and that the lawyer will get in touch with him when the time comes for disbursement of the property.*

This didn't quite work out that way. The lawyer had trouble getting in touch with him and preferred that I be the contact for him because he was aware of C's troubles. I managed to get it all worked out to everyone's satisfaction. C passed away three years later from several issues related to his lifestyle.

November 17, 2016

Yes. Let's speak of commitment. Commitment to what you are doing and need to do. It's important to be fully committed to your endeavors. Not wishy-washy. Spend the time to get things done. No procrastination. As you do what is required, it works on your overall plan. Your Universe expands as it would according to the plan that was projected before your incarnation. Procrastination sets the purpose back, and some of those setbacks can become lengthy. If you are thinking it, then get it done. You are not thinking it on a whim, and it could be us reminding you. Make your choice, and then commit your resources to it. Time, money, whatever. It was meant to be. And, remember there are no wrong choices. It all comes to fruition in the end.

Thank you, as always, for your guidance. I need to hear these words from you and sometimes need that kick in the backside.

We are here to help you. Here to remind you. And always here to love you.

November 18, 2016

Phillip, do I have any health issues about which I should be concerned? I'm losing weight, but I have been trying to lose weight.

However, I remember this happened to my dad; he suddenly lost weight and was diagnosed with inoperable cancer.

Yes. That is not what is occurring with you. Your health is excellent, though again, I would caution that it will benefit you greatly to increase your vegetable intake, along with fruits, and cut back on the red meat. Everything in moderation. You know what needs doing. It's okay to have a splurge day here and there but stay with what is good for you. The benefits are enormous. You can have a long and productive life, if you want, by eating healthy.

November 19, 2016

Yes. I would like to discuss C.

Okay.

I am aware of his situation. He has definite problems. But they are not your problems. He is a negative energy to you. Send out your "light" when you are with him. Keep your positive flow going. The more light, the brighter, the more it will deflect his energy, the less likely he will want to be around you.

Unless he can switch over and change, the likelihood of him not wanting to be in contact with you will be great. Stay your course. Again, be polite but firm. He controls nothing. All you can do is wish him "well." Send good thoughts his way. Don't let that negativity get to you. You are in control of yourself. You decide to be positive and happy. Anything dark or negative bounces off you. Put up that shield of positive and glowing light. You are love. You are light. You are the beacon.

November 20, 2016

Yes. I would like to speak on "meditation." The importance of meditation cannot be overstated, as you know. I am happy that you are so aware of the benefits of meditation. Calming the mind does so much for the physical body and the spiritual body.

You are where you are at through meditation.

There will come a time when the population of the planet becomes aware of this, and it will do so much for healing the planet of so many of the ills that it is experiencing from mankind. This is already starting now. More and more teachers are expounding the virtues of meditation, as are you.

We, here, cannot stress enough how important this ritual is for all of you.

You, yourself, know how much it helps you. Body, mind, and spirit. Spread the word whenever you can. Be a messenger. Extol the virtues. You have mentioned it in your book. Let's get that book and the word out there. Continue your writing. Start thinking of the next book. Believe it will happen. You have much to do.

Do you see me going to England any time soon?

We do see that happening. The resources will be there. It is your decision.

November 24, 2016

I'm not sure if I asked this before but are you speaking from your energy, or are you speaking as a combination of guides?

I speak as a collection of like-minded spirit guides that are here for you. Rather than have different guides all trying to communicate with you, it is easier to have one source of information. We are all of a similar vibration. The name "Phillip" was one that popped into your head when we were conversing. One that we placed there and one that we were comfortable with—we thought it was a good name. But you can think of us as an individual if you like. It may make it easier that way. You have many guides, which include animal guides and totems.

One day we should get a deeper explanation of this.

For sure. There is much that needs to be discussed. Many topics and lengthier explanations. For now, we have been keeping it short while you get used to the process. Again, as you become more intuitive and better with the process, then we will expand the discussions. This is why it is important for you to keep up with this every day. Get used to writing more and longer. Set aside more time.

Okay. I will try and set aside 10:00 a.m. for this. Sometimes other obligations get in the way.

That is understandable. Life goes on.

November 25, 2016

Is there something you wish to say? First, though, I'm kind of off-balance this morning, almost dizzy. Can you tell me what is causing this?

Michael, you need to take better care of yourself eating-wise. I've said this before. You have to be concerned about your blood sugar levels. This is a wake-up call. You don't want to wind up diabetic. Time to do something about it.

You're right, as always. I know you have been putting this thought through to me. I will get on it. Too much sugar. Thank you.

November 26, 2016

Yes. Hi, Michael. I would like to talk about your session (Merkabah) tomorrow. Be open to what is happening. Let yourself go with it. Relax and enjoy the process and the journey. Do not be fearful. It is safe, and we are with you. This can help you to open up and accept the premises.*

We will be there with you. Feel our presence. Feel our energy. Be open to the experience. It is all advantageous to you.

Okay, I will try to relax and let it happen.

Good. Feel the love. Be the love.

*This had been an ongoing issue with me. I had a hard time letting go completely. I seem to hold back just a bit from detaching all the way.

November 29, 2016.

Phillip, how do you think the workshop went on Sunday?

The workshops are useful to you. You get the benefit from all the energies in the room. You couldn't gain as much on your own. You are progressing. Keep up with the workshops and the homework you get from Claudette. I know you don't like the drive, but that's just the way it is. We will watch over you and be there to help.

Do you think I made a mistake in signing that car insurance form for C?

It wouldn't have hurt to call the lawyer, but it's done now. Don't worry about it. It will all turn out all right.

Thank you. I was worried that I had done the wrong thing afterward. Sometimes I can be impulsive. I could use help with that.

We are always here to guide you. You can always call on us.

I must remember that. There are definitely times when I can use your guidance.

We will give you a nudge. Look for it. Feel it. Go with your intuition. It is a strong influence.

November 30, 2016

Phillip, can you tell me how I can detach when I am meditating to let the flow of energy come through more easily? I'm having trouble letting go completely.

You just need to keep at it. It may be the hardest of all, that detaching. Go into your heart chakra. Feel the love. Relax, relax, and relax. Let that flow of energy come in. Feel a release from the body. It's one of those things that you have to constantly work on. Eventually, it will become easier, and you will do it without even being conscious that you are. Don't get frustrated. Everything will occur when it is supposed to. Let the Universe do its thing. Trust in the process. Be happy.

December 01, 2016

Good morning Michael. Yes, I would like to speak about your health again. It would be a good time for a physical checkup. There is a concern with your blood circulation. Your leg falling asleep, and some dizziness.

Okay. Is there something I can do to remedy that?

Yes, but talk to your doctor.

December 02, 2016

Hi, Phillip. I am seeing the doctor today. I still feel a little lightheaded. I don't know if this is because of my weight loss.

Your doctor should do a complete physical.

I thought you had said that my weight loss is not a concern, as I have been trying to lose weight.

You don't want to lose it too fast, though. It should be in moderation. Eat often but in small amounts.

Are there any major problems you can tell me about?

No. You may need more iron in your diet.

December 04, 2016

Yes. I am always ready to pass on some thoughts.

Let me speak on your vibration. It is slowly getting better and better. You can feel it much more readily now than a couple of years ago, even six months ago. This is good. Keep working on improving that.

I had a vivid dream last night. Simply put, it was that Verine's death could or should have been prevented. Even though she had health issues, this shouldn't have happened. There were mistakes made, and there is an awareness of that, and now I get the word "cover-up." Do you wish to comment on this?

I believe that more could have been done, and yes, there were problems that shouldn't have happened. I don't like to use the word "ineptitude," but there are issues. They are aware that it could or should have been prevented, and they are not sure how to go about closing this problem. You could say "cover-up."

How do I handle this issue?

I would let it be known that you are sensitive and not happy with the way this has gone and see how they respond.

Verine is in a good place, and she knew that her days were being counted down, but she would have liked that extra time, especially with you moving into her complex. She does appreciate all that you have done for her.

In the end, I told the doctor how I felt, stating that Verine's infections went unnoticed because she was heavily sedated. I believe, in the future, the doctors and staff will be more conscious of looking into this as a possibility. I left it at that. I didn't want to get embroiled in any controversy. "Cover-up" might have been a little harsh, but it did come through to me that way.

December 05, 2016

Yes. As you give, so shall you receive. What you put out there, you get back tenfold. Be generous in all your attributes. Give to others, whether it be monetary or even just a smile. And, don't be concerned if others don't reciprocate. That's on them, not on you. Give and expect nothing in return. It's the giving that defines who you are. Be all that you can, and, in doing so, you make the world a better place.

December 06, 2016

Yes. Be careful and alert today with the road conditions. We will watch over you during this travel. Just be vigilant and take it slow and steady.

Okay. Anything else?

Yes. It's time to get back to the painting and writing. You have the time now that a lot of the other stuff has been done. Time to let creativity flow again.

December 08, 2016

I would like to discuss Meditation again. We have said how important it can be, but there is so much more to it. Aside from the feeling of well-being, there is also the benefit of aligning all three of your presences—the body, mind, and spirit—to function together for your overall benefit. This brings you to a place which is like no other. A Oneness. God-like. And that is not a blasphemy but a part of who you are. You are a part of the whole, and though many might not believe it, you have within you all that you need to be that. You are the Universe. You are Source Energy. You just don't realize it or believe that that could be possible.

*When you quiet the mind in meditation, you can go deeply into that space where the Universe resides. It is within you. And that **is** you. Don't doubt it. You are an all-powerful being but barely tapping into the potential that lies within you because most of you can't imagine that something like that is there.*

So continue your meditation. Find that place where the Universe is waiting for you. Believe it. Trust it. Welcome it. Love it. Then you will have accomplished something. And the world will be a better place.

Wow. Thank you, Phillip.

All that has been said so far, especially after that, can leave no doubt at all in my mind that this is Higher Guidance. Beautiful words. Insightful teaching.

December 12, 2016

Yes. As I mentioned previously, it is time to get back to painting. Set up your schedule. Get into the habit of painting every day, if possible. This is another thing that you have to put on your agenda. You don't realize it, but it is important to you. It is important to who you are. Don't let it slide. Get on with it.

We've mentioned "creativity" before. This is you creating. Once you get in the habit, then you will really start seeing the improvement, and you will begin to miss it if you aren't doing it.

December 13, 2016

Yes. I would like to talk on your Christmas. It may seem lonely for you, but there are many who love you. Don't fret. We are here for you. Enjoy the season. Think of the many good things that are a part of you. Really, it is a holiday for the children, and you have family both here and there that care about you.

Thank you, Phillip. I'm okay with it all.

December 15, 2016

Yes. You know that this is not in your best interest.

(Speaking about my occasional cigar use.)

But I don't inhale, and I get such a nice relaxation from it. I enjoy it and only do it down at Birch Bay.

Yes, I realize that, but there is still an element of harm in this. We are here for your well-being, body, mind, and spirit. We want you to succeed.

Man, that kind of bums me out. It's too bad when you must give up everything that brings you some pleasure.

We understand. We are simply pointing out what can cause problems. We are here for your guidance along all lines, and it would be neglectful of us if we didn't point out all possibilities.

I appreciate that, Phillip, and will take it under advisement. I will try and cut back and maybe even quit. But it is peaceful for me to sit outside, look at nature, and enjoy a cigar.

We understand.

December 19, 2016

Let's talk about Birch Bay. It is a good place for you. You find your inner self there. It relaxes you and gives you a sense of peace. There is a "vortex" there, which makes it easier to connect to spirit. You have had some wonderful meditations there and some interesting experiences. You do love Nature, and you get to experience that much more so there.

Verine says "hello" and "thank you" for all that you are doing for her (working with the lawyer on her will). She is sorry she couldn't have been around a little longer now that you are there (I moved into a suite in her complex just before she passed), *but she is grateful for all the wonderful family and friends that are here. She says you were right in much that you had told her, and it was an easy transition. She is so happy to be with Lisa* (her daughter) *again and Toby* (our dog), *who was very excited to see her. Her mom, dad, and Mark* (her brother) *say "hello," and they are very proud of you and thankful for all that you have done, as is your family.*

There are many good days ahead for you. Enjoy your life and all that the Universe brings to you. It is filled with abundance and the Universe wants you to have it and be happy. Have a great Christmas, and look forward to all the wonderful things that are waiting for you in the New Year.

December 22, 2016

Phillip, I just thought I would ask you to help me remember the words for Verine's inurnment. Help me do a good job.

Absolutely, Michael.

Will Verine be there or know what's happening?

For sure. She will be watching and grateful for this, as will her family and friends.

December 23, 2016

Yes. Very good job on Verine's inurnment. The emotion only added to it. It was right. Verine was very happy and thanks all of you for your efforts. Now it is time to get back to you. It is important to stay with what you are or should be doing. (There was quite a bit of snow on the ground the day of her internment. It was a small group of family and close friends. Her wishes were to have her ashes placed in with her father's, as her brother's had been placed with the mom. I gave the eulogy and was fine until I got a little ways in and looked at those around who loved her and started choking up. I did get through it all right.)

I want to get into more profound discussions on the things people are interested in.

Yes, we can do that. Be prepared for more.

Because I am thinking of another book, I would like it to be longer and have better coverage of different topics.

Absolutely. It is in the works to be done.

I still have administrative stuff to do with Verine's estate, but I will work on getting into a routine again.

Good.

December 25, 2016

Yes, Michael. Merry Christmas from all of us.

Thank you.

You are getting close to a new year, and it is time to make this coming one a very productive one in everything that you do. Creatively, Spiritually, and Physically. This will be a good year for you. There will be a lot going on. There's the possibility of travel and new discoveries for you. Open yourself up to all of these exciting occurrences.

December 28, 2016

Keep doing what you are doing. Your cold will go away. (I rarely get colds and can't remember the last time I had the flu.)

Also, treat every day as a holiday, not just at certain days of the year. You need to have that festive feeling all the time, and then you will notice good things happening.

Remember, it is that good-feeling emotion that increases your vibration and increasing your vibration gets you into the place of manifestation. Every day is Christmas, or whatever your favorite holiday may be. Then watch your life change.

December 30, 2016

Yes. Go for a walk. You like walking, and it is important for you to get out, plus the exercise is good for you, not to mention the fresh air. This is something else that you can get into the habit of doing, weather permitting. You have an abundance of fine places for walking now.

Just start compartmentalizing your time for diverse activities. Try to cut back on your TV watching.

Good advice, as always, Phillip. I do like to walk and will be doing more of that now that I am here. Thank you.

2017

January 01, 2017

Well, Phillip, here we are in a new year. Is there anything you wish to say?

Yes, Michael. A new year, and now it is the time to consider setting up your schedule for the different activities you are to be doing. Painting, writing, walking, eating properly, less TV. You should consider three days a week for a good walk. More fruits and veggies.

Okay. What about 2017?

It is a good year for you. You can progress in many areas. Improve your sensitivity greatly. There are a number of things in the works for you. Don't waver in your resolve. Stick to your guns, as they say. Stick to the plan. There are numerous good days ahead, starting almost immediately. Look for the signs. Be aware. Open up to the possibilities. Fear not. Let the energy flow.

January 02, 2017

I am not here to berate you or tell you that you are wrong. I am here to guide you. You have free will and can do what you want. If you ask for my advice or guidance, I will provide it. I will tell you what will work best for you on any given item. You can follow my advice or not. That doesn't mean I am displeased or upset with you. We cannot live your life for you. The decisions you make have consequences. We love you and are here to help in every way possible. You know that there are many roads to get where you are going. We are here to guide you along the roads that benefit you, that make the journey more fun, and keep you on your path. The reason you are here.

Thank you, Phillip. I am always grateful to you and my guides and angels for all you do for me. I love you all.

January 04, 2017

Yes, Michael. Can you feel our presence?

I am getting an intense tingling in my forehead.

We want you to start feeling us more, along with hearing us. We want you to tap into your sense.

Okay.

If you think you are feeling us but aren't sure, then ask for our response. We have to get into this two-way communication. You have been trying it occasionally; now we need you to do it more.

All right. I will try to remember to do it more often.

Good. It is time now to start moving forward and expanding your abilities and moving up in the process.

Right.

January 09, 2017

Yes. Let's talk about increasing the length of these communications. It is time for us to start discussing different topics in more detail.

Okay, I'm ready for that.

Let's talk about the soul. This magnificent part of "All That Is" and that which is a part of you.

All your lives add to the experience of your soul and, therefore, the All That Is. Through you, God gets to experience all these wonders that make up every living thing. I should say everything, which means the rocks, the waters, the earth, the stars, the planets—the All.

So, you may feel small in the enormity of it all, but you are just as important to the whole. Your lives, your escapades, all add to the flavor of the overall dish. Without you and your soul, it would be incomplete.

Know that your day-to-day existence and all the little parts of your day are what make up who you are, and who you are is important to the whole, just as everyone is.

There isn't anything or anyone who is more important than another. Remember this when it comes to judging others. Their existence may not seem like much, but they are a part of the whole and may live many different lives. This particular existence may be for a reason for them or us. Judge not. God does not judge. God loves all. Something to keep in mind. It is easy to criticize. Try to catch yourself, and a lot of this has to do with the way you were brought up from family and friends. Be the example. Be the change. Be the glorious soul you are meant to be. Then will you be a Master.

When I finished typing this, I got chills. This had been the best message yet. What wonderful words. What truth. How quick we are to judge someone because of some action or word that doesn't agree with our philosophy or way of living. I am getting better at catching myself but still occasionally fail when someone, say, cuts me off in traffic, and I call them an asshole. I know nothing about that person or what is going on in their day, but I am quick to judge. Now, having said that, maybe they are just an asshole, but it isn't for me to say. I think this is one of the hardest guidelines to adhere to, and, as Phillip expressed, it has a lot to do with how we were raised and probably more so with the people we associated with.

January 11, 2017

How committed are you to those things you should be doing?

Well, I thought I was fairly committed to that, but I need to have a life too. It's okay to do those things, but can't I relax a bit, or do they all have to be done constantly?

Definitely, you can take it easy, but don't waste time when you are really doing nothing, and you could be doing something positive.

Okay.

And age is just a number. You are in good health, and you are getting yourself in better physical condition. There isn't anything you can't accomplish, but you have to put your mind in it and keep your projects in focus.

Okay.

You are here to accomplish certain goals. We don't want to see you fall by the wayside and not meet the standards you set for this physical incarnation.

Okay. Keep on me if I start slipping, and thank you, as always, for your guidance.

January 12, 2017

Yes, Michael. You have the ability to contact those who have passed—family and friends. It is something you have to practice. You can do it as we are, writing what comes through. The more you practice, the better and easier it will get. Eventually, you will be able to hear the contact without writing. So, something else for you to practice and work on.

January 15, 2017

I am glad you are pursuing your art again. Keep doing it. It is a part of who you are.

Does Mom help out or see me doing this art?*

Yes. She is very proud of how far you have come. Try and feel her presence while you are painting. She is there to help you and partake in some of what you are doing. She enjoys watching you while you are painting and will provide inspiration for you.

*My mother loved painting and was a wonderful artist but couldn't get into it until everyone in the family had grown up and left home.

I had my grandkids over one rainy day and brought out some cheap paints and brushes I had bought to keep them busy. They said, "Come on, Pampa, you paint too." So, I sat down and joined them in the painting. After they left, I started playing around a little more and found I enjoyed it. I had never considered art a hobby or something I might be interested in. While I was talking to my mom on the phone not long after, I mentioned this, and, of course, she got very excited. The next time I visited her, she gave me some extra paints and brushes and a couple of books she had on watercolor painting, her preferred medium. That's how it all started for me. I read several books on the subject, bought how-to videos, and was hooked. That was in 2004, and I have been painting ever since.

It's nice to know that she is watching me paint and is there for inspiration. She was very talented, and I know I must have inherited some of that from her.

January 16, 2017

Mom, is that you?

Yes, son, Michael. I am thrilled to see you doing this. It is so nice to be able to communicate with you. I am so happy for you. Everything here is so wonderful. You can't even imagine.

Have you seen Verine?

Absolutely. We were all here for her when she arrived. It was a shock for her at first, but it was an easy transition. She is still getting to see everyone, all her family and friends. She is so proud of you. You helped her so much, and it was very much how you had told her about transitioning from one place to the next. For that, she is grateful. Live your life to the fullest. I am with you when you paint. Please keep doing that. You are getting so good at it. I couldn't be prouder of you. Dad is here and says hello.

Maybe I will try him next time.

He looks forward to that. We all love you so much. Be well. Be happy. There are many good days ahead for you. We are glad you have connected with Kay and Kathleen (cousins). I hope you get to visit with them. And please, get to England. This can happen.

I love you, Mom, and all my family and friends. Have you met John and Katie?

Oh, yes. They are beautiful and love you so much. They are with you often.

Wonderful. I love them so much, and I am grateful for their presence, even if I don't say it aloud. I know they are around. I will talk to them soon.

Be well, son.

January 17, 2017

Yes, Laundry.

Laundry?

Yes. It is one of those household chores that need to be done every so often. Just like the others you have—cleaning, vacuuming, etc. These are mundane tasks that require your time and effort. It is a part of your physical existence. All these things are a part of your experience, even if it doesn't seem like much. It may seem trivial, but it is not. All these little experiences make up who you are.

It seems a little funny, but I understand what you are getting at.

Enjoy all that is going on, including the little things that you take for granted. When you can love the whole process, then you are moving towards "Mastery."

Okay. Got it. You may have to remind me of this every so often.

Of course. It doesn't happen just like that. You have to be conscious and aware.

January 18, 2017

Dad, are you there?

I am here, son, and excited to be able to communicate with you directly.

Me too. I can feel your presence.

Good.

So how are you doing?

Everything here is amazing. I am helping out with those who pass quickly and may be unsure of what has taken place. It is all very rewarding when you can help others. There is tremendous love here for everyone and everything.

Wonderful.

I am so very proud of you, son. You have come such a long way and are so far ahead of anything I could have imagined.

I am very grateful for your presence and everything you and my family and friends do for me.

We want the best for you, and you can do it all. Never waver in your decisions.

Is there anything else you wish to say?

Just keep up with what you are doing. We will talk more, and it will be easier. We are all here for you.

Thank you, Dad. I love you.

Love you too, son. Always.

January 20, 2017

Phillip, yesterday I had lunch with K.* He had some questions that I hope you will address. The most important was how he could advance himself spiritually. And then he had some family concerns.

Okay, Michael. K. needs to find someone who can help him energy-wise. One of the ways that he can try on his own is through paper and pen. Placing the pen on the paper and just doing little circles. He has to free his mind. He has to detach. Very important. When thoughts interrupt, write down the thought, then go back to the circle. He has to put aside twenty minutes a day for this. It won't occur overnight, which is why he needs to find someone he can work with to increase that energy flow.

He knows deep inside that he should be channeling. This is something he has set for himself. To ignore it is a waste and a loss to those he could be helping. The greatest gift anyone can give is to be of service to others. If that is who he is, and it is, then not to do it is a disservice to himself and others.

As for family, each must live their own life. Each has their own journey. You cannot live another's life. That is their journey. You have your own agenda. You need to love yourself first, even though that may seem selfish. Then give your love and wishes for well-being to others. As you send this love their way, then notice the changes.

Also, be on the lookout for inspiration. Little signs that may show up. It could be words from a song or words on a billboard. Your angels and guides are there for you. Ask for their help every day, and then look for those signs. They want you to succeed and will do all within their power to see that happen.

Okay, Phillip. Thank you. Can we come back to this again tomorrow?

Of course. There is more to be said.

*K is a friend who is very interested and well-read in spirituality, but he is hesitant to move it forward mostly because his family is not comfortable with that philosophy.

January 21, 2017

I would like to continue with the questions from yesterday for K.

Okay. You had a glimpse of something during your meditation. That is, when K. is trying his meditation, by writing down his thoughts, he can then let them go, knowing he can come back to them later.

Yes, I got that.

Also, he should know that he can get help from his guides. He has to be open to the possibilities and accept what is coming through to him, make notes, and, just like you have been doing, Michael, he should start journaling, writing down whatever comes into his head, even if it doesn't make sense. As in your case, the more he does this, the better he will get at it, and the better are his chances at opening the doorway to other possibilities like his channeling.

Very good. Thank you as always, Phillip. I want to pass along as much information as possible to K.

We can pass along some guidance; as always, it is up to the individual. Free choice.

January 22, 2017

Is there anything you would like to add to K before I email him?

I don't think so. Pass on these words and see if there is any kind of response. See if he feels this helps. See if this resonates with him.

He knows that he needs to do something. Let's see if he follows through.

January 25, 2017

Phillip, K is very grateful for your guidance.

He is most welcome. I hope he gets what he wants and follows the guidelines.

Is there anything you would like to say?

Yes. Continue to read over past writings. It confirms a lot for you and will help the process.

January 26, 2017

Is there something you wish to speak about today? Right off the bat, I got the subject "fear."

Yes. Fear not. You know there is more than just the physical. You know you are so much more than this physical body. You know you have lived many lives. So, what is there to fear? Fear is a negative energy and accomplishes nothing good for you. Release that emotion. In many cases, your fear is ill-founded, and what you fear doesn't materialize, and, if it does, it is usually less than what you imagined, and you say, "What was I so worried about?"

Give whatever you fear over to the "angels" to deal with and free yourself from the negativity that brings you down, lowering your energy. Tell yourself, "I have nothing to fear. What's the worst that can happen?" and let it go. Troubles can lead to greater things and can strengthen you. Stay positive and keep happy. Good things are waiting for you. Look forward to them arriving and know that they are coming. You are above such lower emotions.

January 27, 2017

Yes. Just as physical exercise is important, so is rest. Your body needs to revitalize itself. The cells need to restore. The brain needs some downtime from all the constant activity. Resting promotes self-healing, another reason why meditating is important. A lot is going on while you are sleeping or quiet.

January 27, 2017

(Morning meditation)

I am getting "Nanny." Is that you, Nanny?

Yes. How wonderful to speak with you in person. I am so happy to be here with you. You make me so proud. I love you so much. All your family is so proud of you and all that you are doing. We are here for you.

I love you, Nanny.

Thank you, grandson. I loved the time we had together. You were such a wonderful baby—the best ever and such an adventurous boy. You have come such a long way, and you still have much to do.

Thank you, Nanny. I loved having you around when I was young. I wished you could have stayed longer.

It's just the way it presented itself. Everything happens for a reason.

I am glad you are always there for me. We will talk some more.

Yes. Love you always.

Thank you. I love you too.

January 30, 2017

Yes. Kryon.* I know it would be a good idea for you to attend that meeting in March. There will be much energy there which will benefit you. You will get a lot out of that, much more than just reading the book.

Okay. I will set something up.

*Kryon is an entity channeled by Lee Carroll. Lee Carroll is an American channeller, speaker, and author. I had read some of Lee Carroll's books, and he was coming to a nearby town for a weekend forum. I thought I would like to attend and asked Phillip his thoughts.

> He describes Kryon as an angelic loving entity from the Source (or "Central Sun") who has been with the Earth "since the beginning" and belongs to the same "Family" of Archangel Michael. He claims the information he publishes, both printed and online, is intended to help humans "ascend to a higher vibrational level," which, according to his books, is synonymous with overall mental, spiritual and physical evolution. – *Wikipedia*

You can learn a lot more about Kryon by going to *Kryon.com*.

January 30, 2017

(Morning meditation)

Toby and Buster, two of my dogs who had passed many years apart, had come through.

Hi, father. We will call you "father," for that is the way you feel to us. We are so happy to have this joining with you.

I miss you both.

We are around here and there. We look forward to when we are together again. Stay well. We are both very happy and enjoy where we are and all the wonderful energies here. We are good friends and enjoy a good run together and exploring. Bye for now.

January 31, 2017

Yes. Illumination. The Light within. You have this Light within you. The Universe (God) beats, glows, vibrates in your being. It is part of you. It is part of the All. You can share this Light. You can broadcast this Light to the world and, by doing so, make the world a better place, making those around you better. So use that Light whenever you can. It is also a part of who you are. A Light Worker. Yes, as are many who are here to take the planet in its next step forward. A new era is upon everyone. Many have incarnated just for this reason. Change is happening, and it is for the better. So remember, use your Light for the betterment of all.

February 03, 2017

Yes. Do everything in moderation. It is not recommended to overdo anything that can become harmful to you. This especially applies to eating and your cigar smoking. Also, as you start aging, it is even more important to do things in moderation. It is okay for your physical activities, walking, exercising, but you don't need to go to extremes.

February 06, 2017

I had a little more going on with the Merkabah today. Usually, not much happens. Does this mean it's getting better? I know I ask for help with it.

Yes. Keep doing it. You will start to experience more and even get to traveling. Like everything you do, the more you practice, the more improved you will get, and the more improved you get, the bigger help it is to you energy-wise for the rest of your vibrational matter.

Okay. I will keep at it.

Yes. Good. You are starting to feel more vibrations, and you are getting there. We are here for you, as you know, and we see improvement.

February 08, 2017

Hi, Phillip. I had a very intense feeling this morning when I did the Merkabah and when I was doing my premeditation routine before that. Can you explain this, please?

Hi, Michael. Yes. It means you are progressing. You are getting comfortable with the process, and now you are at a place where different occurrences will start to happen. Good for you. You are at a place where it will be easier to make transitions, to get in touch with spirit, and to experience other dimensions. This is very exciting. We are proud of where you have come from.

That is exciting news. I am looking forward to this exploration.

Yes. A good way to look at it. New sensations. New vibrations. New energies.

Since the Merkabah started coming up more often in some of my questions with my guides, I wanted to give you a deeper explanation of it.

> Merkabah, also spelled Merkaba, is the divine light vehicle allegedly used by ascended masters to connect with and reach those in tune with the higher realms. "Mer" means Light. "Ka" means Spirit. "Ba" means Body. Mer-Ka-Ba means the spirit/body surrounded by counter-rotating fields of light (wheels within wheels), spirals of energy as in DNA, which transport spirit/body from one dimension to another. –crystalinks.com

> *The MerKaBa is a spinning structure of light similar to the chakras. It is similar in that when spinning properly it works as an inter-dimensional gateway—kind of a Star Gate—so that higher consciousness may incarnate into the physical body.* –spiritualhealing-now.com

Claudette formed a Merkabah group where we go through the Merkabah meditation together with a sequence of breaths, finger movements, and visualizations. Our circle is often joined by Archangels, Ascended Masters, and other Highly Evolved Beings interested in helping us raise our vibration and evolve the planet. The Merkabah is a vehicle that can transport our spiritual self anywhere.

February 10, 2017

Is there something you wish to say? But first, I just thought of something. As I was about to start my meditation, I sensed my friend Bill* coming through to say hello. Was this true?

Yes. That was your friend connecting with you. Very Good.

I told him I would try and meet with him later.

Yes. You can do that. As I've stated, the more that you do this connecting with us, the more effective you will become.

Right. I will keep working on that.

Not working. Enjoying.

Yes. Sorry. I agree; it is not work.

Good. You are coming along.

What do you see with this Kryon meeting?

There will be excellent energy there for you to feed off. All these endeavors help you to get where you need to be. You are starting to communicate a little without the writing. That is good.

I am feeling more energy/vibrations lately.

Yes. That is a sign that you are getting stronger.

*Bill was a good friend when I was in my early teens living back east. We were a group of close buddies, and we had many adventures together. The early sixties were a different time. We had great music and dancing, outdoor rinks in the winter, swimming in the summer, and always on the lookout for girls, lol, with little time for TV.

February 10, 2017

(Morning meditation)

Hi, Bill. Are you there?

Yes. Here, Mike. Wonderful to communicate with you. It's been a long time.

Yes. Has it ever. How are you?

Excellent. I've been here a while. Longer in your time. Not so long here.

How was your journey over?

It was okay. I wasn't sure what to be expecting. I had help, and there were energies here to meet me and help me with the transformation.

I'm sorry. I didn't think of you at the time in that session. I'm gathering that was you.*

Yes. I wish we had communicated then. Doesn't matter. This is good.

How was your life?

Interesting, to be sure. Lots of ups and downs. I experienced all that I needed. It all worked out the way it was meant to, for me and others.

I am here to help you in any way I can if you need anything. I can add my energy to assist you.

Thank you so much, Bill. It makes me nostalgic for those good old days we had together.

Yes. They were great. What a wonderful time and a good bunch of guys. Good times.

I appreciate this, and I'm glad we could connect. Thanks for being there for me. I can use all the help I can get.

You are doing great. Keep at it. You have lots of interesting things to come.

Thanks, Bill. I send you my love and gratitude.

And I, you. Be well.

*In one of my sessions with Claudette, several words came through: William, married, Las Vegas, and Elvis. At the time, I couldn't put it all together, but a few days later, I thought of Bill and that it could have possibly been him. I had heard that he had passed.

February 14, 2017

Yes. Valentine's Day. So love. There is much to be said about relationships, especially between two people in love. Obviously, it is a give-and-take proposition. One must let the other be who they are. It is not one's job to try and change the other into what they think that person should be. For it to work well, it involves loving that person with all their quirks and personality and to be responded in kind.

It was foretold that I would meet and marry someone. That was a while ago. Do you still see that happening?

Absolutely. You know there were circumstances that hindered that development. You were told a few times that it was necessary to cut the binds with another. You didn't do that, so it stopped the possibility of anything in that regard progressing. Now that the other scenario has changed, the possibility is there again and should happen. Your choices dictate what occurs in your life. You know that.

Yes, I do, and I know that is why everything happened the way it did.

One of the things Claudette told me was that she saw me getting married again. However, before that happened, I would have to cut my ties with Verine. Even though Verine and I had been separated for several years, we were still married. I had to divorce Verine, which I was hesitant to do for reasons I'm still not sure about. We were on excellent terms, more like very good friends, and spoke to each other often. Whether I thought it might hurt her feelings, I don't know. After Verine passed away, it opened the door again for me to meet that special person. This is what Phillip was talking about.

February 16, 2017

Yes. I would like to talk about "Romance." Romance doesn't just have to be about two people. You can have romance with many things. You can have a relationship with Nature.

One automatically assumes "people" when you speak of romance, so I was checking that it was you and not me again.

(The word "romance" popped into my head, and I was thinking that it was merely me thinking that.)

You have to trust, Michael. You are in communication with spirit. You are still having doubts. You are not making this up.

Sorry. Yes, I know.

Okay, back to "Romance." It is the "love," the excitement of something or someone, usually a person, but many times a place, as in a romantic getaway but not with another person. A place that inspires, that you have a love for, and an excitement to be there. You have had such places; Heffley Creek (Interior Lake in B.C.), the west coast of the Island (Vancouver Island), Birch Bay, when you were younger, Lac La Peche (Gatineau, Quebec). There was a romance with being in these locations. There was a special feeling when you were there—an emotional attachment. There is romance in your life even though you are associating this word with a person. As always, be thankful for another blessing that you have. Gratitude is a strong emotion that can help you in many ways. Be thankful for all that you have and all that is coming your way. And don't doubt.

February 18, 2017

Phillip, sometimes I think I am catching slight movements out of the corner of my eye, just for a split second. Is that anything, or just my imagination?

You are catching spirit energy. It could be angels or a guide. It is an energy that is making itself known that you may become aware of. This is another stage of your progression. Little bit by little bit. Tiny steps. Just as you are feeling energies around you at times. There is always a presence there. Don't be concerned about embarrassing moments. (Pheww!). Spirit isn't concerned with your human characteristics. It is aware of such necessities. Spirit is there for your "awakening," and, as always, it is there for your benefit.

February 19, 2017

Yes. I would like to talk about Meditation again. You need to find that place that really lets you go, deeper, deeper, where there are no thoughts interrupting. Where the essence (soul) can arrive. You are still holding an attachment to the physical place where you are at.

You have to let go of this last bit of attachment. Let spirit in. Let spirit take over for you to experience so much more. There may be some fear of letting go to this extent. You can do it. This is the last step for you to accomplish, to move into these many realms, these other dimensions. It is the hardest but will be the most rewarding. You have angels and guides to protect you, who are always with you. They won't let anything happen to you. Like the movie says, "Let the Force be with you." This will open all the doorways to what you have been seeking.

Okay. Good. Thank you, Phillip. Is there something I can do to help me let go?

Just trust in the process. Trust in your guides. Trust. Trust. Trust.

February 21, 2017

Last night while I was outside, one of the lights started flickering. Was that someone trying to get my attention?*

Yes, it was John and Katie saying hello.

I thought it might be. I am grateful for them doing that and grateful for their presence.

They were very happy that you acknowledged them and were glad to be with you.

*Okay, I know what you're thinking, it was just a light flickering, and they do that all the time. Let me describe this a little further. There were four solar lights in a row. The second from the right started flickering. Then it went off completely, and I thought they must be cheap solar lights. Then it started flickering again. That's when I thought it might be someone trying to get my attention, so I said aloud, "Is that you, John and Katie?" The light went out again. I started talking to them, thanking them for visiting me. When I stopped talking with them, the light came back on and stayed on.

It never went out or flickered again. I knew it was them, but I still wanted to confirm it with Phillip.

I have another Merkabah session with Claudette on Sunday.

Yes. Good. Again, all these sessions are helping you. The combined energies in the room will strengthen you, and you get to see others and their gifts. It's another confirmation for you of what you can do.

February 24, 2017

You've got the trailer on your mind, Michael.

Yes.

Don't be concerned with what others think or say. You know in your heart what is right. Others will think what they want. That is for them.

Right.

Remember, worry serves no one. Don't succumb to it. Don't let your imagination take over.

February 25, 2017

Yes, Michael. I would talk about the Merkabah. You are starting to get there. As always, the more you do it, the better will the experience be. Keep at it. It will come.

Maybe you can address some other subjects a little deeper. I am prepared to write longer.

Okay. We can do that. Is there something you would like to start with?

No. I will let you pick something, and we can go with it. How about we begin on Monday?

That is a good plan. We will do that then.

February 26, 2017

Yes. I would speak on letting go. You are getting into a deeper trance state, but you must also be conscious. You don't want to get to a sleep state. You need to be in that dream state. If you go too deep, try and get yourself aware, and then go just that bit deeper. It's fine-tuning the state. It's a balancing act. Something for you to work on. You are getting there, and you will find that place, and then it will get easier to accomplish.

February 28, 2017

Yes. I would like to discuss Meditation. I know we have spoken on this before, but it is an important topic, and there is a lot to be said on it.

Meditation is freeing the mind and body. You have a body, a mind, and a soul. It is about giving over to the soul. When you relax the body and mind, you are letting the soul free. You are letting the soul dance. And when you let the soul dance, good things happen. The body is suddenly able to start healing itself, getting back to where it wants to be. The mind is suddenly open to many possibilities. It is not tied down to the normal quantities of what usually occupies it with the regular day-to-day occurrences from the past, the future, or at the moment. This can lead to opening up to new dimensions, new Universes to explore. All of this doesn't happen overnight. It takes practice, dedication, and a willingness to let go. You want the body totally relaxed and the mind in a deeper state of being. You can do this as you do, Michael, by starting out saying to yourself, "Deeper, deeper, deeper, more relaxed" and so forth. You want to feel your body relaxing and growing heavier—all your muscles unwinding. You want to empty your mind of those normal daily thoughts, which is probably the hardest thing to do. The best and easiest way to do this is to concentrate on your breathing.

Breathing is a big part of meditation. You want to try and slow down your breathing. Start with a few deep breaths, usually in through the nose and out through the mouth. You want those breaths to expand your lungs and stomach (diaphragm). Then breathe normally through your nose but slowing down, still bigger breaths. Now when those thoughts creep in, you can acknowledge them and let them go. Concentrate on your breaths. In and out. In and out. Again, when those thoughts creep in, which they will do, think "in and out" (breaths). This takes lots of practice. You will get better at it and find it easier as you do this. Eventually, you want to get to that dream state. The body is completely relaxed, as is the mind. Your mind is in a place where it is in limbo, between wakefulness and sleep. It is that state just before sleep, where you are almost asleep, but you still have that awareness of your state. It is here where the soul has the freedom to take you on new adventures. You have heard of "out of body experiences?" It is in this state where this can happen. All of you have these experiences while you are sleeping. You just don't remember them, or you have a dream that seems very vivid, which you do remember. Oftentimes that is an OBE. You just don't know it as that. Body and mind are completely at rest, and the soul is dancing, moving somewhere else. The soul is always tied to the body. Sometimes you awaken with a start, like a thump. This can be the soul returning in a hurry and coming back too fast.

We will continue this discussion again.

March 02, 2017

Hi, Phillip. What do you see happening with Claudette's interest in a book and my role?*

I see you doing the actual writing, with her telling her story and you putting it on paper.

*Claudette expressed an interest in doing a book and telling her story. I told her I would help in any way I could.

Okay, thanks. Is there anything you would like to pass on today?

Yes. I am your Higher Guidance, as you were wondering (as opposed to Higher Self—the two are separate). There are many guides here to help you in all aspects of your physical existence on the planet. I am here for that and to help you with your development to a higher state of being, to fulfilling your reason for coming here—to fulfill your contract, to help you expand and experience all that you need.

Yes, I was wondering about that.

You may call on your many guides for assistance in everyday dealings like your art, music, or anything else. There are guides to help you with it all. There are guides for anything you can think of.

March 03, 2017

Have you any thoughts with regards to the meeting with Claudette yesterday?

I think it went very well, and you are both on the same page. I see this getting done and being very successful. I see a lot coming out of this joint venture for you both. It is something that both of you will have to work at. It will be beneficial.

You should continue to order books (my first book), so you always have a few on hand.

March 07, 2017

Yes. I would like to talk to you about our connection. I would like to see this speed up a bit. Patience is always a key, but I feel maybe there is a bit of a lull now, like it is stuck in one place. I would like to see it start moving forward more. We need a jump start. We need more vibration, more energy.

Okay. How do we do that?

Again, we have to let go and open up to spirit. See spirit taking over in a good way. Spirit is here for you as always, and we are here to help.

Do not fear that we are taking over your life. No. We are simply trying to lift you towards a more comprehensive state of being with spirit. When you are meditating, feel the energy inside you. This is loving energy. Let it in. Let it take you. Then you will be in a place where you will hear and see.

I feel you now.

Yes. Confirmation. You can do this. It is time to move forward with your experiences.

Okay. Good. I will work on that.

March 10, 2017

Hi, Michael. I am excited to think that you could go to Scotland for the ISF (International Spiritualist Federation) convention. This would be a wonderful opportunity for you for many reasons. The energy there would be a big boost to you. Seeing others from around the world with these many gifts and sensitivities and the different areas they work in. Also, there would be the opportunity afterward to visit with relatives and see where you are from—your ancestry. This is high up there on your to-do list.

I am also excited about doing this. It would be very interesting.

Claudette mentioned that it would be a good idea for me to join the ISF, which I did. They hold a congress every year in different countries where members come from all over the world for a week. Members get to observe and partake in a variety of spiritual enterprises.

March 15, 2017

Infatuation. Don't let your imagination go so far as to take away from reality. There is the importance of being sensible when it comes to finding that special person. Yes, anything is possible and can happen, but it is also prudent to be realistic. Keep an open mind to the possibility that it can happen, but you should be considering within realistic boundaries. You are in good physical condition, but don't go way out of normal expectations. Be happy knowing that the right person is there for you and will show up. Keep an open mind.

March 20, 2017

Hi, Phillip. There seems to be much more in the works for Claudette than just this book, which is what came through to her in today's session.*

Yes. There is a lot more to this collaboration. As she stated, it's on a need-to-know basis, and you are not ready yet. All will become apparent at the right time. It is a very interesting situation. You have the possibility to do some great things. You just have to get to that level. I know you are trying, and we, of course, are there to help. It will happen. Be patient and continue with your lessons, continue to open up, work on letting go, and see things begin to change for you. Do not worry about age or time. There is all that is needed. Be expectant. Be grateful. Be ready, and always be happy.

I believe I am sensing you now.

You are indeed.

I look forward to what is coming. I see it as an adventure.

That is a wonderful way to look at it, for that is what it will be.

*Claudette and I had set up Skype sessions every two weeks to start working on a book. It consisted of me asking her questions and letting her run with it. She has vast knowledge and infinite experiences regarding spirit and spiritual matters. She said she felt there was a reason the two of us had come together on this project.

March 23, 2017

Hi, Phillip. I've got my 70th birthday on Monday. Is there anything you would like to say about that, I mean any effects you would like to talk about?

Hi, Michael. Only that it is just a number. It is nothing to dwell on. It gives a timeline for your physical being, but no more. It is up to you to decide how you want to be. You have the power to be whatever you want, health-wise, how you look, how you feel. Nothing more than a number. You have many years ahead of you, if you wish, in which you can accomplish a lot. It is your decision as always.

I am curious about something, and I don't know if you can answer it. Would Claudette's guides be interested in adding something to the book? I don't know if you are in a position to answer something like that.

Yes, that is something you would have to discuss with her. We are here for you, and her guides are there for her. It is an interesting thought, though.

I would be interested in doing a book with you at some point.

That can happen.

March 25, 2017

Hi, Phillip. I have the Merkabah class tomorrow.

Very good. We will be there with you. Let go and enjoy the experience.

Thank you. Do you know and can you tell me what Claudette was saying about my mother and me being a part of the Galactic Federation?*

Yes. I do know of it. You are a member of this Federation. Your mother took you there. You have to do as Claudette said and ask to be taken there when you meditate. There you will find your answers.

We will discuss this again when you have made this connection. We do not always give you answers to your questions right away, but only when the moment is right for you, when you get the most benefit from it.

Okay, I hope I can do that.

It will happen.

*Claudette said that my mother was part of a Galactic Body and that I also had some part in it, but I have no idea what that is or entails. I still need to find out more about this.

March 29, 2017

I would like to speak about your brow chakra. It is your dominant chakra, and it is responsible for your sensitivity. It is very strong in you, and you should continue to strengthen it. It is where your third eye is located, and this is something that will open for you, opening up many senses. Work on that and continue with your Merkabah. Don't be so concerned if you aren't experiencing as much as others. Your time will come. It is all unfolding as it should. Know that it will happen.

Be thankful in advance. We are proud of you and excited for what lies ahead.

April 04, 2017

Hi, Michael. Do not forget that when you are doing certain things, you can ask for assistance from your many guides here or other guides who will make themselves available for you, as in your art, for instance. There is nothing wrong in asking for some help when you are doing your art. This doesn't mean that a guide will take over, but merely help in the creative prospect and guiding you if you are experiencing some difficulty. All here are to help make life easier. You only need to ask, and we are there to provide assistance.

April 06, 2017

Hi, Michael. I would like to speak on family. Your family is very important to you. Don't worry about whether they believe the same way that you do. Each of them has to come to awareness in their own way and at their own time. That is not your concern. All you can do is send loving thoughts their way. You are all about yourself and how you are progressing – continuing with your studies, meditations, workshops, and focusing on happiness and love. Each has their own path.

April 10, 2017

Yes. You know you are surrounded by angels. Not only your Guardian Angels, who are there to watch over you but a vast number, an army of angels who are there to help you in all sorts of ways. They are singing your praises, sending you love, and helping in every way possible. I know you are always thanking them and remembering them, and that is a good way to show your love, and there is tremendous appreciation here for that. Call on them often. They will hear and are ready to step in and be of assistance.

I will. I am here in Birch Bay. This is a place that is important to me. I love being able to come here.

Yes. You have a definite bond with that place. It is your bond with Nature. The trees, flowers, and birds all keep you in a good mind.

April 11, 2017

Hi, Phillip. I was just thinking about some things for the book's introduction, and I had some really good thoughts. I am sure you and my guides gave me this information. I ask that you help me remember these thoughts so that I can get them down on paper later.

Hi, Michael. Yes. You felt our presence, and yes, it was us giving you some guidance. We will be there when you wish to put these thoughts down. It will be good stuff for you to use. Keep at it. It is coming along. We will continue to provide you with assistance in writing this book, along with the interesting thoughts and words that Claudette will provide.

April 14, 2017

Hi, Phillip. May I ask if you see anything happening soon as far as resources or sensitivity goes? I feel this will be a good year for me, with many possibilities. I don't want to squander them.

Hi, Michael. This is a good year for you. There is a lot that will be happening, moving you forward towards your goals, both spiritually and financially. Again, don't be impatient. All of this will happen, and happen when and as it is supposed to.

Thank you. I know I can get impatient. I think it's my personality. I like to see things taking place. I want to see progress.

It will be there. It will show. You have a lot going on. Take it day by day. Stay the course. Know that it is coming. Be happy in the knowledge. There are many great days ahead.

April 20, 2017

Hi, Phillip. I may need some inspiration when it comes to Monday's session with Claudette, asking for new material or new questions.

We can help with that. Look for something coming your way.

I know you are thinking about the loss of the trailer. Never give up on that dream. Don't admit defeat just yet. There is always time. As the saying goes, "It's never over until it's over." "Keep the faith, baby."

Haha. I will continue to hold out hope, and I will continue along my way working towards my goals.

That is the way. It is all there before you, waiting to manifest. Everything occurs when it is supposed to.

April 22, 2017

Yes. I would like to talk about the soul. The soul is a part of the Divine. You've read this before. Just as a drop of the ocean is a part of the Ocean. It is the Ocean and always will be. Your soul, which has all your experiences from all your lives imprinted upon it, expands the Universe. The Universe, or God, or Source, expands and lives through you and all the souls throughout Infinity. Every rock that you or anyone touches is like being touched by God.

You cannot take one drop of the ocean and say it is not the Ocean. You cannot take one soul and say it is not God or Source Energy. All of you are such. Stop killing yourselves.

When you hate, kill, love, help, belittle another, you are hating, killing, loving, helping, and belittling yourself. As you treat another, so do you treat yourself. Let your soul expand with Love. Nothing else matters.

May 1, 2017

Hi, Phillip. Since I've been doing the Merkabah, have I entered the embryo* stage? Most of the time, I'm not seeing or feeling anything.

You have entered it many times. Your sensitivities are just not refined to the point where you can enjoy the experience. As I have said, you have to keep at it. Be persistent, and it will happen.

I don't want to feel like I am holding the group back from their traveling goals.

You are not. You are actually an important part of the energy. Having a male in this group strengthens all of them and makes it better. Don't put yourself down. Feel empowered.

Is asking Master St. Germaine** for assistance something I should continue doing?

Absolutely. He is a strong Master and one that you would love to have in your corner. Continue to seek his guidance.

*There are several required steps when doing the Merkabah meditation. When one finishes doing the required steps, the person then enters the "golden embryo," which is the 13th Universe, the embryo of the Earth.

**Master St. Germaine is one of many Ascended Masters.

The following reference is taken from www.alphaimaging.co.nz/meet-the-ascended-masters:

An Ascended Master is a Being of Light who is not in body. An Ascended Master has had many lives in a physical body, and through these lives and their free will and hard work have raised their vibration and consciousness to such a state as to have cleared all their karma and dross from their chakras and bodies. The Ascended Master is not the past life person; it is not the lower-self person who ascended. In truth, the Ascended Master is the Higher Self of the person who strived to ascend.

They have all walked the Earth in many lifetimes, such as you. They have had lives of suffering, lives of illness, lives with children and families, and more. All that you have experienced, they have too. In this personal and human way, they stand before you, not as someone on a pedestal, but as someone who has walked in your shoes. They now stand beside you, helping and guiding you in your life and towards your ascension.

May 3, 2017

Yes, the importance of keeping up this dialogue. We should be doing this every day. Lately, it's been hit and miss.

Yes. I know you are right. I must make more of an effort.

Good.

I am working on getting myself in a place of "Love" and feeling it more when I do my meditation.

Excellent. That makes all the difference. It will help a lot in progressing you to feel and see what you have been hoping for. It is, after all, the greatest emotion, and the more you can stay in that place of "love," the greater your life will be, and all your desires fulfilled. You may even find that your desires change and what you once wanted suddenly isn't as important anymore.

May 4, 2017

Question. I am interested in contacting Master St. Germaine. Will he make himself known to me? Can I connect with him? It's important as far as the group goes.

Yes. You can connect with him. He will answer you. Keep asking for the connection. Feel his presence when you are meditating. He will be there to assist you and join with you in your travels.

Do you know Master St. Germaine?

I know of him. There is power there that can be a huge benefit to you. It will be a wonderful partnership. There is no end to what you can accomplish when you have energies like that helping you.

May 5, 2017

Yes. Your health. You need to cut out the sugar. I've said this before.

Yes. I know I do. I've been thinking about that. It isn't easy.

I know. When you get the urge, you need to willfully let it pass. It will take concentration and commitment. Once you get by three days without it, it will get easier. But you must stick with it. And try and give up all the sweetness also, like your coffee cream and cereals. You can cut those out gradually, but try and let them all go.

May 7, 2017

Hi, Phillip. I'm curious; would you ever contact me to beware of a situation that would be harmful to me? Or, do you only answer when I have questions?

We would send you a feeling of unease for a situation which you are considering. It would be intuition or that gut feeling that something isn't right. If you then asked us, we would advise you to a particular course of action or inaction.

Okay. What about angels stepping in to help?

Angels can definitely be there to protect you. But not always. It may be that a particular circumstance is your actual exit point—your time to leave. In that case, they would not interfere. But if is not your time and you are in a perilous situation, angels can step in. Angels have been there for you in the past when you have done something dangerous when you weren't really being too smart in your choices.

Yes. I believe that. I know I have had times when things could have gone badly for me and didn't. I believe angels were there to help me.

May 9, 2017

Hi, Michael. Yes, I would like to talk about Purity. The Purity of the Soul. It is God. God resides there. He/She is a part of you. It is all Goodness and Love. You should realize that you are that Purity. You have that as a part of you. No matter what is happening in your earthly plane, physical environment, you always have that Soul Purity with you.

We may have to return to this at some time.

Yes. It needs to be explained further, longer, and more succinctly. We will visit this at another time when the connection is stronger.

May 10, 2017

I was very excited to see that I had sold two books with good reviews.

Yes. It's a start. Well received. It will continue to sell, picking up momentum.

Thank you. That's great. Anything else?

Yes. I would like to see you get that bike and start riding. You are doing your physical exercises, but this would add another dimension. Also, keep vigilant with your sugarless diet. Very important. If you feel yourself slipping, do a quick meditation. It only takes a few minutes, and the craving will pass. Don't put yourself in a place where those desserts are available. Pass it by. Once you can keep off it for a couple of weeks, it will become much easier. After a month, you won't even notice. This is going to help you in many ways. And more fruits and veggies.

May 11, 2017

Hi, Phillip. I want to get this off my chest because it has been bothering me. The trailer has been put up for sale. It was offered to me first, but I wasn't in a position financially to buy it.* Somehow, I always thought I would have it. Now I understand that there may be something better out there for me, and I'm okay with that. But it seems that everything must line up properly, and I must do everything perfectly, which seems highly unlikely, for me to receive what I want. Years ago, it was foretold that I would get married again, but I didn't. I thought I would get the trailer, but I didn't. The odds do not seem to be in my favor for these predictions to come true if I have to have all of the planets aligning perfectly and me living a life that perfectly coincides with what is needed.

*Their son didn't use the place and was also happy to have me go down and look after it. I had the pleasure of using it for a few years. I helped with expenses and made sure the place always looked good. I knew at some point the day would come when he would want to sell, and I always held out hope that I would be able to buy it. He was more than considerate with me and was even willing to let me work on a payment plan, but I didn't want to put myself in that position.

When I posed this question to Phillip, I was in a discouraged mood.

Hi, Michael. It does seem that way to you now because you are disappointed. Yes, you do have to be a vibrational match to manifest your desires, and that can be tricky and not easily accomplished. But having said that, it is in the stars for these effects to take place, but it is all about timing. You may not be ready for these things to happen or, as you said, there is an even better something waiting for you. Don't be discouraged. Don't be put off. And don't give up. Remember, it isn't all about what you have or can get, but what you can give. You have a lot of that, and it's what is important, not the other stuff. Be happy. Be grateful for all that you have, and you have a great deal. Be that Love above all else.

I understand, Phillip. I just had to let that out and get that off my chest.

I understand. It is good to speak out.

May 13, 2017

Yes. How are you doing? Do you feel like you are getting somewhere with your Merkabah meditation?

I feel like I am moving forward, albeit slowly. I am getting into that detached state, and I am working on that "Love" feeling.

Good. Stay with the "Love." Open your heart. Quiet the mind. Let go. Release yourself to the Energies that are there for you. You can do it. It is time for you to move forward and get closer to spirit. There is much help here for you. Let those energies in.

Okay. Good. I am ready for this next move. I want to explore everything available out there.

Let's make it happen.

May 16, 2017

Yes. Be aware of those little things around you. Those little odd noises. Those movements you think you catch out of the corner of your eye. Those are all small hints that spirit is around you, making itself known. Stay vigilant because at some time, there will be a manifestation of voice or even sight. Prepare yourself for this occurrence.

May 19, 2017

Hi, Michael. Yes. I know you are sad about the trailer. Let it go. Know that everything happens for a reason. There is something else in the works for you. Keep up with your writing and your painting. You are in a good place. Be happy. Be grateful. I know I have said that before, but it is good to reinforce these messages. It is of prime importance. It will be said to you many times until it is in your nature and a part of you.

May 23, 2017

Yes. I would like to speak some more on "Love." Let your love flow from your heart. Feel the joyous emotion of Love. Feel it radiate from you, and feel all the Love that is flowing to you from everywhere. Feel this Love surround you. Bask in its glory. When you can experience this Love in all its splendor, then there isn't anything that can hurt you or trouble you. You are part of the Divine, and this Love feeling is proof of that. Send out this Love to the planet and all living things, for it will change the world. "All we need is Love."

May 29, 2017

Hi, Phillip. I would like to hear your thoughts on the Merkabah session we had on Saturday. I had the feeling of traveling, but I'm never sure if it was just my imagination.

Hi, Michael. Yes. You were there, and it was happening. The sensations, feelings, and impressions will get better as you get better. The group energy is a big plus for you.

Don't, whatever you do, bring yourself down. You also bring your energy and particular aspects to the group, and this is recognized by all. There will be wonderful experiences and days ahead.

Good. It looks like the Scotland trip won't be happening this year. Much of what I am hoping for seems to be falling by the wayside.

It only means that there is something else that will occur that will better serve you.

I did feel that Master St. Germaine was there helping me.

He is just the Master that you need now and will be very beneficial to you in the days and weeks ahead. We are extremely happy for you that he is there for you.

May 31, 2017

Yes. It would be to your benefit to cut back on the amount of TV you are watching. You could be doing so much more by cutting back. Fill up that time with your other interests – painting, writing, walking, riding, and reading. You don't really need a lot of that other mindfulness.

All these things we have spoken about are moving you in the right direction. To who you really are and what you are meant to be. Fulfilling those desires. Seeing those dreams come true.

June 5, 2017

Hi, Michael. I am glad that you recognize the importance of these communications. An excellent time is right after your meditation. You are in a good state then for this. It will get better and better, as will your Merkabah. You are already aware of a change in your perception as you do it. Again, it will get better and better. You have guides, angels, Archangels, teachers, family, and friends, and now Ascended Masters, who are all there for you. Know this. Allow this. What wondrous journeys are waiting for you. What knowledge and experiences you will glean from this. You are now doing what you were meant to do—the reason you are here now at this time. Bless you.

We are grateful for you and your commitment to come to this place for the betterment of it and the expansion of the Universe. Thank you.

June 6, 2017

Yes. Again, I would just like to touch on the Merkabah. You are feeling it. You can sense the travel. You can sense the Masters. You are also getting close to that Third Eye activation. You feel it also, right?

Yes, I believe so.

Good. Any time now. Stay with all that you are doing. We can't wait for you and this experience, which is so close.

June 7, 2017

Yes. Art. Again, this is your creativity. This is your release. We would love to see you let go and just let the paint flow. Let the inner you come out, and we would love to see you pursue the psychic art. Let spirit work through you.

Yes. I mean to try that. When I finish this current painting, I will try it.

Good. It can be very rewarding. Very liberating, and you will see some amazing results. We believe you will get a lot from this process.

June 10, 2017

Hi, Michael. Yes. The Hathors.* You will have an opportunity at some point to interface with them. This will be another amazing experience for you. There are so many possibilities coming your way. Such an awakening. It is very exciting. Keep up with all your meditations. Keep up with "opening your mind and heart." You are getting there.

> *The Hathors are a group of interdimensional, intergalactic beings who were connected to ancient Egypt through the Temples of the Goddess Hathor, as well as several other prehistory cultures. "We are an intergalactic civilization with outposts that span parts of your known Universe and beyond." –taken from Tom Kenyon's website (www.tomkenyon.com), where you can learn much more about the Hathors. Tom Kenyon has a connection with The Hathors and channels some of their sounds and tones. (See also YouTube)

<u>Hathors, Pleiadians, Arcturians and Lemurians, Galactic Federation</u>

I want to take a moment to talk about these Higher Beings as they will become part of the story here and there. Below are very brief descriptions of who they are and what they are about. There is a lot of information for further study on the internet.

Hathors:

> The Hathors are Ancient Masters of sound and light here now to assist us with our planetary evolution and ascension. They are the "Healers of Healers," an ascended civilization of inter-dimensional masters who embody Unconditional Love. The Hathors have served our planet's evolution and ascension for over 850,000 years.
>
> –OkinHealth.com

Pleiadians:

> The Pleiadians are a group of multidimensional off-world beings from the Pleiades star system who are concerned about the future of our planet and who are helping us with our spiritual shift moving from 3D into 5D (expanded consciousness) which began in 2012. (Many aboriginal cultures have spoken of the year 2012, most notably the Mayans. The prophecy was taken to be the "end of the world," but what it was foretelling was the end of one era and the beginning of a new one. This was a shifting of old planetary awareness into a new age of spiritual rebirth, an elevation of consciousness.)

Arcturians:

> Edgar Cayce has said in his teachings that Arcturus is one of the most advanced civilizations in this galaxy. *It is a fifth-dimensional civilization that is a prototype of Earth's future. Its energy works as an emotional, mental, and spiritual healer for humanity.* Arcturus

> itself is the brightest star in the Bootes constellation, approximately thirty-six light-years from Earth.
>
> The Arcturians teach that the most fundamental ingredient for living in the fifth dimension is love. Negativity, fear, and guilt must be overcome and exchanged for love and light.
>
> The Arcturians work in close connection with the Ascended Masters whom they call the Brotherhood of the All. They also work closely with the Galactic Federation. The Arcturians travel the Universe in their starships, which are some of the most advanced in the entire Universe. —*The Arcturians by Clifford Stone*

I have also read that their spaceships guard our planet, protecting it from negative extraterrestrials as part of the Galactic Federation.

<u>Lemurians:</u>

> Lemuria was an ancient civilization that existed before and during the time of Atlantis. They are both highly evolved and spiritual beings of pure love and light, vibrating at the highest frequency.
>
> The Lemurian beings are the Earth Keepers, the protectors of Earth Mother's land and her natural resources.
>
> They are the intuitive, the mystics, the healers, the kind, the generous, the peaceful, and the loving. — *lemurianshaman.com; lemuria.net*

<u>The Galactic Federation:</u>

> The Galactic Federation is a cooperation of space-traveling civilizations in our Milky Way Galaxy. The

Federation consists of hundreds of thousands of members and was founded millions of years ago. The Federation has an enormous fleet of spaceships at its disposal to mediate or intervene in any impending conflicts. Commanders of some of these ships have become well known, like Ashtar, and have been channeled by mediums for the last fifty years. More and more mediums are said to be channeling representatives of the Galactic Federation. — *greaterpicture.com*

These HEBs (Highly Evolved Beings) are interested in seeing this planet evolve into a higher frequency, which means a more civilized way of existing. They are joining their "Love" vibration to the many lightworkers who have incarnated at this time of the Earth's evolution to bring about positive change to the planet. More and more people are awakening to this new era in our shift from 3D to a 5D reality, which means more oneness, unconditional love, and forgiveness. The future of the planet is in our hands. They will help wherever possible, but in the end, it is up to us, which is always the case.

June 11, 2017

Yes. You got an insight yesterday about better using your time during the day, split between painting and writing. This was your guides sending this to you. We would like to see you being more productive and getting more out of your hours. This doesn't mean that you can't have time for other things or for your enjoyment. It just means that we would like to see less of the wasted time where you are losing out on your creativity. We would like to see you fulfill your true potential.

Yes. I kind of figured that message or thought was coming from you. I will try to do a better job focusing on that.

Good. We are only trying to help. Remember, you have free will and are free to do what you like. These are suggestions from us, who are looking out for your betterment and fulfilling your destiny, realizing why you are here.

June 13, 2017

Hi, Michael. I am looking at the possibility of you starting to hear spirit. Getting yourself to that point where you will begin to see your sensitivity to spirit increase. Where you will notice more, experience more. Increase your vibration, thereby increasing your awareness.

Cool. I look forward to that.

Good. It's on the way. Be ready.

June 14, 2017

Yes. Sleep. Sleep is very important, both for your physical and spiritual well-being. You should be getting at least seven hours of sleep each night along with that little nap* you take in the afternoon. This is a recharging of your batteries. There is much going on while you are sleeping. You have your dreams, the ones you remember and ones that you don't remember. It is a time for your guides to give you information that will help you progress and assist you in your daily duties. You need that period of rest. Again, it is important to you. Don't downplay it.

*I worked most of my life in the Stock Brokerage business and was used to getting up early in the morning to be at work by 6:00 am, which coincided with the markets opening back east at 9:30 EST. Because we finished early, I got in the habit of having a nap in the afternoon to make up for less sleep at night. I did this my whole life, and I still do it.

June 16, 2017

Have you thought of journaling your dreams? It is an excellent way of remembering them.

I should consider it because I do forget most of them and only remember little snippets of them.

This will help, and as with everything else, you will get better at it. Plus, your remembered dreams give you something to think on.

June 19, 2017

Hi, Phillip. Is there something you would like to say? Also, was that my imagination, or did Master St. Germaine show me that room?

(As of this writing, I'm unsure exactly what I'm referring to here as it's been a few years.)

Hi, Michael. Master St. Germaine did show you that room. It was brief, but it is slowly advancing this communication with you. It is building up a rapport with you. You will get these little visions until Master St. Germaine feels you are ready for bigger things. Trust what you see and feel.

June 21, 2017

It was nice to see the favorable reviews from those who bought the book on Amazon.

Yes, it's a good book. It's all about getting the word out. It may take a little bit of time, but it has only been a year. It will pick up.

June 22, 2017

Hi, Phillip. Is that an accurate vision I just had during the Merkabah?

(Again, as of this writing, I don't know what that vision was as a few years have passed since, and I wasn't in the habit then of writing everything down.)

Yes. You continue to have doubts about these experiences. You must believe and trust what you are seeing. You are being shown these so you can get familiar with the experiences and trust in what is given to you. Eventually, hopefully soon, you will know these and be very comfortable with them.

I appreciate the experiences. I sometimes wonder whether I am not just imagining something I have made up.

You are imagining, but not something you have made up, but imagining what is taking place. Revel in the experience and continue to appreciate what is being given to you and how this is expanding your sensitivities.

I am grateful for it all. Thank you, Phillip, as always.

June 24, 2017

As usual, I would appreciate your help in detaching and getting in touch with spirit in today's class. I know Master St. Germaine will be there to help. I hope I can connect with him.

Of course, we will be there, as always, with you. Your Guided Master will be there and will be assisting you with your work. "Work" isn't the right word; your path, your teachings. Remember, enjoy the process. Don't fret. Relax and go with the flow.

June 26, 2017

Hi, Phillip. I gave it a try with the "psychic art," but I am gathering that this is something that I have to keep trying.

Yes. Stick with it. Just get yourself in that trance state. Give spirit permission to use your hand, and then wait. Stay that way for as long as you deem right. Like many of these things, they don't happen right away. But if you stick with it, it will happen.

Okay, good. Is there anything else you would like to say? I am curious about the "Lords of Light."* Did that help me, or was I too conscious? I am never sure if I am holding back.

It did help you. Everything that you have taking place is helping you. We would still like to see you 'let go' more.

I seem to have a hard time with that.

Again. Just keep with it, and it will happen one day, and when it does, you will then realize how easy it is, and it will be easier every time after.

Everyone else had such amazing experiences. I wish I could experience something like that.

They have been doing it a lot longer and may have had their abilities for a much longer period of time. You are still very new with this. Don't get frustrated. Remember, it is going to happen, and you still have lots of time to experience all these wonderful things.

*The Lords of Light are made up of seven Archangels and Ascended Masters. They are Spiritually Enlightened, Higher Beings of Light: Aeolus – Cosmic Holy Spirit; Chananda; Lord Adrigon VaCoupe – Lord of the Pleiades; El Morya – Chohan of the First Ray; Lord Jophiel – Archangel of Illumination; Lord Rananda Kumara; and Archangel Ezekiel.

June 28, 2017

Hi, Michael. Can you hear my voice?

No.

Soon this will happen, and your Third Eye is getting close to opening. You have been working on that for some time now and the results are very near. This is going to open up a lot of possibilities for you to do with your Clairs. You will begin to hear spirit. You already have a fairly good grasp in feeling spirit. This will really open up your medium abilities. Continue to do what you are doing. Continue with the Merkabah and the other exercises that Claudette gave you. All these are going to be of valuable help.

Okay. Thank you, Phillip. I am excited about this. It feels like it has been a long time coming, but I understand what you have told me in the past about going through the process and all.

Good.

Any thoughts on the new book?

It is coming along. There is still a good ways to go. Again, just take it a bit at a time. It will get done and will be well received when it is done.

June 30, 2017

Hi, Michael. Yes. The Merkabah. Are you noticing anything different while you are doing it now?

Not really, but I do get the feeling of spirit with me; I sense this presence.

Yes. You are. They are here for you and assisting you, guiding you, and downloading assistance to you in order that you can let go more and more and begin to experience the many wondrous travels that you will partake in and that are ahead for you. Continue with the other exercises that Claudette gave you. All these will help to get you there.

Okay.

We just want to reinforce your possibilities. That is why we tell you some of these things over and over—to give you confidence and so that you don't give up. It is all there for you.

July 1, 2017

Hi, Michael. Remember to get back on your vegetables and fruits. You have gotten away from that. It is important for you to look after your physical body by eating better.

Yes, I am going to start in earnest again after this weekend. It's a holiday weekend, so I will enjoy it and get back to proper eating on Tuesday.

Okay. Try to stick with a better diet. You want to maintain a healthy lifestyle, and you don't want to be bothered by health issues that will hinder your development.

Okay. Can I start on Tuesday?

All right, but stay the course. You can do this. Be vigilant. You will see a difference.

July 3, 2017

Yes. You should get back to your painting. Don't neglect that. It is also important to you and a part of who you are. When you are thinking of these things, that is you being aware that this is something you should be undertaking. We drop little thoughts your way to entice you, to awaken you, to point you toward a given situation that you need to undertake or be aware of.

Yes. Thank you, Phillip. I was going to get back to it. I just wanted to get caught up in the writing of the book. As soon as I can get that off, I will return to my painting.

Very well. When you get caught up, see if you can do both. Share your time with both endeavors. Don't let other distractions draw you away from these.

July 4, 2017

Hi, Phillip. I just tried the "Advanced Merkabah Activate."* Did it work? Will I know if it worked? And, did I travel somewhere?

Hi, Michael. No, you did not activate the Merkabah. You need some further practice for this to happen. It will happen, and you will know it when it does. You did have an experience, however, though it wasn't where you asked to go. It was more like a dream state that you would have when sleeping. Keep working on this. Eventually, you will be taken to that place. I know you are feeling some frustration. Again, it is getting closer. Again, "Stay the course." You are going to get there. Try and be patient. I realize that this seems like it is taking a long time, but really it isn't. You have tremendous potential, but it has to come with a process. It just doesn't pop up because you desire it.

*The Advanced Merkabah Activate is a quicker way of getting into the meditation. Once you have done the longer form for an extended period, you can get to a point where you only need to say, "Advanced Merkabah, Activate," and it will set in motion your Merkabah without having to do all the other steps.

July 5, 2017

Hi, Phillip. Are there any questions you might have for me to ask Claudette tomorrow?

Hi, Michael. We will send some thoughts your way. Be open and mindful that these thoughts are coming to you.

Great. Thank you, Phillip. I will return to my painting, and I would like some help with the psychic painting.

Yes. As we said, you have to stick with it.

July 6, 2017

Yes. Let's talk about Religion. Of course, you have your own thoughts on this subject, and they are not wrong. Through guidance and your own experiences, you have come to understand that religion is man-made for his own endeavors. Many have become rich from using religion to preach their views at the expense of those easily led. God and any religion is within you. You do not have to seek out others to find out what is right and wrong. Merely search your heart where God resides. There is the answer. Listen to your heart. There is truth. Listen to your heart. There is everything you need. You have come to understand this. There are some that need to hear, that need to belong to such organizations, and that isn't a bad thing, as long as you take the good parts and aren't persuaded by rantings of "hell" and "damnation." God does not judge, only forgives. All. God is Love. Pure Love. And, Loves All. The Kingdom is there for everyone. You know this.

July 8, 2017

Is it possible to speak to my Guardian Angel?

Of course. It is good to speak to him every so often.

Hi, Ezekiel. I want to thank you for always being there for me. I know you saved me on several occasions. I thank you for that.

Hi, Michael. Thank you for your thoughts. We are here for you, and we were there to make sure that you continued your physical perspective to fulfill what you had planned in this existence. We are pleased with your progression and know that you may call on us at any time for assistance. We send you Love and Protection.

Thank you, Ezekiel, and thank you, Phillip, as always.

July 10, 2017

Yes. Don't give up on your book. Keep trying to promote it wherever you can. All it takes is a little break to get it some attention. This will happen. Keep thinking of ways that you can get the word out there. We will help. We will send you inspiration. Be on the lookout for thoughts that will help. It has only been a year. Lots of time. Sometimes these things do not occur right away. Everything will happen when it is supposed to. Don't get down on yourself because it doesn't seem to be going anywhere. Keep a proactive frame of mind. It will happen.

Thank you, Phillip. I appreciate your encouraging words.

July 12, 2017

Hi, Michael. Yes. I would like to continue our discussion on...

Phillip, I don't feel anything you are saying.

I think that constant noise outside is interrupting the flow of communication. Maybe later would be a better idea.

(An extremely loud lawnmower was being used right outside my room.)

July 13, 2017

Yes. Your grandmother is here.

Hello, Michael. It is so wonderful to communicate with you. I am so proud of you and all that you are accomplishing. You are doing some good work, and you have so much potential for more great things ahead. I love you so much.

Thank you, Nanny. I love you too, and I am so happy to have this chat with you. I appreciate all the love you send my way.

You're so welcome. Keep up all the good things that you are doing. Everyone here is happy for you and proud of you and sends love your way. Your grandfather is very proud of you.

Thank you, Nanny. I send my love to all and appreciate their good wishes.

Stay well. Love you.

Love you also.

Bye for now.

Hi, Phillip. Is there anything you wish to say?

Just to keep the lines of communication open. We would like to see you start sensing more. We are sending along some assistance with that for you. It is time to start expanding your awareness. Be open.

July 15, 2017

Yes. Don't forget your spirit art. We would like to see you continue with this. We would like to see you advance this so that you could do it more and more. It could even be a part of the book. So you need to get on this.

Okay, Phillip. I will try to give it a go, though I didn't feel much the few times I've tried it.

It will come. Relax your mind. Let spirit in. Don't give up just because it didn't happen right away.

July 17, 2017

Hi, Phillip. I just asked for some help during my meditation because I hadn't felt like much was improving in my sensitivity training, and I felt a connection—a stronger connection.

Yes. We heard you and sent some vibrations your way. Again, don't feel down when it seems as though nothing is improving. There are things going on with you, and it may not seem that way, but it is there. One of these days, there will be that breakthrough. Stay with what you are doing. Don't get discouraged. Know it is going to happen. Be ready. It is closer than you think. All is well.

As the reader can see by now, this was a constant theme for me—I would feel I wasn't making any progress, and my guide would continually reaffirm that I was getting there, that I am close. This will go on for some time yet. Again, it was all about needing to line up with the correct vibration and let go completely, which I was hesitant to do. It was as though there was something in my nature that didn't want to give up that control. Even though Philip would say I was getting close, it never seemed fast enough for me, which is when I would get discouraged.

July 18, 2017

Remember, I would like to see you get on with the psychic art and some original painting. We want to see your own artistic expression and the ability to channel art from spirit. This will be another unfolding of sensitivity for you. Free your mind and let spirit take over your hand. We believe this will be a very exciting development for you. But you will have to stay with it.

July 20, 2017

Yes. Again don't get caught up in Religions. They are man-made to help cope with man's own thoughts on what should or should not be done for his/her sake. There are some truths, but there are also many fallacies that govern what constitutes bad advice. There is not a judgmental, wrathful God sending souls to Hell for wrongful acts or bad deeds. God has given you free will and has unconditional love for all that you are, for all that you have done. Just the fact that you incarnated into this harsh environment when compared to where your Higher Self resides is enough for complete love. For God to experience through you, fills God with gratitude and love. If God forgives all, who are you to do otherwise. This may be hard for humans to do when grievous acts have been committed against them, but it is a part of evolving into your Higher Good. You are here to evolve, to better yourself, to expand your soul. It is why you chose to experience this physical existence. You have much guidance and support in spirit, just waiting for you to ask. I know you understand this, Michael, but it is good to go over it and may also be a help when this comes to future writings. We may expand on this at a later time.

July 22, 2017

Call on us to help you with difficulties, as in when you are struggling with your diet. We can help you get through those few important moments when the hunger pangs get you. You just have to ask. We can make a difference.

July 24, 2017

I just did the Merkabah and felt I traveled to a building where I saw people in cubicles. Then everything went dark. Was this the Federation I had been asking to visit?

Yes. That was a part of the building you saw. Just a small part. You aren't ready yet to experience anymore. It was to show you that what you have been asking for is possible and that these things will happen. More and more will be shown as you get more comfortable and better at it.

July 25, 2017

The other night I had a dream of meeting Barron.* Was this a dream, or was it an Out of Body Experience where I was actually with him on another plane of existence?

You were with him on the astral plane. You know that while you sleep, your soul travels and oftentimes meets up with those who have passed, and sometimes with other souls whose presence are still in the physical who are also traveling. This can be to communicate information or just to meet and socialize as a friend or relative would, as in crossing paths. This will come through to your physical self as a dream. The acuteness of the meeting with Barron would have been an O.B.E. It may have been Barron saying "thank you" or just showing that he had crossed, was there, and was okay, as well.

*Barron was a friend of the family and Verine's boss. He passed a few years after having suffered a stroke.

July 26, 2017

Yes. You are concerned about the "spasms" in your back.

Yes. I'm not sure what is causing this. I hope it is not my kidneys.

Well, there is something there. Continue with drinking water. Stay with the fruits and vegetables, and your exercising, but don't overdo it. Walking is good. If this continues, you should see your physician.

Is this serious?

It could be if left unattended. Your body is starting to show signs of weakening with age. But, it doesn't have to if you look after it. And remember to keep a positive outlook. You are the Master of what happens. Visualize and confirm that your body is healthy and strong. There is no reason why it can't sustain and keep you in good standing for many years to come.

July 27, 2017

Hi, Phillip. Near the end of the Merkabah, I felt myself in a place of whiteness; I believe I was under. And was that you who said, "We are all here."?

Yes. You visited with us very briefly but not long enough for us to be perceived. That was us/me responding to your question. You will visit more often and for longer periods. Excellent. We are filled with joy for this for you. Again, you are getting there bit by bit. Every time you get stronger, It will not be long now for your experiences to expand.

July 29, 2017

I will ask for your help for tomorrow's class to help me connect, detach, and let go.

Of course. We will be there for you. The group's combined energy, as usual, will be of great benefit to you, and you will add your energy to the group as well. Be clear. You are important to the group's overall energy as well.

July 30, 2017

Do you have anything I can add to my "Guided Messages from the Other Side" Facebook page for a quotation?

Yes. I have something for you. "Always be true to yourself. You are unique, and you matter. You are a part of the Whole, and the All is a part of you. You make a difference whether you realize it or not."

That's great, Phillip. Thank you.

You are welcome. We are happy to pass on this information.

July 31, 2017

Well, that was a wonderful workshop yesterday; the energies were incredible. I could feel the "Lords of Light" and Master St. Germaine. I think that did a lot for me. I appreciate everything they did for me.

Yes, there was a great benefit to you being there. Alignment was very good for you, and the added energies of the group, along with the Masters, was also very helpful in bringing you forward. Master St. Germaine raising your vibration so you could travel was excellent.

It was interesting that A saw me on the Ashtar Command ship.* I will have to ask them about that, how they saw me, and in what capacity.

(Our group traveled to this command ship. I remember seeing a large picture window looking out at space. A is part of our group and lives near me, and I drive them to the workshops. This person has very good abilities. Whenever the group returns from a Merkabah experience, we relate what we observed to the others. This person had seen me on the ship, which was quite amazing to me.)

There is more to this, but not right now. More will be revealed later with regards to this.

Good. Well, I was taken with the whole thing. Some of the others had tremendous visionary pictures, very vivid. I look forward to a time when I can have that experience.

Remember, they have been doing this a lot longer than you. You are coming along. Your vibrations are getting stronger. A breakthrough is imminent. Enjoy all that you are experiencing, and have eager anticipation for what lies ahead.

> *The Ashtar Command is an etheric group of extraterrestrials, angels, light beings, and millions of "starships" working as coordinators of the activities of the space fleet over the western hemisphere. Ashtar, the commander of the galactic fleet and representative for the Universal Council of the Confederation of Planets, is currently engaged in Earth's ascension process, moving us into the 5th dimension. –Ashtar Command website.

August 2, 2017

Any thoughts on my book as far as sales go? Is it just me and my usual impatience? I know it is something I must learn to get over.

Yes. That is something that you should learn to adjust to. Your book is going to find a niche. As you get more requests for it, you will be slowly getting it out to more people. Eventually, it will get noticed by that certain person who will get the word out to a broader audience. Then you will see the results you hoped for.

That is good news. How do you see the book that Claudette and I are working on?

It is coming along. There is still a lot of work to be done. It also will get there and will reach a number of people. It has been said that this will also promote your own book. Keep at it. Good things are ahead.

August 3, 2017

Good morning, Michael. Yes. Your back alignment is feeling better. The upside-down position (inverter bed) allows blood to flow to your head; this also decompresses your vertebrae. There are a lot of benefits to this for your well-being. Continue to use this. It will help you in many ways. We know the apparatus is in the way*, but keep it anyway. All these things come to you for a reason. You want to progress. This is another helping hand in that direction. All the little things add up to bigger improvements. Be open to our suggestions. When you are getting continuous thoughts about something, it is our way of getting through to you. Time for you to act.

Got it. Great. Thank you, Phillip.

*This apparatus stood in the middle of my living room, and I used it to help with my back issues. I have a pretty small apartment, which is fine for me, and this is standing in the living room. I had brought it out of storage to help with my back. I don't get a lot of company. Lol

August 4, 2017

Don't be concerned if you do not feel like anything is happening in your Merkabah meditations. It won't be there every day, where something is occurring. Sometimes it's merely you receiving guidance from spirit energies, even if you don't sense it. It doesn't mean that nothing is happening. Every time that you do it is a bonus for you. You are obtaining good vibrations. Good energy. Nothing is wasted. Receive it with gratitude, and feel the love that is coming to you.

August 5, 2017

Hi, Phillip. I just thought I would touch base with you today and say hello.

Hi, Michael. Very well. It is good to always keep the lines of communication open.

Do you see anything happening soon with regards to hearing or seeing spirit?

It is going to take effect. I can't tell you exactly when. It all depends on you and the vibrations you are giving off and receiving. You must continue to do what you are doing. Focus on your third eye. Increase that Love vibration. Feel the spirit that is your Higher Self. Remember who you are before you incarnated through your meditations. Continue to ask for guidance and help from your guides, teachers, angels, and Masters, and know deep down that this is coming. Everything arrives when it is supposed to.

August 6, 2017

Don't forget about your walking. You should try and get out some more. There are many benefits to you – physically and mentally.

Yes. As always, you are right. Good advice. I've been meaning to do that. I will start tomorrow.

Good. It is just a matter of setting aside an hour or an hour and a half and doing it at least twice a week if you can.

(I do like to walk, so this is not a problem.)

August 10, 2017

We are glad you are back to your painting. We had a mind connection with you last evening, which is good practice for you. We want you to get to that point where you will hear us, but that doesn't mean the written conversation needs to stop.

Okay. Good. I will continue with "mind" communication as well.

August 12, 2017

Yes. Dialogue. Keep the transmissions going, either in your mind or through writing. It's important to touch base every day if only for a short time.

If I don't write, I do usually think of you, but I will try harder to communicate instead of just thinking about you when I do.

Good. Because we can talk, like I said, if only briefly. We want you to get used to having a dialogue with us, to be comfortable with it so that it is simply a normal part of your day as if we were there beside you, which we are when you want us. As Claudette said, it would get boring if we were there beside you every moment, but only a thought of us and we are there.

August 14, 2017

Watch your shopping today. Keep in mind healthy choices. You don't need to go overboard expense-wise on unhealthy purchases. Get the things that you need and some little food items, but stay away from those things that are not in your best interests.

August 15, 2017

Again, we have gone on about this several times now, but you need to eat better. More vegetables, more fruit. Less sugar. Less fast food.

I know, but it is not easy. There is the convenience of fast food and the enjoyment. Not much enjoyment in vegetables, but I know you are right.

You have the ability to live a good long life, but you must take better care of your body. You can't just wish it to be well. You must provide the nutrients it needs to keep it running properly.

Okay. Let me finish what I have, and I will give it another go.

All right. A few more days and then get on with it.

August 16, 2017

During the last Merkabah, I believe I was taken back to Ashtar Command by Master St. Germaine. I feel I have a connection to this ship. Can you confirm that?

Yes, you do have a connection to it, and this will be shown to you when the time is right.

Why do I get shown snippets of these things without being given the whole picture?

Remember, you are still very new to this even though it may not feel so to you. There are processes. You have to match your vibration to that which you are seeking.

Does that mean those who have this ability without any problems already have a higher vibration to start with?

Yes. But remember again that they also have to go through their own processes. Each of you is different. Each of you will take your own path to getting there. Some may seem easier than others, but not necessarily so. That may be your own perspective. You may not know all the facts. Trust that the Universe knows what It is doing and what is best for you.

August 17, 2017

Let's talk about children. There are new incarnations happening all the time, and those energies manifesting themselves on the planet at this time are bringing their new energies filled with positiveness and light, heralding in this new age, bringing about positive change that is shaping the earth and all that abide there with their love and light and a new perspective. There will be new inventions that will greatly enhance the environment, getting away from the previous ways of accomplishing things. There will be a fresh, positive outlook that will overtake the planet, ridding itself of negative energies. It has already started. New generations are questioning the ways of old to bring about change. All of this is getting help from other dimensions. It is in the Universe's best interest to have this planet succeed.

Thank you, Phillip. That is good to hear.

August 19, 2017

Is there anything I can do when I go to bed at night that will help me improve my sensitivity?

Hi, Michael. Yes. You want to clear your mind and then see yourself as brilliant white light—surrounded by brilliant white light. Hold that picture if you can until you fall asleep. You can invite your guides and angels to help you while you sleep. When you find yourself semi-conscious during the night, try to get back to that place of white light. The more you do it, the easier it will become. This will enhance *your vibration and help you along with increasing your sensitivity. See yourself in that place, as that white light, whenever you can. You also want to bring that "Love" feeling into your place of being.*

August 20, 2017

Is it possible to remember any part of me before I incarnated?

That it is. You may remember some part of yourself. But also part of your transcendence to this dimension was to forget who you are in order for you to try and remember through your life experiences. All of your living was to get you to this point. You are finally getting closer. The fact that you asked this question shows that you are finding your Self. The opening of your third eye will assist in this remembrance.

Thank you. I am always thinking about opening my third eye.

Good. So it shall be.

August 22, 2017

Do you think Master St. Germaine would speak to me?

He will. You need only to ask.

Okay. One day, I will do that. I had another experience while doing the Merkabah that felt as though I was back on the Ashtar ship. I feel I have a connection there for sure.

Yes, Michael. You do. You will continue to visit it until you get a clear understanding of why.

Okay. Good. I have a session with Claudette and a class coming up this week.

Claudette may have an answer for that thought you had, and we expect another exceptional class on Saturday.

August 23, 2017

I wondered if you could explain my thoughts on the many dimensions or universes where another "me" exists. Is this because of choices that I didn't make? This is what I want to talk to Claudette about, but I thought you might add something to it. Can you shed some light on this? I am ready to write if this takes a while.

Hi, Michael. You are right in thinking it's involved. There is much to this. There are many of you across a multitude of dimensions, doing many different things. Rich ones, poor ones, married, divorced with children and without, some with disabilities and some healthy. Some daring and some not. Every aspect you could imagine, there is one of you, all in the "Now" moment.

So when I pass, do the others become a part of me?

Yes. Some may pass before you, and some may continue to live longer, but remember, time is inconsequential. You will be aware of all of it. This explains why, say, someone who had no musical abilities in this life find that, when they transition, they have the capability to play certain musical instruments, as an example. You have the capacity to tap into your doppelganger, if you like, by meditating and asking that individual who possesses the ability you seek to help you attain that power or attribute.

Okay, I think I get it without needing to go deeper into it.

August 24, 2017

Yes. Cousins. Try to keep in touch with your cousins.

Okay. We are not what you would call close.

Well, yes, that's true, but they are a part of your family. There is history there—if not with you, then with your parents—and it is good to keep that open.

August 25, 2017

Claudette asked me to meditate on whether I was around at the time of Jesus, which I did.* I also asked Master St. Germaine to take me back there, which he did. I got a brief glimpse of being a shepherd in a desert area. So, I believe I was there, though I don't think I knew or had seen Jesus. However, I believe I knew of Him. Would you comment on this, please?

That was very good. You are starting to get results with that brief picture. Now you can begin to see what it is going to be like. Yes. I am excited. So yes, you were there when Jesus was. I am not sure if the time is right to reveal any more than that. This is something that we can return to once your abilities are stronger. Good job.

*Claudette had told me that she knew she was around in a past life during that time. She was curious to know whether I could get any information through meditation about also being there. I should mention that she had done a past life regression and discovered that she was also in Atlantis in another life.

We have all lived many lives. Past life regression is a method of taking a person back to a past life and is usually done by a trained therapist or a medium trained in this technique through hypnosis or a trance state where the person visualizes themselves in a different time. If you are interested in learning more on this subject, pick up *Many Lives Many Masters* by Dr. Brian Weiss.

August 27, 2017

That was an unbelievable class yesterday—the energy, the vibrations, the Lords of Light. It felt amazing. I hope that everything that happened wasn't just my imagination. It was very powerful, and I believe that it will help me in a big way.

Yes. Exceptional and of tremendous help to you. Those kinds of sessions will benefit you immensely. Don't consider "just my imagination." You did feel the wonderful vibrations and energies. That was real. You were there and participated in all of that. We were thrilled for you. You are on your way to more fantastic experiences. We couldn't be happier for you.

August 29, 2017

Hi, Phillip. I am heading out to my brother's place. I'm not sure I will get any meditating done, but I will try to keep in contact with you. Do you have any words about this trip?

Yes. Be careful.

Of what?

Just be overly cautious while driving and with your activities. Be aware.

Are you recommending that I don't go because something might happen?

No. Go, but as I said, be cautious.

Okay. I hope all of you will be watching over me.

Yes, to be sure. We will be there and give you a nudge if we are concerned.

Thank you.

September 3, 2017

Hi, Phillip. So it has been a while. It was nice to have a break at my brother's. Thank you for the forewarning. I was trying to be aware of any potential problems.

Hi, Michael. Yes, you were. That was good, as there could have been some periods where problems might have arisen. This was a good break for you. You sometimes need a break. Your human side took over and gave you some free time where you weren't concerned with spirituality, which can sometimes take over. You don't want to get to a place where you get tired or fed up with always practicing spirituality, and you wind up dismissing it completely. You are both human and spirit, and as much as we want to see your spirit side get stronger, we don't want it to overwhelm you to the point where you ignore it altogether.

September 4, 2017

Yes. Prayers. You do a good practice with your prayers, but occasionally the brain gets in the way, and you begin thinking of other things while you are praying. Try to concentrate on the words and feel the emotion while you are saying them. This gives them strength, and now there is conviction present that makes the words more powerful, which gives meaning of a higher order.

Okay. I will try to be more aware.

September 5, 2017

Hi, Phillip. That was a good meditation today; I thought I had found that sacred place in the heart. I felt that vibration of "Love."

Yes. Very well done. You did get there. That is something for you to continue to visit. You will realize more and more emotions, feelings, and this is another way of increasing and expanding your vibration. Good job.

Thank you, Phillip. I am excited about this.

That is good. That's the way you should feel. That is the way you get better and better.

September 6, 2017

Yes. That was another good meditation today. There was more "help" sent to you. The Lords of Light came at your request and bestowed gifts to you to assist you to expand your sensitivity. Very good.

That's wonderful. I know I am getting help, but I thought I would ask Them particularly if They would assist me.

And They did. They are there for you and anyone who wants to expand their awareness for the betterment of All.

I love the Merkabah; it is a great meditation. I feel it more and more.

Wonderful. Keep at it. There are some amazing journeys that lie ahead and excellent experiences.

September 7, 2017

Hi, Phillip. I telepathically sent you a message about something I might ask Claudette about today in our session because I didn't have anything. And, I received this response: "No, not really." Right?

Yes. That's right. You have a lot of information already, and you don't need to have something every session. She might have something, but don't worry about it. You still have a lot of transcribing to do.

Yes. It is a lot of work.

It will get done. Just hang with it and keep at it.

September 11, 2017

I'm not sure what's going on with me right now. I usually look forward to my meditations, but lately, I am becoming restless during them, almost as though I wish they were over before they even start. I'm not sure why this is?

Yes, I can see and feel that. I think that possibly the meditations you are doing are becoming too routine. Maybe it is time to try something different and of a shorter length, to get you back on track.

September 13, 2017

I know you are feeling discouraged. Don't be. The routine is getting to you a bit. You will get through this. It is merely one of those things that comes by every once in a while. Something will happen that will get you back on track stronger than ever. Don't fret about it. It happens. Take it day by day, and it will all work out.

Phillip was aware that I felt in a funk because I felt as though nothing was happening in my meditations. There seemed to be no movement or new insights—I felt I was going around in circles. This happened to me periodically, but something would happen to get me going again, and my enthusiasm would return.

September 15, 2017

Okay, I'm back from my period of "fickleness" and ready to get back in touch with my meditations, etc.

Good. All that was told to you was said before. Sometimes reinforcement is needed when you feel like you are not getting further in your quest. Amazing experiences await. It will be worth it to go through this process and don't give up on your psychic art. It is there for you.

September 16, 2017

Oftentimes in the physical, you let your imagination set up situations which are completely out of anything that would take place, creating worry, fear, and it's usually beyond your control anyway. Relax. Just do whatever you can and let it unfold the way it was always going to.

September 18, 2017

That was a good Merkabah meditation—good sensations, and I felt I went deeper than I usually do without losing consciousness.

Yes. Very good. You did indeed. It proves that all is working. That you are coming along. That you are getting there. As your experiences get better you will finally realize that you can do this, and you will look forward to sensing more and more as you grow into this.

September 19, 2017

Yes. Again, a friendly reminder to watch your diet. It's time to get back to veggies and fruits. Also, watch your sugar intake. It is for your health and well-being.

Yes. Okay. Why is all the stuff we like bad for us, while the other things that are more expensive and less tasty good for us?

Yes. Well, it is too bad it is that way, especially when it comes to expenses. You would think that what is good for you would be more affordable. And, as taste goes, you just have to give it more of a chance and get used to it. You want to get into that routine of fixing and eating what is best for you, especially as you become older.

I know. I will try to add better food choices. I have done much better by drinking mostly water.

That is a big improvement and has definitely benefitted you.

September 23, 2017

I thought I would check in with you before going to today's workshop.

Have a good experience. Relax. Enjoy. It will be good as always. The combined energies of the group help you. It is all good for you.

September 24, 2017

Well, that was an extraordinary workshop with Claudette and the Merkabah group yesterday—nature spirits, faeries, Hathors, healings from the Hathors, visiting the Hathors' home. It was unexpected that Claudette asked me to channel. I'm not sure I did it very well. I'm not even sure if it wasn't just me talking.

Yes. It was a wonderful experience for you. We are so excited for you. Don't worry about the channeling. It is Claudette's way as a teacher to give you the experience and to help you with your confidence. She knows that you can do this, and it is her way of advancing you. You are an important part of the group. Your energy adds to the overall effect.

All are important, and they know that. They have been doing this much longer than you. Just go with it. Enjoy these experiences, which will get better and better, and watch yourself expand and grow. We are so thrilled for you, and you know you have so much support here among all the other Energies that are here to help you. Be the Love.

September 25, 2017

At the beginning of my Merkabah meditation, I sensed several people as I walked up some stairs who I believe may have been guides of mine. Is that correct?

Yes, those were some of your guides. The energy that you refer to as Phillip is the conglomeration of all these like energies. We are a similar vibrational energy. We speak as one. We all have our own specialty, if you will, to assist you while you are in the physical.

That is what I believed, but it was nice to finally see you, even if it was only a glimpse.

It is a good beginning.

September 26, 2017

I have the psychic art of Mother Joseph. Is she here to help me somehow?*

Yes. She will be there with you and will help you with your sensitivity to spirit. She will be another guide to assist you. Don't get freaked out by the art. It is not who she is. It is a reminder that she will be there for you. And don't worry about the pastel dust. It has pretty much dissipated.

Okay. I am happy to have her assist me. I need all the help I can get.

You are doing fine. You are coming along at a pace that is right for you. Don't beat yourself up. Enjoy the process.

*In our Merkabah class, made up of four students, our teacher had four psychic art paintings she decided to give to each of us. They were to be an additional guide for us. She asked us to choose the painting we felt drawn to. I didn't feel drawn to any, so I waited until the other three had made their choice, leaving the remaining one to me. It was a pastel painting of a woman I learned was named Mother Joseph.

Mother Joseph was the Founder of the French Catholic Order of Nuns. She spent time among the sick and got the name "Mother Joseph." The French Catholic Order of Nuns grew their own food and distributed it among the needy. Mother Joseph was very pious but had a sharp tongue when necessary. She never asked the other sisters under her care to do anything she would not have done herself. The nuns helped each other make their coffins for their burials. She argued with the hierarchy (a most unseemingly thing at that time) for the sake of the poor; she felt the money spent on churches could have been better spent on the poor instead. She said that "Jesus preferred the humble Church to the ostentatious Church." She developed arthritis in her later years but still knelt for long periods in the chapel, praying for mankind. She asks for prayers to be said for her.

September 28, 2017

I am trying to fight off a cold, which I don't get very often.

Yes, you have a pretty good immune system. Meditation helps with that. You forgot to use the bacterial hand sanitizer, which you usually do when you returned home, which is how this cold took place. Picture yourself well. Stay with your meditation and use that to shorten this cold. You won't have it long.

September 30, 2017

Hi, Phillip. You have been answering my questions lately, but is there anything you would like to say?

Yes. I know you haven't been feeling well with this cold, but try to keep up with your normal routines when it comes to diet, exercise, your painting, and writing. Just don't overdo it. Rest is important when your body is ill. It needs to fix itself. You will be back to normal very quickly.

Okay, good. I am already starting to feel a little better. I am not sneezing as much as I was yesterday.

You are on the mend. Gradually begin your routines. It is time to move forward.

October 1, 2017

I would like to talk about Abstinence. You can let go of certain things for your betterment. Abstaining from certain foods, abstaining from physical goings-on that are a part of your routine, like watching TV. You can pick days where you can fast or decide not to watch TV at all. When you start doing this, it may seem hard, but the more you do it, the more you will notice how much easier it becomes and how much more productive you are. Start by picking one day a week and see how that works for you.

All right, I will give it a try.

October 2, 2017

Hi, Phillip. Terrible tragedy in Las Vegas.* Some bad things are going on in the world lately. Many lives are transitioning.

* On the night of October 1, 2017, Stephen Paddock opened fire on a crowd of concertgoers at the Route 91 Harvest music festival in

Nevada on the Las Vegas Strip. He killed 58 people and wounded 413, with the ensuing panic bringing the injury total to 869. –Wikipedia

Yes, we touched on this during your morning meditation. When transitioning from one phase to another, there is oftentimes chaos. To get to that place of Peace, which most people want, there is the opposite—Chaos and War. It takes what seems like a senseless killing for the populace to rise up in disgust and anger to get the governments to react. There are far too many weapons of destruction (guns) available to anyone. It will take a majority of people sending out "Love and Light" to the entire World, world leaders, countries that have been involved with strife to finally reach a point that will tip over to a place of calm and peace.

This will happen. Unfortunately, it will take more of these catastrophic scenarios to get to that tipping point. Continue to send out unconditional "Love" to the planet and all of life.

October 3, 2017

Yes. We would like to continue to give you inspirational guidance that you can use for your "Guided Messages" page.* The more people that come to your site, the better it will promote your book. It is worth investing more money for promotional purposes. In the days ahead, we will give you more additional words that you can use. This is not only good and applicable to you but to everyone. There are beneficial words to come. You also might want to consider upgrading your website. It would be advantageous to pay someone to do that.

*I have a dedicated page on Facebook for my book *Guided Messages from the Other Side*, where I post informed messages that I have received from spirit.

October 4, 2017

Yes. Vibrations. When you feel that tingling in your body which you associate with the presence of spirit, that is your vibrational frequency being raised to sense spirit. It is a communication with spirit. That is what you are striving for. This will progress from sensing spirit to hearing and even seeing spirit. This is your Clairs* strengthening. Keep going for that vibration. You have that strong bond with your sixth chakra, your brow chakra. This is your third eye coming into being. It is there just waiting for the right time for that veil to be lifted. This should happen soon. Then you will experience those amazing sights and sounds that you have been working towards. It is there. You are doing well. Remember to use your meditations as explorations. You are the explorer, and new worlds await you. Isn't that exciting?

Yes, definitely. I can't wait.

Soon.

*Clairs are your psychic senses, your intuition. The main Clairs in spirituality are clairaudience – the ability to hear spirit; clairvoyance – seeing spirit; clairsentience – sensing or feeling spirit or being empathic; claircognizance – clear knowing or inspired thoughts. Two more go along with our physical senses, and they are clairsalience – clear smelling; and clairgustance – clear tasting, though these may be less prevalent. Occasionally, you may smell the odor of cigarettes or a particular perfume when no one is around. This could be associated with a familiar person who has passed and is trying to make their presence known. Or you may be conversing with someone on the phone and get the taste of a particular beverage only to find that the person on the other line is drinking that beverage. Usually, one of the Clairs will be predominant.

I can sometimes smell cigarette smoke when no one is around, which I associate with my father, though he quit smoking many years before he passed. He was a heavy smoker when I was growing up.

When I smell it and ask if it is him, I get confirmation by the tingling sensation I feel. He's letting me know he is around. I'll say, "Hi, Dad," acknowledging his presence.

October 5, 2017

I might try doing my Merkabah before I go to bed tonight for a change. Also, I hear the lawnmower starting, which is annoying when I'm trying to meditate.

Sure. Try it. See if it does anything for you, and "yes," the lawn care guys do not help when you are seeking peace and quiet, which is the reason you meditate. That quiet inside of you that helps you connect to your Higher Self.

Will it help when I go to sleep, having meditated just previously?

It could, though meditating in the morning does set you up for your day ahead. At night, you will get that relaxation and calmness right as you go to bed, which could be beneficial.

Well, we will see.

October 6, 2017

Hi, Michael. Good morning. Yes, you seem to have given up on your psychic art.

Well, I don't feel anything is happening there. Maybe I need to wait for a time when my sensitivities are stronger.

You have to keep trying. Take half an hour every day that you can, and let yourself go. Detach and see if there is any improvement. It will come. It's like everything; it takes some working at it and putting in the time. Eventually, you will experience results. Once that happens, you are on your way.

Okay. I will try to remember to put some time aside. I may need a nudge now and then.

We will give you that.

October 7, 2017

I had the impression that the Lords of Light visited with me during my meditation and were there to give me something that would help me. Is this correct?

You are correct. You have included them in your "Prayers of Gratitude," and they will visit you every so often to give you downloads, if you like, to assist you with your sensitivity with your Clairs, with your Third Eye. You are noticing a difference even as we write this.

Yes, my brow is still tingling.

Yes, you are going to feel more intense compressions around your head. Your body will also tingle more now when you are doing your meditations and even at times when you are not meditating but merely being quiet. You are shifting your vibrations, or, we should say, your vibrations are shifting you.

I am very grateful to the Lords of Light and all of those who have been there for me.

They want you to succeed. They are there to see you fulfill your destiny. You are now doing what you are here to do. It has taken a while, but it is all happening as it should. There are great forces at work on your behalf.

October 8, 2017

Yes. You saw that red color during your meditation. This is to do with your root chakra. This was balancing your root chakra, which is important. It is the first chakra, and getting it balanced sets up that stability for the rest of your chakras.

Very good. You are continuing to move in the right direction. As your chakras become balanced, you will feel that kundalini* experience which can be very profound, another step in your development. Stay with it, as I know you will.

*Kundalini is a forceful energy located at the base of the spine where the root chakra is found. It is sometimes depicted as a coiled snake. When awakened, this spiritual energy rises through the chakra system, augmenting each of them as it advances. Awakening the kundalini is spiritual development and can be overpowering to some. This raw power can be activated through yoga and meditation.

October 9, 2017

Yes. Happy Thanksgiving (Canadian Thanksgiving). It is good to be grateful for all that you have, even for those who feel they have nothing. If you look deeply, you can find something to be grateful for, even if it is just to be aware in the 'Now' moment and to conjure up thoughts that there are better days ahead.

I have so much to be grateful for, and I express my gratitude every day for all that I have and all that is coming my way.

That is a good way to be. Have that feeling of gratitude to go along with the words, and good things will continue to flow to you.

And I am always grateful to you and all my guides and angels, teachers, Masters, and the Higher Energies that come forth to assist me.

As we are grateful to you.

Thank you, Phillip. I love you all.

As we love you.

October 10, 2017

I vaguely remember a dream last night where my psychic abilities were coming into being. Was that merely a wish from my subconscious or something happening?

That was something happening. There was a slight variation in your vibration. This occurred while you were in that dream state. This goes on even though, most of the time, you will have no memory of it. This time you did. All these occurrences are getting you closer to that breakthrough that we all are waiting for.

There is more going on than you realize. This is not a quick jump to sensitivity. As we have stated before, it is a process, and you have to go through all of the stages to get there.

October 11, 2017

Is there something you would like to say? Also, it will be one year tomorrow since Verine passed. I think she is settling in.

Yes. Again, time is a physical measurement in the linear. Here, no such thing. So it still doesn't feel like she has been here very long. But, yes, she is settling in just fine. She is happy to be with all her loved ones. She is sorry that the Estate is taking so long and has been so much work for you. She is very grateful for all that you have done. She couldn't have asked for anyone better to look after things. She sends her love. You have so many family and friends here that love you, are proud of you and what you have become, and they are excited for the future for you.

Thank you, Phillip. It is nice to hear those lovely words.

They are sincere.

October 13, 2017

Can you hear me?

I don't hear a voice, but I get words pictured in my mind that come to me.

Okay. This is something we can work on. Let's try doing this from now on and see if it can't lead us to that voice unless you would be more comfortable with the way it is now.

No. I would like to have direct communication. I don't mind writing; it is good to have a hard copy of what was said, but I would also like to have you there where I can increase my sensitivity. I want to be a true channeler.

I agree. So we will continue with the writing, but we will also work on that thought communication.

October 15, 2017

Let us talk to you about meditation again. Going into that quiet place, silencing the mind, when a thought creeps in, immediately recognize it and dispel it. It would be best if you were in your heart chakra with no interruptions. Deep, deeper. You want to be in that very thin overlap between the physical plane and the astral plane, from which you can travel to other dimensions. Yes, there are days when it is more difficult because of the frame of mind you were in before the start of the meditation. This would be the time to do the Kadoish* recording. It will help you get in the proper frame of mind for your meditation. Use that recording.

Your mind was too busy in today's meditation, interrupting the process. You were back and forth, never getting into that constant space that you want to be in.

*The Kadoish is a powerful mantra that translates into "Holy, Holy, Holy, is the Lord God of Hosts" and is beneficial when intoned before a meditation. It assists one in getting into the "Love" vibration or zone. There is so much more to this prayer. You can find recordings of the Kadoish on YouTube.

October 16, 2017

I am wondering what to say to my cousin Anne about sending her a healing? How can I put it? I am not sure what her beliefs are. Or should I not do that?

I think you should say something. See how the conversation goes. Just be yourself. See if something along that line comes up. You can mention it, and she can accept it or not. All you can do is try and see if you get any impression as to her being comfortable with the idea.

October 18, 2017

I tried contacting you without writing, but I was not successful.

Yes, we got the connection but not the flow of words. That's okay. We can keep working on that, and we will continue with the writing. There is a much better flow of information. You have been doing this for a while now, and it works very well.

Yes, but I will try to communicate thought-wise also.

Good. It will come about. Don't feel that you have to rush into this. There is all the time in the world.

Okay. Thank you, Phillip. Maybe we can get back to some inspirational words that I can use on my Facebook site. I know I have been asking a lot of questions lately.

Absolutely. We are very into doing that. If someone else reads and gets a benefit from that, then that is a plus.

October 19, 2017

Just don't leave your painting too long. You need to balance the transcribing and the painting.

Yes, I know. It has been on my mind.

That is us giving you a nudge. Pay attention to those consistent thoughts. That is us sending signals to you.

October 20, 2017

Maybe you should try a different medium for your psychic art. Try the oil bars. That may work better, and try it with your left hand. Also, try and do it sitting at a table. Free your mind and let spirit take over. Keep trying this. It will happen. Once it does, then you will get more and more proficient at it.

October 21, 2017

I am going out to my nephew's place later. It is supposed to be a very stormy night. I would like to ask my guides and angels to watch over me and keep me safe while driving if you would please.

Of course, we will. Drive carefully and be aware. Be focused. We will be with you.

October 23, 2017.

Can I communicate with an angel right now through my writing?

Yes.

Okay.

(Angel) I am here for you. Is there something I can do for you?

I thought it would be nice to talk to an angel. Knowing angels are watching over me is very comforting. So thank you for all you do for me.

We thank you for the being that you are. You have our Love. The fact that you chose to incarnate into the physical for your experiences is something to be proud of, and we appreciate the fact that all of you are expanding the "All That Is." We are here for you always and are ready to assist you. You need only to ask.

Thank you so much.

Thank you. You have our Love.

October 24, 2017

You are concerned with the Estate matters. Do not worry. Everything is going to be fine. You are doing and have done everything you can. It is going to be all right. Worrying needlessly isn't helping you. The process is up to others. You have no control over that. Let it be.

Yes. You are right. I tried activating the Merkabah without using the guided CD. I am not sure whether it worked.

It did, but you should keep using the tape. Eventually, you will not have to, but there's a little more time needed to be spent with it yet.

October 25, 2017

So I am working on this psychic art. I feel as though it is more me than being guided by spirit.

That's okay. It is a start. The more you do, the more you will give over to your guide. One day you will feel and see a difference. Like all these things, you have to keep at it. Once it starts, then it will skyrocket. Good job. I am happy to see you opening up to this.

October 26, 2017

Yes, with regards to the upcoming workshop, do not be concerned about how well you are doing and where you are with regards to others in the group. Most of them have been where you are and have been doing this for some time. You have to relax and let yourself go. Detach and let it happen. And you know what, if nothing happens, that's okay. You are getting the benefit of all the energies that are present. Every time you go to one of these, it benefits you. You get stronger. One day you will be in their place, and they also benefit from you being there. You have an energy, and all of them realize it and appreciate it.

Okay. Thanks for the pep talk.

It's what you need to hear.

October 28, 2017

Workshop today.

It is going to be a good class today. Enjoy. Let go. We are with you. As always, there is the blessing of the energies, which is important for you. It is all good.

October 29, 2017

Well, another awesome class. I felt several energies, and I appreciated the Lords of Light being there and aligning us. But again, I'm not sure if I am sensing these places we visit or just making them up. The others have such amazing visions and even communications with these energies, whereas I am mostly blank.

I understand your frustration, Michael, but you are getting huge benefits, and you are partaking in these travels. You are just not getting the full experience as the others because they are more advanced than you are and have been doing this longer. You are still pretty new with all of this and, as we have said a number of times, you are becoming better every time you participate. You are experiencing much more than you give yourself credit for, and you are still holding back from your fear of not getting the understanding that the others do. Don't worry about them and what they are perceiving, and don't worry about what you are noticing. Just 'Let It Happen.' You are doing very well. The Universe appreciates you and what you are doing. You are recognized by the Higher Evolved Beings. Be happy and grateful for what you are accomplishing.

Thank you for the pep talk, Phillip.

You are getting there. Think of all the wonderful experiences that are ahead of you and all that you are going to accomplish.

November 1, 2017

I have Verine here.

Hi, Mikey. I am thrilled to be able to converse with you. Thank you so much for all that you told me about what it was like coming here and being here. It is very much like what you said it would be. This really is home, and I am very happy here with all of my family and friends. Your dad says hello. We are all so very proud of you and what you are accomplishing. I wasn't always sure about what you were doing and saying, but I sure understand so much more now. You are doing great things, and I understand that there is much more that you will be accomplishing. There are so many here that would like to talk to you, but right now, we all just pass on our love to you. You have so many friends here, it is incredible. Thank you again for all that you are doing with my estate. It is much more work than I thought. Give my love to Stephanie and Tyler. Toby says hello. That's it for now. We are watching your accomplishments. Your book will do better. All my love.

Thank you, Verine. My love to you and all my family and friends there. Thanks, Dad. Thanks, Toby.

November 2, 2017

You are getting close to the Estate being done. It will be good to be finished with it. No more dealing with those unfortunate distractions. You will be able to put that behind you and get on with your own endeavors.

Can't wait. I'm looking forward to getting it over with.

Just a few more steps to do. You are very close.

November 3, 2017

Hi, Michael. You had communication with Mother Joseph, and she explained why she is there for you, right?

Yes, she is there to help me overcome my tendency to get impatient, help me when I wish things would move along faster than they do, and enjoy the process.

Very good. It is part of your makeup. But there is also a reason why things take longer than you wish. You can't jump over the process. If *everything happened as soon as you wanted, you would miss out. You would skip over details that are important, and you might not be ready for the accomplishment or gift.*

Okay. I understand, and I realize that I am a great one for starting something and then getting to a point where I start looking ahead to the next project before finishing the one at hand.

It is good that you recognize that. She is there to remind you when that occurs.

November 4, 2017

Could you give me something to post on my Facebook page, please?

Good morning, Michael. Okay. "Be the person that you would like to see others being. See the good in others and try not to dwell on anything that doesn't resonate with you. When you see the good in others, then bring that goodness into you and make that a part of who you are. Let your light shine so that others can sense that part of you. Then they can appreciate it or not, that is up to them. As your light shines, that positive energy affects everything around you, everyone and everything. The world needs that light. As your light draws light to you, it has a domino effect and rebounds outward around the world. Can you appreciate how much good that does? There are many more lightworkers doing just that, at this time, on this planet. It is needed now to herald in this energy that will change the world and all who reside there."

November 6, 2017

Yes. Continue to work on your eyes. You can feel that energy across your eyes. This is a precursor to your third eye-opening, something you have been working on for a long time. This may be getting ready to open. Relax and see that happening as you feel that energy. Look for pictures to start appearing.

November 9, 2017

Yes. Merkabah. Do you feel as if you are getting more vibration? Can you feel that energy across your eyes?

Yes.

Good. It is getting closer for you to experience more. Keep at it. Continue feeling that energy grow and expand. There will come a tipping point. It is near.

I am excited about that.

You have many energies working with you to see that happen, and they will continue to work with you. There will be many great experiences to come.

November 10, 2017

Do you want to talk about the Estate?

Well, I am happy that we are close to a resolution. And I am very happy with the accounting and what everyone is getting.

Yes. It is turning out very well for everyone. This is finally getting close to being done. You did very well and deserve applause for all that you did. Verine picked the right person and is very happy and pleased with the outcome. She thanks you for all your hard work and wishes there was more in it for you, but there is more coming your way. This is just another experience for you.

November 12, 2017

How do you see my healing helping my cousin Anne?

You are doing all you can for her. She also has to believe that something good is occurring. She has to have faith. If she can see the slightest positive result, it will give her hope and faith. Then changes can happen. All that you can do is trust the process and continue to send love her way and ask the Divine Light to do what They do. We shall see. We cannot predict because there is free will, and the person has that choice.*

*You may ask, "Well, if the person has a choice, why wouldn't they choose to get better?" The answer is that every soul has a plan in place when we incarnate. It is what each soul desires to experience and, in some cases, for other souls to experience with them. Did the person go through whatever trauma for themselves or for others? While on the other side, souls may be asked or may volunteer to incarnate merely to help another soul experience an ordeal. It makes you wonder, doesn't it?

We also decide on our transition period. We choose our exit points beforehand, though sometimes there is more than one. If things become too difficult, we may choose an earlier one, or if we wind up accomplishing all that is needed in this life, we may depart early.

These blueprints are created with any number of guides who assist with what the soul wants to experience, wants to do over if not satisfied, or rectify unresolved issues from a previous existence. Sometimes it is necessary to rein in the soul's plans if the guide feels there is more adversity than the soul can handle. The soul may desire a specific experience and then set such a Herculean task that it is too much to handle, resulting in an early abandonment. The guides are there to recommend lessening the circumstances or changing the situation to a much more attainable one.

November 13, 2017

Dreams. You are having some vivid dreams.

Yes.

This is all a part of your sensitivity training. As you are getting stronger, your dreams are more vivid. You are dreaming in colors, and you are more cognizant of them, and you are experiencing more dreams during your sleeping hours. Eventually, what you experience as dreams will show up in your meditations. This is how you will start to experience the other planes.

I see. Sounds good. I am looking forward to that.

It is all coming together.

November 14, 2017

Let's talk about your vibration, which is becoming stronger. You are so close now. Stay with the Merkabah, and try to be a little more conscious of what you are seeing. Right now, you are getting brief visuals, but they are flitting out like a dream that you can't remember. You will get better at this—always getting stronger in your visuals and experiences. Wonderful. As you develop this, your Clairs are also expanding.

Very good. It seems like a long journey.

Not really, and the journey never ends. It just gets more interesting and, as they say, "Enjoy the journey and all that it brings you."

November 15, 2017

I find the Goddess of Angels* meditation very overwhelming. I can really feel it. It is one of my favorites.

*YouTube. Guardian Angel, Guided Meditation by Jason Stephenson. (I get quite affected by this guided meditation. It brings on the emotions.)

Yes. It definitely has an effect on you. You are there. You are experiencing what is being related. You are feeling the energies and the alignment. It is a beautiful experience. There is so much joy and love. It is a good one to do every once in a while, especially when you enjoy it so much.

November 17, 2017

You have a little bit of money now, which gives you some security. There are bigger things to come. Wonderful days in many ways ahead. We are excited for you. You can look forward to some very happy moments. Just know that they are there for you.

November 20, 2017

Don't let any problems you have with another or any thoughts which may be disparaging to another affect who you are. You are not that person. They are who they are. Be the best that you can be. Let your love flow. Let your love be for that person regardless of what they do; otherwise, you are letting another diminish the best that you are attempting to be. There must be love for all for you to attain the place that you are striving for. We want you to reach for those goals which you have set for yourself.

November 21, 2017

I don't know about continuing with the psychic art. I'm sure it's just me who is creating it, and the result doesn't look all that good.

As in all these things, it's a process. Continue doing what you are, and it will come. Suddenly you will know when spirit takes over, and you will see amazing results. Don't get discouraged.

November 22, 2017

I was wondering if I could speak to John and Katie?

Of course. Any time. Here they are.

Hi, Dad. We are here.

It's good to talk to you both. Although I think of you, I haven't spoken with you for a while. How are you?

We are fine. It is wonderful to talk to you. We are always excited to talk to you. We are happy to see you and see what you are doing. We love you and are always here for you.

I love you both, and I am so happy to know you are around me.

Always.

How are Buster and Toby doing?

They are always good. Running around and having fun.

Good. Are you involved in other things there?

Yes. You know we are your Joy guides, and we are interested in seeing some of the many wonderful art pieces and the fantastic music. There are concerts here that we enjoy. We also like being around others that share our interests and, of course, meeting your family and friends. Your mother is really something. She makes us laugh.

Well, she is your grandmother, and she made everyone here laugh too.

We love her and Granddad too.

Okay, kids. It was good to talk with you. I love you both. We will do this again. You are in my thoughts.

We love you, Dad, and are always with you. Bye for now.

November 23, 2017

We have an interesting class this Saturday with the Hathors. They are doing a healing, and I am looking forward to that.

This will be very powerful. Again, there will be energies that will be present that, as always, will benefit you. We can't express enough how important these sessions are for you. Your potential is unlimited. Let these energies flow to you. Be grateful for all that comes your way.

Our Merkabah group has had several sessions where the Hathors presented themselves to our circle. Claudette always made sure the group was focused and in the "Love" vibration when we would start.

I have since come to a place in my meditations where I have had contact with the Hathors, but always when I start purposely with "Love" and "Light" in my heart. I get confirmation of this when my body begins tingling all over—this is my sign that spirit is present.

November 26, 2017

That was an incredible experience yesterday—very powerful and with a lot of energy. I am most grateful to you and all the energies that were present.

Yes, it was magnificent, and it was pretty much all to do with the Hathors—their Love and Healing. We look forward to you having further interactions along the way with these wonderful beings.

Me too.

It is so important for you to be at these sessions. Every time you attend, it increases your vibrational energy and moves you further along your development path.

Yes. I understand.

Good. We are very happy for you.

These are my notes from that session:

> Merkabah meditation. Strong energy and a peaceful experience. I felt the presence of the Hathors behind me. The Hathors were present to help us send healing to someone who could use one. I sent this healing to my cousin Anne who is suffering from ALS. They helped us connect with the person. I teared up as I felt the sheer joy that emanated from her spirit. There was an overwhelming feeling of "Love." The vibration coming from the Hathors was wonderful. There was powerful energy flowing as we chanted.

November 27, 2017

I know occasionally you have doubts. Know that you are having these experiences. Let there be no doubt. You are meant to be moving forward with all that is happening with you. And all these experiences are truly occurring. Trust in the process. Trust in all the energies that are there preparing and bringing these events to you. Just as you had your initial doubts about this process that we are doing together and you are now comfortable with it, all these other procedures are happening. Believe it. You will become just as comfortable with them as you are now with this.

Thank you. Again, it was something I needed to hear.

December 01, 2017

Did I do a good job closing the mirror's portal in my bedroom?*

Yes. It is closed and guarded. You are always protected, but this is an added safeguard against any negative energy that may come through, and even though you are protected, you don't need negativity in your home. This stops that from entering.

Very good.

*In a conversation with Claudette, she asked whether I had any mirrors in the house and where they were located. I told her they were in the usual places, like the bathroom, but that I had recently taken one from Verine's belongings because it was nice and long, and I placed it in my bedroom. She was slightly bothered by this, saying that negativity can come through mirrors, especially in bedrooms, and that they can act as portals. She said it was wise to protect myself from that happening by placing a sentinel (a spiritual guardian) there to guard the mirror from negative energy entering. She also gave me some symbols to place on the mirror as added protection. I did this, but as Phillip said, I am always protected. Yet an extra safeguard can't hurt.

December 03, 2017

Glad to see you are working on your psychic art. Continue to do this. You will get better, and spirit is connecting with you. This is helping with your mediumship abilities. Practice. Practice. Practice. Do not doubt that what you are doing is just you. Spirit is connecting. Spirit wants a voice, wants to be heard. You can be that voice.

December 5, 2017

Could I speak to Archangel Michael?

Yes.

I would like to speak to Archangel Michael.

Yes. I am here.

Do you have any words of guidance for me?

I am happy to see you are finally on your path. It took a while and a lot of coaxing. You are doing well, but there is much for you to learn and very much more for you to experience. You have already had some wonderful experiences, which has given you a taste of what is out there for you. You must continue to work towards your destiny. You have wonderful teachers and guides, including angels, Archangels, and other energies, all who are there to see you succeed. Don't disappoint yourself. There is much love from the Universe for you and all beings no matter what. There is great potential within you. You have more power than you believe. I know you sometimes have doubts. Put those doubts aside. It is as it is. Go forth and be. There is much Love here for you.

Thank you, Lord. I thank all of you for all that you do for me and your love.

Whenever I read this, I get that tingling sensation, which confirms that Archangel Michael is present and acknowledging my effort.

Archangels are the primary messengers of God and work closely with our guardian angels to help us with unconditional love. They are highly evolved celestial beings, each having their own characteristics. I have heard the name of fifteen Archangels, but there may be many more. The main four are Michael, Raphael, Gabriel, and Uriel. Archangel/Lord Metatron is also a very powerful Archangel.

Archangel Michael is known as the Protector. His name means "He who is like God." We can call on the Archangels at any time for help. We call on Archangel Michael for protection and fearlessness. He is the preeminent Archangel.

Raphael means "He who heals." You can call on Him for healing and health issues.

Gabriel means "Messenger of God." He is there for those needing help with communication, either spoken or written.

Uriel means the "Light of God" and provides us with clarity and solutions to obstacles that may be causing us troubles.

December 6, 2017

We like where you are going with the psychic art. Draw. Let it happen, and then feel what comes through. You are letting yourself go. This is the way. Let those thoughts materialize, then put them down. Very good. You will become proficient at this. It is similar to your written communication—putting it down on paper. Good job.

December 7, 2017

You are having some back issues. You know you can fix this. Diet, exercise, and keep a positive attitude. See yourself free from this problem—healthy and well. Be happy with yourself and full of gratitude for the wonderful body that is you. You can have a long life pain-free. It is your choice, and you have everything in you to have that.

December 9, 2017

I had a very good meditation this morning. I felt the love and presence of John and Katie.

Yes, they were with you, and you did feel them. Lots of energy, and you felt that love because you were going with the heart rather than the mind. You might want to continue this in the future.

December 10, 2017

Yesterday, when I asked John and Katie to join me in my meditation, I felt their presence. Yet, when I ask other energies to join me and come closer to feel their spirit, I don't sense it nearly as much, if at all. Can you explain, please?

Part of it is that your children are with you much more and have a closer bond with you. There is so much love for their father that it transfers to you quickly and easily. That is not to say that there isn't great love for you from the other energies. Keep opening your heart and exploit that heart chakra more than the mind and keep asking them to come closer so you can feel them. They will, and you will get that tingling sensation so that you will know they are there. You will feel that energy, and it will be powerful. You are always learning. You are always experiencing new ways and means to enhance those experiences. It never ends.

December 11, 2017

It's easy to overindulge at this time of year. Try and be vigilant about what you want. Stay the course. Curb those desires. You can do it. This is mind control. You don't really need that much. Let your body process the good stuff. Your body knows. Listen to it.

December 13, 2017

Hi, Michael. Mother Joseph is there for you. We are glad you are including her in your thoughts. She is another energy assisting you in bettering your connection with the energies of spirit.

December 14, 2017

I'm starting to feel more positive about my psychic art.

Yes. Very good. You are seeing results, and again no doubts. You are wondering if what you are seeing is really spirit coming through, or just you drawing. Believe in what is occurring. It is there. It is really happening, and it is working. Keep with this. This is something that can be very special and not only interesting for you but also will become beneficial to others.

As always, the more you are participating in these kinds of things, the better you will get. Don't waver. Have faith. It is all there.

December 18, 2017

Do you see any good coming from my ads for Guided Messages from the Other Side in the United Kingdom?

It is good to expand your advertising. There is a big spiritualist movement in the U.K., so this could help in getting the word out there. All it takes is one little boost to get the ball rolling, and then when it starts, off it goes.

December 19, 2017

At this time of year, most people are in a giving way—more generous to others. Buying presents and giving. It would be well if this was carried on during the rest of the year. Not necessarily buying presents, but being in that giving vibration and in that receiving vibration which is also important. You always have the yin and yang. It is balance, and everyone needs that balance. Receiving with gratitude for what comes your way is just as fulfilling as the joy of giving.

December 23, 2017

I am curious about the sensation I had a couple of nights ago while sleeping, where it felt as if someone had their hands around my throat. This felt very real to me. Can you explain this, please?

This was a way of letting go of a negative experience. It did feel scary for you at the time. Past energies of a negative type can reside in you and may have been there for years. These can be from bad experiences or a buildup of negative energy. This was a releasing of negativity, and this was how it came through. All in all, it was a benefit to you of letting go of this, even though it didn't seem like it at the time.

December 25, 2017

Merry Christmas to you. Have a great day with your family. It is good to get together. Don't worry. Everything is good and will work out.*

*I was concerned about the weather and driving. I was spending Christmas at my brother's place with other family members.

December 27, 2017

You are going into a new year shortly. It is time to step it up a notch and get busier doing all the things that you have been doing, only better. More orderly. More writing. More painting. More. More. More. And try not to waste time with trivial incidental things that are not helping you. Better diet. Better physical activity. More. More. There is no reason why you can't start now. At least get yourself prepared for this in the coming days. Oh, yes, and more psychic art. You must keep practicing that. You are robbing yourself of important matters that you should be doing, therefore not fulfilling your designed life.

Okay, Phillip. I get it. Thank you. (Said lovingly, if that wasn't coming across, lol.)

December 29, 2017

Thank you for your prayers of gratitude. It means more than you think. It puts you in a place of well-being, which brings the flow of Abundance to you. So many good things emanate your way when you are in a place of thankfulness. Be grateful for all that you have, including what seems like something you don't want, because by knowing what you don't want, you then know what it is that you do want. So, even that is something to be grateful for. The unwanted leads you to the wanted. And your desires keep the flow moving—keeps the world turning. All of it leads to betterment and the Universe experiencing itself through you. That is an amazing quality and gift to have and is the reason all of you are here.

December 30, 2017

You had the thought of doing a video and adding it to your site explaining your book. You are getting a bit of traffic. You should try that. It may add a different flavor to your site and may create interest. At the very least, it would be good practice for a future time.

2018

January 1, 2018

Well, a new year. I hope there will be some good progress with the book this year and with my progression.

There will be. It's all about your participation. What you put in, you get back. It is your effort that decides what will occur, but I see good things happening this year for you.

Very good, Phillip. I am looking forward to that. Thank you.

January 3, 2018

I seem to be in that place where not much is going on with my meditations. I'm not feeling it.

I can see that. Sometimes you reach these plateaus, and there is something happening; you just are not aware of it. You must stay with it, and you will move on to the next level if you like. Again, don't get discouraged. I know it seems as if it is merely becoming routine, but it will change, and you will notice it when it happens. Maintain your gratitude for whatever you are experiencing. It is all good.

January 4, 2018

Wisdom. Be wise enough to know when you are in a place of danger. Be wise enough to realize that not everything is there to hurt you. Because you have freedom of will and are there to experience, don't be afraid to try something you may not be comfortable with. If you try it and fail, you still get that experience, and not everything is attained the first time. The old adage, "Try and try again." It may take several times, but there is a feeling of accomplishment when it has been realized that is wonderful. And if you never attain that goal, if you did your best, then that is all that can be asked. That is not a failure; it merely means that it was never meant to be, and there is something else that is better waiting for you. Go for the gold.

January 5, 2018

How am I doing with moving forward with my sensitivity? I don't see much changing.

There are subtle shifts taking place. You seem to do better when you have that group energy that carries on with you. You have been missing that this last month.* You are near, even though it may not seem like much is going on. As always, stay with it. You are to be rewarded with your efforts. It is there, and there is a lot of support around you.

*There were no workshops because of the holidays.

January 08, 2018

Keep the Merkabah going. It is very important for you to keep up with that meditation. I know you get a little bored with the beginning of it because you have done it so often, but it is a process, and you need that process to get where you want to be.

January 9, 2018

We are glad to see you with this new diet of fruits and vegetables. Do your very best to stay with this. You will reap big benefits, and you are trying to cut out sugar. Your body will greatly appreciate this and, if you can keep it up, you will notice the difference. You will get to where you want to be. Good stuff.

January 10, 2018

Let's continue our discussion about Religion. You are your own religion. All that you have read, all that you have realized, has helped you to form your own opinions. This is your religion. These are your beliefs. This is your spirituality, and it is good. Others have their own religion according to their own experiences, and that is good for them. Appreciate yourself and your religion, and appreciate others and their religion. It's what works best for you and them. All can be in harmony with each other, and there is no need to force your religion on others, just as they do not need to force theirs on you. No discord. Be happy with all. When everyone realizes this, there will be harmony in the world.

January 11, 2018

Sorry, Phillip. I'm having computer problems—frustration with technology. I have a love/hate relationship with computers. I love all they do for me, but I also waste a lot of time with the problems they bring, which frustrates me to no end.

Don't let that get to you. Remember where you want to be. In a place of joy, regardless of what's happening.

Yes, although it's hard sometimes.

Yes. Physical can do that.

(Ha. You know it.) **Okay. Got to go.**

January 12, 2018

I asked Ascended Master St. Germaine if he would take me to the Celestial Realm. I feel like he did, but I didn't experience a lot, just some brief visions in my head. Can you talk about that, please?

Hi, Michael. You did go there with Master St. Germaine. Your abilities are still not there yet where you could experience the whole of it. Though they are coming along, they still have to improve, and that will happen. The biggest thing you can do for yourself is to get yourself into that 'Love'* vibration and hold it. This will help you tremendously. It's going to occur. Don't give up. Don't be disheartened. All move at the pace that is right for you.

*This had been and continues to be a theme with all of my guides, as it should be. We cannot hear this enough.

January 15, 2018

Is the healing session I am doing accomplishing anything?

Of course. The mere fact that you are thinking of that person (my cousin who has ALS) in a loving way is good for them. The energies you are sending are helping even though they may not seem so. That person is benefitting from that energy. Remember, all that you do should have that 'Love' vibration, and only good can come from that. Miracles do happen.

January 18, 2018

I understand your feeling that way*, even though there is more going on than you may realize. I think when you get back with the group, it will re-energize you and help you to move forward. A little break is not *a bad thing*. Sometimes you just need to step back from a situation. It's all good.

*I felt I wasn't progressing in the Merkabah workshops. Impatience is something I still need to work on, and Mother Joseph is there to help me.

January 19, 2018

You are doing well with this diet. Your eating is so much better. Little sugar and lots of fruits and vegetables. AND you are seeing a difference. You can improve your eyesight. You are losing weight and improving your hair and nails. You are feeling good. This is something that you want to keep at, and it is okay to have a day where you let go a little and indulge yourself. But now that you see the benefits, this is something that you will want to continue. Young is a state of mind. Have that state of mind, and so it shall be.

January 21, 2018

We hope to see you back to your meditation routine. It is important, as well as your painting, and so forth. Time is not the same from our perspective and yours. Don't let time dissuade you from what you are looking towards. Take time away from the equation and just continue on your road of exploration. Be thankful for where you are and look forward to what lies ahead. It could be right around the corner.

(Note: I was taking a break from everything.)

January 25, 2018

When you did your "Advanced Merkabah" meditation, you pictured this beautiful garden. Know that you were visiting that place. That was not a daydream. You were there. It was a travel. You pictured flowers, a path, trees, and waters. You thought of the Elementals.* All of that was a part of your experience. Do not write it off as imagination. You are able to do this, and you have a lot of help.

That's good to know, Phillip. I am always grateful for your positivity in helping me remove that doubt.

It is a part of our mission. We are here for you for those very reasons, to assist you in your journey, and we will continue to press those words on you until you no longer have those misgivings, until you have complete confidence in what you are experiencing.

> *The Elementals are Earth spirits/Nature Beings that are here to support and heal the Earth. They come in many different sizes, and each has its role to play in helping the planet. They get their name from the four elements—earth, water, fire, and air, and each carries aspects of those energies. –Justin Andries, the Keeper of al Shante website.

January 28, 2018

Well, another wonderful class yesterday. Again, I hope I am not making things up, but I sensed the presence of Higher Energy Beings. I wish I could see what the others are witnessing.

Yesterday was better. You let yourself go into that "Love" vibration. That is the secret. That and just letting go and accepting whatever takes place, and if you don't experience anything, that is okay. Accept that. It doesn't mean that nothing is taking place. It just means that you aren't seeing or feeling it. Again, that is okay. You don't need to make anything up. And, tell it like it is, whatever that may be. It may be something that is particularly pertinent to you, which is good. Always, always, get yourself into that 'Love' state, that 'Love' vibration, and you will see and feel much more, hastening your development. It is the key. It is important, which is why Claudette stresses that so much.

January 29, 2018

Time to get back to the psychic art. This is something that you need to keep up with. Don't let it slip. You should try to do this at least every other day. You will become more proficient at it. This is a big part of your mediumship, so you must keep at it.

January 31, 2018

We like the look of your paintings even more now that they have been framed. These will make very nice gifts to people. It is a nice thing that you are doing.*

*I framed four of my paintings and gave one to each of the four people in my Merkabah class.

February 1, 2018

Do you have anything spiritual that you would like to pass on?

Yes. We could discuss the soul. What an incredible infinite energy that is you. All of you in all your incarnations. Now and forever. Your being. Your essence, here and now and in the hereafter. Always was. Always will be. Ever-expanding and joined to the All That Is. You know this but probably don't comprehend the immensity of it all. It is beyond words. It is Love, and your physical experience is a part of it. Go deep inside yourself and see the purity of who you are – that Higher Essence. You can feel a little bit of it right now as you write these words. It is in your heart.

February 2, 2018

Hi, Michael. Your mother wants to let you know how proud she is of you and especially with what you do for the family.

Okay, Mom. Thank you. I will always try my best to keep us together. Thank you, Phillip, for passing that on.

You're welcome.

February 4, 2018

It is all about your vibration, which is why you want to be in that "Love" state. That is what is important. If you constantly get yourself in that "Love" vibration, then things will begin to happen, and they will happen fast. So that is what you must do. Always be aware of that feeling of "joy" and "love." We will always stress that for you. It's going to be there. Do not doubt that.

February 6, 2018

Can you tell me anything about the drawing (psychic art) that I just did? I didn't get much with it.

That may happen sometimes. It may not be a strong connection. All the energies that are coming through are there to help you improve on the technique and the drawing abilities, along with strengthening your mediumship abilities. It is good that you are thanking them. The last one was not bad and was a fair depiction of what that energy once was. Keep at it, and at some time, you can look back at where you were in the process and see how far you have come. You will see a noticeable improvement.

February 8, 2018

Is there anything you wish to say today? Also, I just had the thought that there may be another guide working with me. Anything to add to that?

Hi, Michael. Yes. Guides will come in according to what you are needing at the time. I have been here for you and will always be available, but now there is another who will continue with your guidance.

I am getting the name Harold. (I get a name that pops into my head, and that is what we go with. I have to call him/them something. It just as easily could have been a feminine name.)

That is fine. Harold is here to work with you.

Okay. I don't have the words to express my most profound gratitude for everything you have done for me, Phillip.

(There is a sadness within me.*)

Do not be sad. I am here always as part of your group of guides. You may call on me at any time, and I will be there. This is good. This is how it works. It is a sign that you are progressing. Be happy.

Can I meet Harold now?

Of course.

Hi, Harold. Welcome. I am happy to have you here to guide me. I look forward to our joining together and your assistance.

Hi, Michael. I am very happy and proud of how far you have come. I have been part of your group of guides and have been following your progress. So now it is time to move that along. It is time for the next phase.

Very good. I look forward to this with you. Thank you, and a very, very great thank you to Phillip for all your guidance, love, and assistance. I am where I am because of you.

You are welcome, Michael. Continue to do good work and progress. Love, Phillip.

I love you too. Harold, we will continue this tomorrow, okay?

Very good, Michael. Talk to you then.

Thank you.

*I was truly sad when I heard Phillip was stepping aside for Harold. Phillip and I had started my journey together. As I stated at the very beginning, our guides tend to change approximately every couple of years, and as we progress, new guides come forward to help move us further along in our spiritual advancement.

All the discussions Phillip and I had, all the guidance he had given me, and the knowledge he had passed down daily were suddenly gone, and I felt like I was losing a very close friend. Suddenly, he was not there, and I missed him. However, I know he is always available to me; I merely need to ask.

February 9, 2018

Hi, Harold. I would like to say it is a pleasure to have you here with me. I look forward to your assistance. Welcome.

Hi, Michael. Thank you. I am aware of what you and Phillip have accomplished and am here to carry on with your development.

Good. Is there anything you would like to say today?

Yes. So during your meditation, you had glimpses of ways you might promote your book. These you should follow up on. This is inspiration from your guides. We would like to see your book succeed. We are here to help you with that.

Very good. In the next week, I will follow up on that and get it going.

Okay. We will remind you if you start procrastinating. It is time to move ahead with some of what you want to see happen in your life.

February 10, 2018

You are doing well with your psychic art. Do you notice an improvement?

I think I see myself getting a little better with it.

Good. You are going to be surprised when you see how much better you will get at this, and your sensitivity will greatly improve. Good work.

February 12, 2018

Yes. Angels are around you always. Take time out once in a while and see if you can feel their presence. They are filled with love for you and all others, and they are there to fill you with that love that is benefitting you greatly if you take a moment to feel it and acknowledge them. There are a host of angels. Be grateful for their existence and presence for you. They can help in so many ways. There are many realms and many Highly Evolved Beings but remember the angels. Look for them. Feel them. They are for you and all mankind.

February 13, 2018

I don't know what it is, but I'm not feeling like doing the meditations, although I did have a very good vibration when I asked for the Divine Waterfall* this morning.

Yes, I sense that hesitation in you lately. I would like to see you keep up with this, though, so maybe space it out a bit. You did feel that cleansing from the Divine Waterfall. That is good. You are right now still feeling that vibration. Keep aware of it. Hold on to it. Your exuberance will return once you start feeling, sensing all of it stronger. Don't give up.

I'm not going to give up; I just feel lackluster about it lately.

Okay. Don't let that weigh on you. Acknowledge it and let it go, knowing that it will get better.

*I call on The Divine Waterfall of the Sacred Garden to cleanse my chakras before starting my meditation in the morning. I picture this beautiful Waterfall of Light flowing down from the top of my head through my body and exiting at my feet, flowing down to Mother Earth. It cleanses my chakras with Divine Light, especially my Third Eye, as it cascades down.

February 15, 2018

How was that mental connection yesterday?

It was good. How did it feel for you?

I sensed thoughts coming through to me.

Good. It is something we should continue to work on. As Phillip has said to you, the more you try these different things, the better you will get. The more comfortable you will be with it, thereby improving. Always improving to get to where you want to be.

February 17, 2018

Is there anything you would like to say about my upcoming trip?* I probably won't be doing much meditation.

Yes. It will be hard, but try to get in a few quiet moments if the opportunity presents itself. It is a recharging for you. It will help. We, of course, will be there for you.

*I went to Las Vegas with some family members and friends for four days to watch the Canucks play and visit my sister and nephew, who live there. It was a great trip. I came back with less money [duh], but it was worth it. Loads of memories and fun.

Good. It is always nice to have protection when I am in a different environment.

You have many guardians there for you. Continue to picture the Golden Flower of Life Sphere* surrounding you and the environment you are in. Try not to overdo it, although that may be difficult when you are with a group.

* The "Golden Flower of Life" symbol goes back millennia and consists of concentric overlapping circles in a flower pattern. Pagans considered it "sacred geometry" with connections through all aware beings. It has a deep spiritual meaning in the "New Age" movement. It is a part of our Merkabah meditation, and we are also advised that it is a powerful protection tool that you can surround yourself or your property with.

Yes, I will need to cleanse myself when I get home. (Oh yeah.)

Diet and some fasting and lots of water. Try to drink a lot of water while you are away. It will help to flush out the toxins.

February 18, 2018

When you return from your trip, we would like to see you step it up a bit with your practices. It is time now for you to increase all the things that you are doing. More art. More writing. More of the homework that you have been getting, and also to start implementing some of those things that can move you along.

Okay, I understand, and I will need your guidance on some of this.

That is why I am here. There are a lot of energies here to assist you, but you have to be ready to do your part. It is not just going to be handed to you.

I understand. I need a boost or reminder every so often, or I can get complacent.

Yes. We will be on you.

February 19, 2018

Keep us in your thoughts while you are away. If you get the chance, spend a little time in quiet mind. We would like to be in contact with you communication-wise even though it will not be written. You can still use thought and, if possible, words to keep the lines with us open. You will have the opportunity for this.

Okay. I need to have that and know you and my guardians are around me.

Good.

February 20, 2018

This will be our last communication for a few days.

Try to use moderation in all that you do while you are away. (That didn't quite work out.) This will serve you well. It is your first trip in a long while, so enjoy yourself. Enjoy meeting up with your sister and nephew. Have a good time. Stay happy and positive. We are with you.

February 26, 2018

Well, I'm back. Thank you all for watching over me and keeping me safe.

It was a very good family get-together. It is always good to connect with those close to you. You didn't do too badly. A little overdone a couple of days, but that is the nature of the place. (Insert smiley face here.) Get sorted out today and back to your art and writing tomorrow. Routine is good. It is your time to get on with it.

February 27, 2018

Hi, Harold. On Saturday, there was a moment when I felt that tingling sensation, which is always a sign that spirit is present. Was that you that I felt?

Hi, Michael. Yes, it was. You thought of me, and I came through to validate your thought. There were things going on in Claudette's class where she included you in the mix, but with all that was going on where you were, with the noise and people, you probably didn't notice anything, but it was there for you. Gratitude is good. Always. Now back to your practices. Time to move forward with your progression.

Right. I will get on it.

Good. There is much to do. Time is wasting.

February 28, 2018

Okay, so that's a valid response to your artwork. Again, it's about the routine.*

*I had said aloud that I wanted to finish the writing session and then spend a whole week on my art, especially with the oils, which tend to dry out if I didn't constantly use them. It's easier stopping and going with watercolors.

March 3, 2018

I should set aside more time for us to converse in the coming week, although you may have put that idea in my head.

Yes, we did set that thought there. I think that would be a good idea. Let's see what happens. There is always a lot that we can say and pass on. We could cover more than our usual short responses.

Okay. Sounds good. I will let you know which morning we can do that.

March 5, 2018

I am ready to give you whatever time you need to pass on anything you would like to say.

Okay, let's see where this takes us. Previously Phillip guided you on many subjects that were beneficial to you, which had to do with health and well-being and your creative side—your art and writing. He covered it very well, and I don't think I need to add anything to what he communicated except to say that you should continue with what he said to you. All of that is important, and you should be diligent and aware of all of it.

I am here to move along with your development. You have an obvious interest in your book, but that has stalled. There are things that you can do to promote that, and we have slipped some suggestions into your consciousness. It is up to you to follow through with that. It is your will. You can do it or not. Success, however, doesn't hinge solely on that. Success can still come with help from the Universe even without you taking action, but it will take longer. Keep a positive outlook. See it happening. Get into that vibration, and any sort of action will move it forward.

You are improving on your psychic art; even you are noticing it getting better. Keep up that practice, and you will really see that also come forward. That is your mediumship. That is where you will shine.

Okay. Good.

Now, about the ISF and New York.* It can only be beneficial to you. You are concerned with certain aches and pains, travel, and finances. All of this will work itself out. Yes, you are getting older, but your health and stamina are excellent. Don't even consider yourself as that age. Think of yourself as much younger, and that is what you are. You can do this trip, and it will be a great benefit to you.

All right.

*The ISF's annual congress was taking place in New York that year, and I thought about attending. I made it to New York, but not for this meeting. My nephew from Las Vegas asked me if I would like to meet him in New York for a few days right around the same time. It's his favorite place. His father had passed away a few years earlier, so I thought it would be fun to connect with him and spend some family time together. We spent four fun-filled days together. I loved the "Big Apple" and the time with my nephew. Claudette had seen me going to New York in one of the sessions I had with her (in my first book), so another prediction is realized.

In the future, we will discuss other topics that you may have questions about. We are here for you. Ask, and if you don't get a satisfactory answer or feel that nothing is coming through, then ask again. And remember, continue writing these thoughts and feelings. Not only is this a way of communicating, but it is also a record of what has transpired between us. You already know that rereading some of these transcripts continues to help you, and you have the distinct possibility of another book from all these words.

Yes. Very good.

Now you can also communicate with others on this side, which you are aware of. And believe me, there are many who are ready for that communication and would be very happy for the opportunity.

Yes. Maybe I can set aside some more time for that type of thing.

That would be a good idea. It also strengthens your capabilities.

You are concerned lately that you are not getting enough out of your meditations. You hit a plateau, but it is changing now. You may notice a more vibrant feeling taking place, and that is what is occurring.

That's good to hear.

So we have covered some wonderful stuff in this discussion today. What do you think?

Yes. Very good. That is what I needed to hear.

I know.

We should try this again; I mean, setting aside more time for longer discussions every once in a while.

Sounds like an excellent idea.

March 7, 2018

I'm here to remind you of what you should be doing. You are aware of this. Sometimes other things get in the way. Attend to them, and then get back to your routine. You are having concerns about your meditations. This is the most important exercise for you. Don't give up because you aren't experiencing anything or there is too much happening with your thoughts. You can get through this. Let it all go for those moments when you are in meditation. Release everything else. Blank your mind. There is nothing urgent that you need to be concerned with. Most of it is trivial stuff.

March 8, 2018

There is someone here who would like to talk to you.

Hi, honey. How are you doing with everything? I am great and very happy here with all my family, friends, and pets. Everyone is so proud of you and what you are doing. I didn't understand or really believe a lot of what you were passing on to me at the time, but now I know that you were right in so much. You are much more advanced in your thinking than I was or many of those around you. Keep on doing what you are doing. Everyone says hello, including Mom and Dad and Mark. I just wanted to say thank you for all that you did for me. It made my passing so much easier, and you were right in your thinking.* Be well. Pass on my love to the children. They are doing so well.

Thank you for coming through. It is good to communicate with you. Give my love to everyone.

I will. Bye for now.

Bye. Love you.

Love you too.

*My wife and I had talked about what happens when we die. I gave her my view: which was that it was like walking through a doorway and all our family and friends greet us on the other side, with our parents being the first to welcome us. This is what she was referring to. I had done a lot of reading on metaphysical matters and sometimes would discuss my thoughts with her. I could tell she wasn't really sure about some of what I was saying by the look she had or her "hmmm" answer, and I could understand that because there was much that I spoke on that was pretty fantastic. I'm glad she had an easy transition. I believe it must be a very magical and overwhelming moment when we take that journey—so much love combined with the incredible feeling of being "home" again.

March 9, 2018

We want you to lift yourself up. Get back into that positive mood. We want you to become excited again for the many experiences that are on your horizon. Do not give way to any thoughts that can hold you back. Everything is happening. Everything is going accordingly. So go with the flow. Be happy. Be grateful and know that all is well.

Thank you, Harold. I needed to hear that. I was getting down on myself because it all felt like the same thing day in and day out.*

Well, that's where you are mistaken. It is not the same at all. It may seem that way to you, but changes are taking place even though you may not see them. Be of good faith. It is happening.

Thank you, Harold. I hear you.

*When you do these meditations every day and have specific experiences (especially with the Merkabah meditation), and suddenly the meditations become routine, you feel let down. You feel that you're not progressing or moving forward. This is referred to as "hitting a plateau." This has happened to me a few times when I would start to question what I was doing. I would usually take a break from meditating and communicating with my guide until I would get my enthusiasm back. Occasionally, my guide would be on me about it, which would be enough to get me back on my path. I have since found out that it usually means you are progressing or moving up the vibration scale when this happens. And, you don't always need to have something happening. The fact that you are quieting the mind and going into that place of peace and love is wonderful as it is. There are immense benefits from that alone. I have had some incredible experiences in meditation.

March 13, 2018

All these things that you are doing, you need to be more positive about and try not to expect too much. Just let whatever may happen, happen. Let it be. All that is going to occur will do so at the right time. You are doing and being yourself. Be open and be happy knowing it is on its way.

March 15, 2018

Continue to catch any negative thoughts and "erase" them. You are doing that. Erase them and replace them with positive ideas. See the outcome from that affirmative energy. Stay in the "Now" moment. As always, continue to express your gratitude for all that comes your way.

March 16, 2018

(I had done some psychic art portraits and had shown them to Claudette, who immediately pointed out that they were portraits of my guides.)

Is the picture I drew of you?

Yes. I am glad Claudette pointed that out yesterday, along with some other of your guides.

Wow. When I drew that and got the name Harold, I didn't connect that with you. I didn't know I could draw guides.

Which is why I am glad that you showed those to Claudette. Continue to look at those drawings and feel a greater connection with us.

Yes.

Very good.

You feel us now.

Yes.

Now you understand why continuing with this type of art is important to you and why you need to keep doing it.

Yes, I see.

As I've said many times, it will get better, and you will draw much from it. Pun intended.

I will. Thank you, Harold.

March 17, 2018

You are getting more of a feeling, a sense of spirit with your art. Are you not? You can feel more than you have in the past. This will get stronger. You are on the threshold.

Yes, I felt more rapport today.

Yes. Very good. Stay with this for a little longer and hold that sensation.

March 19, 2018

Hi, Michael. We see you doing both your art and writing during the day and moving forward with both, filling your time creating. This is fulfilling for you. This is you.

I understand and will work on that. Sorry, work is the wrong word. I will endeavor with pleasure on that.

Very good. A proper frame of mind.

March 20, 2018

Don't give up on your fruits and vegetables. You've gotten away from them the last few days. You were doing so well. Time to get back to them.

You are right. I will. Thank you.

March 21, 2018

Hi, Harold. I had a noticeable vibration in my throat during meditation today. Can you explain this?

Yes. The activation of your chakras has been moving from your crown chakra downward. You have always had a strong brow chakra. Now you will be noticing the throat chakra more. This is your communication with spirit. This is good. As this strengthens, you may begin to hear spirit. You are feeling it now.

Yes. It is still there.

Work on that vibration.

March 23, 2018

It seems I am not ready to communicate very well with my mind.

Yes. This is still the best way (writing) for you now, though it doesn't hurt to keep trying the other way from time to time. When you are writing or drawing, it is almost like a meditation. You are freeing your mind and just doing it. Just letting it happen. So far, that is working for you.

Okay. Good. We have a class tomorrow.

We will be there for you, and it will be another amazing class, always of immense benefit to the participants.

March 25, 2018

Hi, Harold. Another excellent experience in class yesterday. However, the back pain caused by the chairs takes away from it all. I will ask Higher Guidance to ease my pain.

An excellent class indeed, and you do need to rid the feeling of soreness during those classes. Spirit will work with you to make it more comfortable while you are participating. I know you sometimes have doubts as to whether you really are a part of those travels. Know that you are. You may not be receiving the clearer picture. That will come about. Right now, it is like there is a filter obscuring a part of it. It will improve, and you will see more vividly.

I can't wait for that.

Know that it will happen. Meantime, as always, relax and enjoy what you are getting.

March 26, 2018

Hi, Harold. I would like to know about the voice I heard just as I fell asleep last night. Can you tell me what that was, please?

Hi, Michael. Yes. That was spirit coming through. This can happen when you are in that state between wakefulness and sleep. I know it surprised you. This was also when your soul was leaving your body, and when the voice came through your soul shot back into your body too fast, which caused you to shoot up into a sitting position, which wouldn't have happened if your soul was still with you. Look for this to occur again, but without the shock value when you will hear a voice. This is what you have been asking for and working towards.

Okay. Thank you. I hope this hasn't hindered this from happening again.

No. Don't worry. Next time will be better and soon.

March 27, 2018

I felt much love today from the Other Side and many well wishes on my birthday, which was nice.

Happy birthday, Michael. Yes. There was much love sent to you from everyone here.

Thank you to everyone.

Have a good day. We will talk tomorrow.

March 28, 2018

We were glad to hear what you said about moving forward and about your thoughts on your eating when you go out. Those are "our thoughts" exactly, and you would do well to heed that advice. As you know, we have mentioned this many times in the past.

Yes, you are right. I'm always disappointed with my choices afterward, which seem okay when I'm hungry.

Try to discourage that hunger by eating something small ahead of time. This will help.

March 31, 2018

You can concentrate on your throat chakra. You can use the Golden Rose* to clear the voice box and the shoulder tube. Keep those clean and be expectant of voice coming through, especially at night when you are relaxed and in the delta state where things can happen.

Also, while I am here, consider that fasting diet that you read about and was brought to your attention. Fasting at least one day, and even more, so two days a week would be something that you should be trying.

Yes, I felt you brought that to me, and I will try that.

We did, and it will be good for you.

*In one of our mediumship classes, we were told to picture a Golden Rose during meditation to cleanse specific areas of the head and upper body, i.e., pineal gland, pituitary gland, and throat box, and open the crown, brow, and throat chakras. We were told to use as many golden roses as needed until each area was pure and clean.

April 2, 2018

I'd like you to help with my fast today. I want to do it twice a week, but I need your assistance when I get hunger pangs.

We will help you. When the food desires kick in, think of us; drink plenty of water and tea throughout the day. The first few times will be the hardest. After that, it will get easier. Have your juice drink later in the day.

April 3, 2018

I will call on the spirit guide who can help me with my psychic art and try working with my left hand.

Do that and see what occurs. You are already seeing improvements in some of the portraits. This will get better and better.

April 5, 2018

That was a different meditation today.

Yes. You should continue to get into that state (the slow breathing and clearing the mind, getting to that trance state). That's where things will start to happen. Pictures will start appearing. Think of it as a screen and movies playing on it. Keep at it. Very good.

April 7, 2018

Can you confirm that that was my guide Richard* who came through in my psychic art today?

Yes, indeed, that was Richard. When you first realized that that name kept coming through, then we reminded you of that first session when it was told to you that Richard was your guide at the time. He was just saying hello to you and how far you have come over the years. What wonderful progress you have made since then and all that lies in front of you.

As I told him, I am most grateful for his help and everything my guides do for me.

He is always available and will keep tabs on how you are doing. The same with Phillip and the same when I pass you over to a new guide sometime in the future

*In one of my sessions with Claudette, she said that one of my guides was named Richard.

April 10, 2018

Angels are always with you. You can ask them for help with anything. See if you can feel their presence. They love you unconditionally.

April 12, 2018

Yes. Struggle through your complacency. I use the word "struggle" because that is what you are feeling. You are feeling your meditations as becoming a bit of a struggle because they are seemingly routine. Everyday meditations appear the same. You need to work yourself through this. You need to find that joy, that excitement again. Keep yourself open to the thoughts that there are things just waiting to manifest, and they are very close. Don't get down. Stay with it.

April 14, 2018

Your Higher Guidance is not the same as your Higher Self—the part that is the All of you. Every part of you, past lives, the Whole Essence of who you are. The complete Soul Energy. The Infinite you. And it is good for you to connect with that Energy. All that you have ever been is there. It holds the answers that you are seeking. Continue to try connecting to this Source of Knowledge, and do it with profound love.

April 17, 2018

Is there anything you wish to say today?

Yes. Except you are going over in your mind most of what I was about to tell you right now, and you know what that is. The usual things that I bring up that you are neglecting, so no need to write it.

Yes, I hear you.

Okay. Let's keep the lines of communication open.

April 18, 2018

Glad to see you get back to your routine of art and writing, continuing with your Merkabah, and that you are in a better place with that. As we have said so many times, it is important for you to keep with it for your advancement, and the better frame of mind you are in while doing it, the quicker this will happen. Remember, be happy in all that you do and all that you have in this life. Everything grows from that.

Thank you, Harold. Continue to give me a kick in the pants and remind me of that.

Will do.

April 19, 2018

Keep your exercise simple. You have been overdoing it sometimes, which is what is causing your shoulder problems. It needs time to heal. So keep it simple so as not to exacerbate the injury. As you get older, it is good to be fit, but you have to be cautious in how you go about it. Walking is good. Less strenuous movements and, of course, as always, diet. You don't need as much food. Never did. Get into the routine of eating less. It will take a while for your body to process this, but eventually, you will be eating less, and your body will have adapted to that. With eating less and simple exercises with less stress, you can keep yourself fit and healthy.

April 21, 2018

I just worked on my psychic art and felt my mother coming through.* The picture isn't great, but there is something there, and when I asked, I got confirmation in the form of a tingling sensation in my body.

Yes, that was your mother, and you could definitely feel her in the picture. Her essence was there. Good job.

Thank you, Harold. I am excited about that. Although my family may not see the resemblance, I can absolutely see something of her in it.

Good. And you had a good meeting yesterday with old comrades, which was nice for you.

(I attended a memorial for someone that several of us worked with for many years.)

Yes, I enjoyed meeting up with them, though it was a sad occasion.

It's nice for you to get out once in a while to see old acquaintances. It was a huge part of your life.

*I am not a portrait artist. My normal paintings are landscapes. I had no doubt that my mother came through in this drawing; I could feel her essence. However, it's important to know that the resemblance may not always be exact with psychic art, but should be recognizable to the person receiving it. The medium will complement the drawing with the communication coming through, helping to define that person's energy.

Since this was done, I have come a long way with my psychic art. Some were so-so in the first year or so, and others were downright crude drawings. As my guides mentioned time and time again, it is a process. Without their prompting, I don't know if I would have stuck with it. I can see now that this was something I was supposed to do.

April 22, 2018

Again, be gentler with your exercises. You may want to consider yoga or try getting back into your tai chi. Any strenuous exercise now puts too much stress on your body. As we said, walking is good, and you are thinking of a bike. This is also something you should pursue.

April 23, 2018

Yes, we can do that.* Keep asking us to remove that during the class, so you are not in discomfort.

*I had asked Harold to help me with the pain I would experience during the workshops sitting on the uncomfortable chairs, which took away from being in an altered state.

April 24, 2018

Just keep doing what you are doing. When a thought pops into your head, try and go with it when it has to do with what you are trying to attain. Many times those thoughts come to you from spirit. It is spirit trying to help you in your endeavors. So it is worth paying attention to it.

April 26, 2018

Keep reminding yourself of where you want to be with your health, your lifestyle, your painting, and your writing. Stay positive. Be in that place as though it is happening with abundance in all. Remember, you are a powerful being with all that you need. Your dreams can come true and will come true. You have to have that belief that it is so. All is there for you.

Thank you, Harold. I needed to hear that.

Yes, I know. We are here to remind you.

Please keep doing that. It's easy to forget sometimes.

Okay.

April 27, 2018

When I create the psychic art portraits, is spirit coming through to me? And how do I thank them properly, other than saying, "Thank you for doing this for me"?

It is most definitely spirit coming through, and you are getting an essence of who they were. You especially knew this when your mother showed up. Your thank yous are enough. They are in a place of "Love and Light," and they know that they are helping you, and that is enough. You are showing your gratitude, and they appreciate that. Keep at it. This will be your forte. You will get much more from this as you progress.

April 28, 2018

Class today.

Relax. Enjoy the experience. We are with you. Try not to think about your back. Let us help with that.

April 29, 2018

That was a very powerful class yesterday. I always appreciate all your help and the energy that comes through during the class.

It was very good for you. We are happy that we can assist you. Every time you attend one of these classes, you benefit. Each time you get that much more sensitive until you will feel that shift, feel that breakthrough. You are getting there. You probably don't realize it, but there has been an incredible change happening to you, from where you are now to where you were a couple of years ago and where you will be a couple of years from now. If you could see what we see, you would be and should be very excited. Keep with it. It is all there for you.

April 30, 2018

Is the picture (psychic art) I have just drawn of you?

Yes. It is. A fair depiction. I have waited until you had improved before bringing myself forward for you to draw. You are at that point now where I thought you could do that. So...now you have a face to put to me.

Well, that is very good. I guess I could have put a smile on your face.

Haha. Remember, it isn't necessarily about capturing emotions but a general overall likeness of what the spirit looked like in a physical incarnation from a life of many lives. If it was of someone you knew, then the likeness will represent itself like the way you remember that individual, as in the case of your mother; otherwise, it could be from any number of past lives.

Okay, I see. Thank you for coming through to me. It is nice to put a face to the voice.

Good.

Tomorrow, I would like to talk to you about heightened sensations after the last class. *Okay.*

This is the psychic art portrait of Harold. I believe he was being gracious in saying it was a fair depiction. Later, I get a better image.

This drawing is from an early Skype session I had with Claudette. When I showed it to her, she told me it was one of my guides. The name "Alfred" came through with more information, but it resembles my other "Harold" drawings. Did this guide die in World War I, and was that his name at the time? That's what I got.

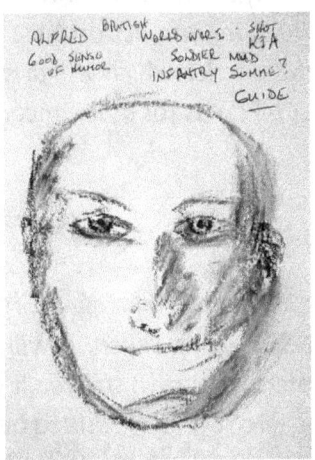

May 1, 2018

I wanted to talk to you about the heightened sensations I experienced while meditating after the last class, but it didn't happen so much today.

Yes, and you know the reason. That chair is not a good one for comfort while meditating. The arms interfere with you.

Yes.

Do your regular Merkabah tomorrow and see the difference. Also, keep working on getting into that 'Love' vibration for the "Activate Merkabah" and try to keep your mind off what is taking place, as Claudette recommended.

It is not easy.

You can do it. Out of the mind. Go with the heart.

May 3, 2018

You got some inspiration this morning about fasting and bettering yourself, ridding yourself of some aches and pains. That is your spirit guides sending this to you. Try and act on this. It will help you. Try to push through the mental barrier which will arise when you get those cravings. You can do it. Call on us for assistance. We will help you.

May 7, 2018

You have been contemplating the bike again. You should do that this week. Don't worry about it being taken. It will be guarded. Put that Golden Flower of Life Sphere around it to keep it safe. This will also be a benefit to you. You get exercise and the added benefit of being outside enjoying the environment that you have. It can be its own meditation.

May 8, 2018

Yes. Doubt can hold you back. Stop doubting and start believing in all that is occurring with you. That psychic art is happening. The travels are happening. You have abilities. Believe it all and have Faith in what you are doing. Have Faith that your desires will be fulfilled. When you doubt, you hold back the vibration, and it will take longer for your progression. Know it. Revel in it. Accept it. It is all there for you.

May 10, 2018

I had an intense feeling doing the Merkabah today. It almost felt like something was going to happen.

Yes. Hold onto that when it occurs. You are very close to a breakthrough. Very good. We are excited for you for this. Plus, it makes you want to continue with these meditations in anticipation of what lies ahead.

May 12, 2018

Now that the weather is getting nicer try to get out more. Get the bicycle and start riding around, enjoying your environment. You might take your camera and acquire some photos you can paint.

That's a good idea. I will get on that this week.

May 14, 2018

Be kind to yourself. Don't beat yourself up if you feel like you are not doing all that you think you should be. It's a new day; start again. Let it go. But don't give up. There are things that you know that you need to realize. If you fall down on those, it doesn't mean that you have failed. Get back at it, and we are here for you. You have lots of help just waiting to be asked.

May 15, 2018

You need to apply sunscreen when you go out now on your walks and when biking. It's not like when you were younger. The sun's rays can be much more harmful. This is something that you need to be made aware of.

Okay. Thank you.

May 17, 2018

You are noticing a change in your meditation, a different feeling.

Yes.

You want to try increasing the recurrence of the Merkabah now that you have that accelerated vibration. It doesn't have to be every day. Maybe two days Merkabah, one day of quiet meditation, and see if this can move you along some more.

May 18, 2018

Your shoulder needs rest. Try not to do anything to exacerbate this situation. Seek gentle movements. No physical exertion. This may take a few weeks. Make it your intention to leave it alone as much as possible. It will get better.

May 20, 2018

You are close to a breakthrough. Again, we say this. You feel this also. You are detaching yourself more now (in meditation). As you do this, things will start to happen. You feel you are close also, don't you?

Yes, I do. I won't press it, but I feel it will happen soon.

Very good. You are right. We will be so thrilled when this takes place. You have been striving for this for a long time, in physical time. Good for you.

May 21, 2018

I was looking forward to the Merkabah this morning, but they are cutting the lawns outside. I thought they were done, but they began again, louder than ever. What the heck?

You had good intentions, but bad timing. Maybe you chose that moment for a reason – to test your detachment, which I gather wasn't that strong.

No.

So this is something you can work on. Imagine being so detached that that bothersome noise doesn't even register with you. Now that is being detached. You just set yourself a test. That's what the bad timing was all about.

Okay. I get it. Work to be done. Thank you, Harold, as always.

May 23, 2018

We would like to see you get out more now that the good weather is here. Enjoy some fresh air. Walk, and when your shoulder is better, bike. You can do this and still have time for your painting and writing. The days are longer. There's more time for all these activities. Find a good time, maybe in the morning before it gets too warm or even in the evenings. Set up a schedule that feels right for you.

May 24, 2018

Open yourself up to all the environment has to offer around you. This is an add-on to what I related yesterday. You have so much near you. Get out and enjoy. Open your eyes to it all and be grateful for the wonders that are there for you.

May 26, 2018

That is a very good likeness of me*. Yes, it is nice for you to have a picture in your mind of who you are conversing with. You can look at that when we are communicating. It may help to bring us closer.

*Another psychic art portrait of Harold had come through. I think he's doing this until I get it close. Lol.

May 29, 2018

As usual, a very wonderful class with the group yesterday. However, I panicked when Claudette asked us to channel the Masters because I felt I couldn't do it.* As much as They (Ascended Masters) tried, I couldn't accommodate Them. I wish I were better at this. My

mediumship abilities only include communicating with you through writing or improving my psychic art.

Don't fret. No one else was concerned with how you did. Even the others, with all their experience, were having a little difficulty. You still have some resistance to letting go completely. Once you get by that (and you are not far off from doing that), then you will be able to channel better. It is all a process. Some come to it easier than others. Some have been doing it much longer than others, and, of course, there are those who can never give up that letting go at all. Lately, you have been noticing more energy, more vibration, and you are in a place where that will happen very soon. Stay positive and enjoy the process. Remember to look at this as an exploration, so revel in the journey. Everyone is rooting for you and is thrilled for you.

*In our monthly meeting, after our group meditation, Claudette asked each of us to connect with one of the Ascended Masters who were present and to channel Their words. Panic barely describes my emotion at that moment. When my turn came, I remained silent. Claudette kindly tried to talk me through it, but with no success. She told me not to worry, saying my doubt was causing me to freeze up, but she reassured me that I had the ability to do it and that I just needed to have more confidence and trust in myself. This wasn't the last time she challenged me to do something like this and get me out of my comfort zone; it was her way of advancing me because she knew I could do it.

June 2, 2018

You are going deeper with your meditation. Good. Now see if you can go deeper but hold on to some awareness.

June 4, 2018

I still have problems with my shoulder (torn rotator cuff, second time). I've tried resting it, but it doesn't seem to be getting any better. What can I do to fix this, please?

Yes. There is an underlining problem. We thought some of the classes you had would take care of this, but you seem to be holding on to something that is deep-rooted. Keep resting it this week, and if it has not improved, then see your doctor. It is a reoccurrence of your previous shoulder injury that you have aggravated.

June 6, 2018

I am wondering about channeling. If I am on my own, can I go deep and channel even though I may not be aware? And if I could, would spirit still come through if I had a recorder?

There would be no point in spirit channeling if you are not aware of it. Spirit could come through though, if you were recording while you were in a trance state.

Is this something I should try?

Yes. Have your recorder, and then when you go deep with that higher vibration, and giving spirit your intention of invitation to them for that purpose, then this could be a viable proposition. Maybe try this on the days when you are not doing the Merkabah, or even do your Merkabah and then try it.

Okay. I will try this.

Very good.

(I only tried this once with no success and decided not to take it any further because I no longer felt the need to experiment with it. I was originally curious about this as a possible viable way of channeling but quickly decided to continue with my normal routines. Sometimes you need to try these things but trust your instinct when it's time to let it go. There's no harm in experimenting.)

June 7, 2018

I have also been thinking about doing Past Life Regression*. I am interested in discovering whether I have known Claudette in a past life. Can you expound on that?

You have known Claudette in a past life. This is something you may want to try. You may want to work on your higher vibration some more and letting yourself go completely to get into that state of mind first.

*Past Life Regression is a trance state that takes you back to a past life and is usually done with the help of a medium. Claudette felt we had a shared past life connection.

June 8, 2018

Do not fret about the Estate. It's all going to work out. Just take it as it comes. Be easy with yourself. Take heed of your thoughts on sugar, sweets.

June 9, 2018

I had a very good feeling today with the Merkabah. It was more intense, if that's the right word. I felt as though I was close to something happening.

You are right. You were close. It won't be long. Try to hold onto that feeling in future meditations, and there will be a sensitivity that you have been hoping for. You are very close, and you are getting the help you are requesting.

June 11, 2018

Hi, Harold. I feel as though I am getting deeper with my meditations with Master St. Germaine and the Alchemist's* help.

Yes. They are helping you to get to that deeper level. Continue with this.

*Spiritual Alchemy is about transforming the inner self. The Alchemist is there to help you do that. Ascended Master St. Germaine is also considered an Alchemist and is one you can call on to help in your spiritual development and in raising your vibration.

Harold, the psychic art that I have done and that I am looking at now, can you tell me about her?*

She is another of your guides. She is there to watch over you and protect you, especially when you are sleeping.

*I had been looking at this picture from two days ago when I asked that question of Harold. I am still trying different tools for doing my portraits. This was done with pastel oils. I have a ways to go yet before I start to see improvement.

June 14, 2018

Keep working on that deeper level of meditation. Claudette will provide you with new insight on that.

What about Past Life Regression?

We think you should try that. It's a new experience that could provide some information that might open up to assist with what you are doing. It is worth looking into.

June 15, 2018

My shoulder is starting to feel better. (Rotator cuff still.)

Yes. Resting them is working. Continue with this. When they are better, do some very light exercises and bring them back slowly. It is a good time to get that bike now that you are feeling better.

Yes, I am going to do that Monday.

Good. You are thinking of the lawyer (Verine's Estate). You have a plan in mind for dealing with that (it seems to be dragging). Go with your plan. This will get resolved. Something is going on there.

June 16, 2018

I want to take the opportunity to say how much I appreciate communicating with my guides. I am grateful for the advice you give me and how much it helps me.

Thank you. We are here for you, and it is our pleasure to be there for you, knowing that your progress and improvement is as much joy to us as it is when you feel good about how everything is going. We are proud of you and what you are accomplishing. Blessings to you.

June 18, 2018

I feel I'm starting to let go more and getting into a deeper trance state.

Yes, you are. Stay with it, but see if you can hold onto what you are experiencing. You are going too deep, to the point where you are not observing the adventure. You want to get there but also be aware of what is happening without the left brain (logical) taking over.

June 19, 2018

It appears that everything keeps pointing me in the direction of New York.

Yes. We are glad that you are considering this. All things happen for a reason. There is a basis for this trip, and it being New York. It will become clear.

June 21, 2018

My shoulder is slowly feeling better after resting it for a while now. However, I don't seem to be losing much weight with this diet.

Continue resting the shoulder. It is improving. You may consider some light exercises. Just raising and lowering your arms. You can eventually increase the action at a slow pace, but remember that particular injury is prone to reoccurrence, so don't overdo it as you have done previously. Once you feel any suggestion of discomfort—Stop.

Stay with what you are doing with your diet. You will notice a sudden significant drop in weight. Without you exercising your upper body mass, it takes longer, but the reduced caloric intake will compensate. You do not need a lot of food input when you are not exercising. Most of you eat more than you need to. You will get there. You know what is good for you and what is not. Walking is good for you. Keep that up, and remember to bike.

June 22, 2018

Our class is tomorrow. I hope you will help me let go and reach that deeper status.

Of course, we will. We will also help to relieve any back issues you may have to go along with that. These classes are so important for you. The added energy is invaluable.

June 24, 2018

Thank you for being with me in the room yesterday. That was another incredible class with the Masters of Rays* and the Lords of Light. There was tremendous energy, and it was very uplifting. I felt I conveyed Master St. Germaine but wasn't sure whether he was speaking through me or merely me. I'm not sure if I was deep enough for him to come through.

Definitely an exceptional class. How wonderful. Take heed to what Claudette said. It is a process. You are just starting with this channeling. You will go deeper. You will let yourself go more, and it will get better.

The energies will work through you. Don't doubt. Stay positive and let it happen. All is taking place. Experience it. We are always happy to be there for you and are proud of how well you are doing.

*Ascended Masters associated with one of the seven Chakras, also known as the Chohan, or Lord of that Ray.

June 25, 2018

I had a very good meditation today. I felt I went deeper, and it was more intense than usual. Very good Merkabah also. There was a nice feeling of movement (spinning).

Yes, very good. That was much better. You are so close to discovery. The energies you received at the class are assisting you. All that you have been experiencing through these classes are moving you forward, raising your vibration and energy. You can see how important they are for you. It would be extremely difficult for you to do this on your own.

Yes, I agree.

June 26, 2018

We are glad to see you continuing with your psychic art. Keep with it. You may want to try it using paints and see if that frees you up. Don't think too much. Just let it flow. Be loose with it.

June 29, 2018

I try to immerse myself in the vibration when meditating, as Claudette suggested.

That is good. Stay with that. Things will start to happen. When you are experiencing, then you are in a state to notice phenomenon. You are in a trance state but not so deep that you lose consciousness of what is going on.

July 1, 2018

Stay with your plan for your diet and exercise. You don't need some of those things you are considering. You can use them another time. Maybe next weekend. You have been doing well. Do not relapse.

July 2, 2018

Writing and painting. Get back on track with these.

Yes, I have been letting them slip lately. I will get back to them. I want to make sure I can get my walks in.

That is good also. There are enough hours in the day for you to accomplish all these. Let go of some of your distractions (TV). You know of what I am speaking.

Yes.

July 4, 2018

If there is something that you have been wanting and it isn't coming your way, it doesn't mean it won't; only that it has been delayed or there is something else out there coming to you that is even better for you. Know that your desires are being fulfilled, and it is only you that may be delaying them, or the Universe has decided when the right moment might be.

July 5, 2018

Well, that was amazing. I would never have thought that might happen.

(I had connected with a Higher Being. I will leave it at that.)

Yes. That is awesome for you. What a thrill. Good for you. This was a wonderful experience for you, and now you know that there are incredible experiences ahead waiting for you, as we have hinted at before. We are the messengers and helpers of which He spoke. We are happy for you.

Thank you. I love you all.

July 7, 2018

I've decided to go to New York as I feel I should go there. I hope you can help me so that everything runs smoothly and without any problems.

Yes, very good. As we said, you are supposed to go there. Everything will work out fine. Don't worry about your physical discomfort on the plane (bad knees). Don't worry about the weather (hot and humid). It is all good.

July 9, 2018

Don't be afraid to relate your experience from a few days ago. You believed that it happened and who you communicated with was who They say They were. That's all that matters. People can make up their own minds whether they wish to believe or not. That is on them. As long as you believe, that's all that is important.

(Here, Harold is referring to my connection with a Higher Being on July 5th and my hesitancy in relating my experience because I feared others' reactions.)

And, yes, it was out of fear. The fear was that people would say, "Okay, he's lost me now. He's gone too far." Let me just say that any of you that have read the *Conversations with God* books by Neale Donald Walsch, well, that was my experience. It seemed as normal as my communication with my guide. The words popped into my head, and they were very special. Here is what I recorded after the meditation:

> Morning meditation (not the Merkabah). I was letting myself go when I saw a beautiful purple color. I decided to try to merge with the color. I saw and felt it envelop me. Then a voice telepathically said, *"This is God."*
>
> **God?**
>
> *Yes.*
>
> **This is amazing.**
>
> *It shouldn't be. I Am always here.*
>
> **I know, but to come through.**
>
> *It was the right time.*
>
> **I have been trying to improve my sensitivity.**
>
> *I know. I have many messengers and helpers for you. You just have to open up some more. You have been doing very well, considering you started later in your life. It was the right time for you. You are moving along your path and getting to where you need to be. We are*

proud of how far you have come and thrilled about what lies ahead. I Am a part of you as you are a part of Me.

Thank you, God. Thank you. Thank you.

Bless you. We will talk again.

(And we did.)

I needed to let go of the fear and share my experience. I believe we can all do this by going to a quiet place in our heads with no distractions and asking God a question. Try it. You may be surprised. And if nothing happens, don't immediately dismiss it. I've been working on receiving spirit now for a few years. If you sense some words coming through, then go with it. My biggest hurdle was always wondering whether I was merely making everything up. My guides had to remind me not to doubt myself constantly.

July 18, 2018

Sorry I missed our talk yesterday. Is there anything you would like to say today?

Yes. Go with what works best for you with your psychic art. It's okay to experiment with other mediums (paints, etc.) but stick with what works for you.

(I've been using oil pastels because they are easy to draw with and blend nicely. I tried watercolors, and the results weren't very good.)

Yes, so I found out.

That's okay. You never know until you try and that may get better in the future.

July 20, 2018

I know I shouldn't be asking because it defeats the purpose. However, do you envision a place where I can grow vegetables and flowers, where I can have a cigar occasionally without worrying about others, and where I can have a dedicated space for my art? I am not complaining; I'm happy to be where I am, but it doesn't give me the flexibility to do these things that interest me.

I do believe that you are going to find that place, and it will happen. Don't concern yourself with age or running out of time. It is all good, and it will turn up when the time is right for you. It may seem as though many years have passed since you first made known your desires in regards to this, but it isn't even a blink in the eye in the greater scheme of things. You have accomplishments ahead of you to fulfill. Concentrate your efforts on those and, remember, be happy for all that is in your life.

As always, very good advice. Thank you.

July 23, 2018

Is it okay if we try communicating by mind sometimes? I won't give up the written conversation.

Yes, that's fine. The written part is very important. It's a solid record, whereas the mind is quickly forgotten. Practicing with the mind is fine, though. There is no reason why you can't do both. I know you wonder if you need to do the written every day, that there is nothing of any significance that will come through every day. But it is essential to keep this line of correspondence open. It is our connection to you and you to us, and you never know what might come through that is meaningful.

Yes, I understand.

July 25, 2018

You can't live another's life for them. You can offer advice if they ask. You can counsel if they ask. But ultimately it is up to them to take their actions. You can help, but that is all. All are responsible for their own decisions, and then what happens will be in accordance with what they choose. You wish them well and send them "Love" and "Light." Don't get caught up in their drama, as then you are making your own decisions to do so, and those actions will have an effect on you.

July 26, 2018

I thought I would try an app that is supposed to pick up several frequencies and help communicate with spirit to see if anything would happen. Is this viable or just a gimmick?

I wouldn't put too much faith in this. You were right to protect yourself first. You would be better served to continue with what you have been doing. You can keep trying this, but don't get too involved with it. You want to be better with your communication, and that will only happen by doing what you have been doing.

Okay, good.

(I let it go.)

July 27, 2018

What do you think of my plan?

This is the right move. They need to take a positive step, one way or the other. Merely doing that will create a release. You can't get caught up in the drama. Try and remove yourself from this toxic situation. Stay with your position and hold on to your positive energy.

I was embroiled with the turmoil of my friend, who was having difficulty making any decisions regarding their daily life. I intended to tell them that I could no longer be involved and to seek professional help. The constant phone calls were draining my energy, with no changes ever made.

July 29, 2018

Let's talk about my failure in removing myself from this situation. It didn't turn out the way it was supposed to.

You had a plan. Part of it worked, but you caved when it came to removing yourself completely. You should distance yourself from this the best way you can. You may have to slowly wean yourself away from this. Remain truthful. They are in a vulnerable state. Don't beat yourself up. You were trying to help, and they are playing on your goodwill.

July 30, 2018

You will be away for a little while and won't be doing your usual meditations (meeting my nephew in New York). See if you can work on some quiet time, even if it's only for several minutes. It is always a benefit to you when you can do this, even if there are a lot of other things going on. As always, we are with you, for you, in every way.

July 31, 2018

I will try to keep you in mind while I am away. There won't be any written contact.

Very good. We will stay in touch. Be aware of the weather with regard to your physical exertion. Hydrate, and don't overdo it. Your health is good, and you can do this. Be aware of all that is around you. Be vigilant. You will have a good experience.

August 6, 2018

I had a wonderful trip. Thank you for watching out for me. Was there a specific reason I thought I should go other than spending time with my nephew?

I had a great time in New York. I met my nephew there, and we had a splendid few days seeing the sights and sampling some fantastic meals—we ate great food in Little Italy, saw the Empire State Building, New York Stock Exchange, 911 Memorials, Central Park, and Coney Island. We used the New York Subway system completely, and it was fine if a little warm. I would definitely go back there again. I wasn't sure if there was supposed to be a special meaning to being there, which had previously been hinted at.

You are welcome. Yes, it was a very good trip. It was special to have some time with your nephew and share some memories. Good for the both of you. It was lovely that you could add your energy to the city. It was also important because it shows you that you can travel comfortably and enjoy someplace different, something you may do more of in the future – as in meeting your relatives in England. New places. New energies. Plus, you had that moving experience connecting with spirit, which you deeply felt at the Memorial.* All of it was as it should be, and it was foretold.**

Yes, that's true.

*I had a profound experience at the National September 11 Memorial World Trade Center. It was an overwhelming sensation of spirit being present. My whole body began tingling, and I felt a deep sadness. It was very emotional. It occurred twice as I approached each memorial, and it stayed with me for a while. The energy of what took place on that tragic day was very present. It was quite remarkable.

**It was foretold that I would go to New York in one of my sessions with Claudette.

August 7, 2018

Just your routine. You know what I mean.

Yes, I do. I am aware of what I need to be doing.

Okay. Just a reminder. A gentle, loving nudge.

Ha Ha. Yes, thank you, and never stop nudging me.

August 9, 2018

That situation has been resolved to your satisfaction. It is all good now.

(Separating myself, I thought, from trying to help my friend.)

Yes, thank you.

You can let that go and get on with your projects. Take care of yourself and get on with things. Your energy is growing stronger. You are moving forward with your aspirations.

Good.

August 17, 2018

It's been a few days. There's been a lot going on the last few mornings, and I'm not good with meditating in the afternoon or evening. I've been in touch with you briefly. It's time to get back to regular routines.

That's fine. Sometimes other things get in the way. You are best with morning meditations. We did come through to you yesterday about regulating your hours better.

Yes, I got that. I must work on that, especially during the week.

All is well.

August 18, 2018

You are in a good place with your exercise; now it's time to work on your diet.

Yes, you must have been channeling me. I thought that this morning.

We were. When you get those inspirational thoughts, it is us sending you reminders.

Right.

Also, John and Katie send their good thoughts and love to you.

Thank you. I will speak to them.

August 19, 2018

Is the healing I am sending doing anything?

(Remote healing for my cousin who has ALS.)

Of course, it is. You are sending energy out to someone. Remember that unconsciously this person chose to have this experience, and ultimately it is them deep down that chooses whether to surrender the experience and return to health or to go on with this illness. That is their choice. All you can do is send that positive healing energy and what happens is up to them. You send your love either way and rejoice knowing they are participating the way they wanted before incarnating here.

(This may be a hard concept for many people to understand, especially those who love this individual. Before incarnating, many energies (spirit) choose the experience of debilitating illness. And the reason may be to see how they handle the condition, but it could also be a collusion between various individuals before coming to the physical to see how they can deal with this crisis. You have the afflicted and the concerned family members and friends handling the problem in their own way. Addiction also plays into this scenario, both for the individual and those closest to them. It is all about how both parties can manage the situation. It can go much farther than this, where many perish from, say, cancer or epidemics. By bringing attention to the disorder, cures are developed or worked on to reduce and finally end public suffering. It is because of their suffering that awareness is brought to bear.)

Yes. That is right. It is hard for people to conceive of this.

Unfortunately, this disease took its toll, and my cousin passed several months after battling this condition for several years, but I'm sure she beat all the doctor's expectations for survival. She briefly came through to me a year later.

August 23, 2018

Don't let your apprehension of what might happen in the class hold you back, which it can do. Let whatever is to be—be. Don't let your concerns take a hold of you. What you are worried about might not even take place, and even if it does, just go with it. Relax and let it flow. All is good.

Thank you, Harold. I get concerned about not being able to channel.

You can only be what you are. No more, no less.

August 26, 2018

Once again, a very good session yesterday. Thank you all for your help and energy.

We are there to help. You are getting better all the time. All these wonderful energies are a big boost to you.

Yes, for sure.

August 29, 2018

Stay with raising your vibration. Let yourself go and feel that inspiration expanding outward. Stay in the "Love" vibration. Feel that merging with the Mike Ellis soul and feel that merge with your Merkabah, as you did today. Keep doing that. You will notice a change. You will sense a shift.

August 30, 2018

We have talked about this situation (my friend who is having personal problems. I know. I'm still dealing with this). *Ease yourself from it without causing any distress to the other party. Again, do so kindly, friendly, but honestly. You are trying to raise your awareness, your vibration, and the distraction which has negativity attached to it right now is not something that is helping you. This may sort itself out in the future, but right now, you need to be in a positive space.*

Yes, I understand. I didn't do very well resolving that issue last time. I will be more determined in the future.

Don't fret about it. The past is behind you, as you have stated. It's all about now and moving forward.

September 2, 2018

I'm off to my brother's place for a few days. I will try to keep in touch, and, as always, I will ask my guides and angels to watch over me.

Good. Commune with Nature. It is good for the soul, and of course, we will be there for you. And a simple reminder to take things easy. Be alert. All is well.

September 6, 2018

I had a very nice time with my brother. Thank you for watching out for me.

Good. Family is important. You have a close rapport with your brother, and it was good for you to get out into Nature and see the trees, waters, and feel the breezes.

Yes. I like that.

It is good for your soul. It is nice to leave the busy streets and bustle behind for a while.

Yes.

Now it is time to get back to your other interests after that pleasant break.

September 8, 2018

Yes. There are some more things you could be working on that would be of benefit to you in getting your book noticed. You have had a few thoughts with regards to this, and you should act on those thoughts.

Yes, I need to spend some time on that.

A little bit of time and a little money will be well spent.

September 11, 2018

Just a reminder to stay with your psychic art. This is important for you. You need to proceed with that. It is a part of your mediumship.

Okay. I will get back to it tomorrow.

September 12, 2018

Am I depicting anyone in these psychic portraits, or is it merely what I happen to put on paper? I'm not sure if I am doing anything.

You are indeed. Again you have that doubt. Be assured that those coming through, whether guides or other spirit energies, are flowing into your hands and portraying a picture on your paper. Remember, spirit art isn't always an exact replica but very close. You should feel an energy there.

September 14, 2018

We have much that we can pass on, as you have been wondering, and we will do so when the time is right. You are taking a lot both from your classes and other readings. We don't want to overload you or give you info that will be overlooked because of all the other material that is coming into you.

September 17, 2018

We are sending thoughts your way of things that you should be trying. These are things that may help you get what you want or get you closer to where you would like to be.

Okay. Thank you for that, and please continue to do that for me. I know I need to keep hearing those things for them to sink in.

We will do that. It's a part of that stubbornness that you have, that and procrastination.

Yes, to be sure.

September 21, 2018

Hi, Harold. Is there anything you would like to say today?

I believe you just heard it. You have to work on that again. You asked to be reminded, so that is what I am doing.

(Harold is referring to my diet.)

Yes. As always, you are right. I need to get better with that. I will try to improve.

It is for your benefit.

September 27, 2018

Hi, Harold. I haven't been communicating with you through writing because there isn't much coming through, just the usual. However, I feel my Merkabah meditations are going well.

Hi, Michael. Well, yes, there hasn't been much to pass on unless, as I said, you have something, in particular, to talk about. But, having said that, we should keep the lines of communication open, even if it's just to say hello. That is important. Maybe not every day, but certainly every other day.

You are having good Merkabah meditations. You are going deeper and starting to hold on to some of what you are experiencing. Very good. Also, the 'Advanced Merkabah Activation' is pretty much there. Also very good. Keep at it. You are making fine progress. That concentration on the third eye is paramount. Stay with that.

October 1, 2018

I have a mediumship class tonight.

Don't worry about the session. Let be what will be. It will be fine. Keep a positive frame of mind.

October 3, 2018

I know you were disappointed by not channeling, but you could have.* You just needed to get started, and it would have continued from there. You had a fear of failure. There is no failure. You need to strive to let go and allow whatever is going to occur, to occur for the highest good. Like everything else, the more you can have the opportunity to experience this, the better you will get. This is what you want, so let it be. It is all good.

Thank you, Harold. I want to be able to do it. I will try to let go of my doubts.

Good. There isn't anything you can't do.

*In class, we were again asked to channel. When my turn came, I sensed the Master with me, and I had words, but they felt like my own. As Harold said, I should have just gone with them. It would have been okay. No one would have judged me.

October 8, 2018

Just wishing my dad a happy birthday.

He appreciates your thought and is watching over you. He is always available for you, as are all your friends and relatives. They send their love. Now that your holiday (Canadian Thanksgiving) is almost over, it is again time to get on with your business. You know of what I talk.

I do. I'm aware that I need to get on that.

You have a lot of help here. Use it.

October 12, 2018

Hi, Harold. I'm sorry I missed the last few days. I will try not to let it go that long again.

Yes. Brief touches of mind, but the daily communication is important to you, even if only for a short moment. The writing is beneficial to you, and you need that connection to us.

There doesn't always have to be words of wisdom, and so forth; it's the contact that matters.

October 15, 2018

Again, I'm unsure whether my psychic art is someone coming through or just my imagination. Plus, some of these faces look like the same person.

Yet you still doubt. This is your subconscious picking up on the vibrations that are coming through to you from spirit, moving through you, and some of these may come through many times, helping you with your process. You may see the same or similar faces more than once. Let go of your doubt. Believe and go with it. Your appreciation is welcome. Feel the love. Look at the eyes. Feel it. This is your medium. Know it and revel in it.

October 17, 2018

No, just glad you are connecting. You are aware of what you should be doing. We are reminding you. You are receiving our thoughts on that.

October 20, 2018

While Skyping with Claudette, she saw a figure behind me. Unfortunately, I lost contact with her and couldn't learn more about who she saw. Was that you?

Yes, it was. I thought it would be a nice surprise for you to know that I was there with you.

Yes, it certainly was. I appreciate that. Was there something you wanted to say?

No, not really. It was merely to let you know we are here for you. We may do that again and maybe bring some more to that communication.

Great. I certainly look forward to that. Also, I could use some guidance to set up some questions for spirit when Claudette is channeling.

We can do that. It will be another great experience for you to be a part of.

Yes, I am excited. Thank you, Harold, for coming through and for everything you do.

October 23, 2018

Press on with your psychic art, and don't be disturbed with what you are rendering. It is a process, and it will show itself with your perseverance. Eventually, you will be amazed at how well you are doing with it. It will be easy, flowing, and you will feel the energy coming through. This is your gift.

October 28, 2018

We have a mediumship class tonight.

Don't worry. Relax. Let whatever happens happen. Try and detach. Don't worry about the others in the class and what they are doing. They have their own thing. You have yours. Be yourself.

October 29, 2018

Another incredible class last night. I had an unbelievable experience. The energy was amazing.

Yes. Incredible is right, and think of what good the group did. Think of what you accomplished with the help of all the other energies that were present. Something to be proud of.*

Yes. It is very humbling to be among all those wonderful beings.

They are very appreciative of what you as a group did. You have their joy and love.

How wonderful to be a Lemurian and know I can always go to their.

Yes, indeed.

I feel blessed, and I hope all the Hathors' and Arcturians' healing will help me in the days ahead.

It definitely will. You will notice a difference.

Great.

*We finished our Merkabah meditation, and Claudette explained the Lemurians were present and what we were being asked to do. I could see in my mind's eye as it was being described.

The Lemurians asked the Merkabah group to assist them, along with others, in closing a fissure that had opened in the Pacific Ocean floor. We were taken to and greeted by the Lemurian Council and given instructions. Each of us was there as inhabitants of the planet to add our energy to close and seal this rift. We stood in a circle on a plate and moved toward a portal, covering the rift with the energies present. Parts of this are a little hazy to me now, but the breach was closed and sealed. This was significant to the planet. We returned to the main courtyard and again met the Lemurian Council, who told us that we were Lemurians. A plaque with our Lemurian symbol was placed in the courtyard. They thanked us and told us we were welcome to return anytime and that they might call on us in the future.

Claudette asked us each to write down what we experienced. This is what I wrote:

It's hard to describe the unbelievable energy radiating through me when they announced that our symbol would be there forever and that we were Lemurians. All of this took approximately half an hour.

November 5, 2018

Yes. Patience. All will present itself when the moment is right. There is no reason to be down if what you are waiting for isn't happening. It merely means that the time isn't right. Hold on to the thought that all will occur when it is the appropriate moment. Let it be.

November 9, 2018

For all that you are doing, the most important is your meditation. Do not forego that for the rest. It benefits you the most. Plan your activities, but make certain that meditation is at the top of that list.

Okay, Harold. I will get back on that and plan better. Sometimes it just seems routine with not much going on.

There are always things going on, even if you don't notice it, and it is all beneficial to you. I cannot stress this enough.

November 13, 2018

Next summer, I intend to go to England for the ISF (International Spiritualist Federation) Congress, provided the necessary funds are available.

This is very much something that should be. It will be a wonderful experience for you and a chance to connect with your birthplace and your relatives. The money will be in place.

November 14, 2018

I overdid the groceries, especially the meat products.

Make sure when eating that you use vegetables with it. Next time eat first before you go for your groceries, so you are not hungry when you are shopping.

November 25, 2018

I have a class today. I hope my guides can help with the aggravating back problems I have sitting in those uncomfortable chairs so that I can attain a deeper level.

We will do that. We will be there as always for you.

November 26, 2018

Hi, Harold. First, thank you for taking care of my back; it didn't bother me during class. We were thrilled to go to the Galactic Federation and for my mom (who is a member) to come through. I sensed her presence, as did others in the class.

Excellent.

Also, I feel I can start letting go a little easier, so I can go deeper. However, I still can't channel anyone. I hope that will get better. It always makes me nervous when Claudette asks me to channel, and I get nothing.

You see how good these classes are for you. So much help there for all of you. You benefit so much every time you attend. Once again, do not fret about the channeling. It will come. You are becoming better all the time, and there will be a breakthrough. If you look back, could you imagine what you are doing now? All is well. Your mother was so pleased to be able to participate in your circle. The others in your group noticed the love coming through. Very moving.

November 29, 2018

I sense that you wish to talk to me about my psychic art.

You are right. Yes. You need to get back to that. You have had a lapse with it. It is a part of your mediumship, so you shouldn't let it fall away.

December 2, 2018

I had a terrific meditation where I felt I was getting great help with channeling, especially from Lord Melchizedek*.

Absolutely, and what a Master to have that happen with. Very powerful for you. Awesome. Let Him lead you, and just let yourself go. You are well protected. Very happy for you. Great!

*Lord Melchizedek is an Ascended Master of the Highest Order who is there to help us with our development and ascension.

December 08, 2018

Was that you who showed up behind me when I spoke to Claudette (via Skype)? And who were the other two she saw?

Yes. They were two of your other guides, Doctor Guides.

Okay, thank you for doing that. Should I be concerned that Doctor Guides were present?

Well, you do ask for doctor guides in your prayers to help you with some matters (my shoulder), so they were there as support for what you were asking for. Also, you know you have to take care of yourself, and as always, we are here to remind you again that diet is important for your health. You know that and need to heed your thoughts.

Okay, thank you all for your help. I will try to do better.

Good.

December 11, 2018

That was wonderful. I felt the Lemurians' presence because I got that tingling sensation. I also felt I could channel. I hope I can improve and become more comfortable with that process. I feel as though Lord Melchizedek is here to help me do that.

Very good indeed. You are right on all counts. You will get better the more you do it. Everything that happens, especially in the classes, strengthens your abilities. Continue to put in the time and effort, and you will see results, some of which you are already seeing. Good job.

December 15, 2018

Yes. Even if there is nothing to pass on, just say hi and keep the lines open between us. It doesn't take long, and you have been verbally saying 'Hi' without the writing, but the written part is an element of your process. We will get to a point where that isn't as important, but right now, it is.

December 19, 2018

Don't worry about any financial matters. Everything is there for you. It all will work out. Go about your time as though everything is in place, which it is. It's that time of year when your expenses rise, but all is well. Be happy.

December 20, 2018

Just a quick hello while I get on to this never-ending Estate matter. I will ask for extra help from my guides and angels to have this work out without any complications if you would, please.

Of course. We are here for you.

December 23, 2018

That was a very good meditation. I felt as though I had gone somewhere. There was a joyful feeling.

Yes. John and Katie were sending that joy to you. You went deeper and had some experiences. You are sensing more.

December 29, 2018

It is a busy time of year, and normal routines slip by the wayside. With a new year approaching, we remind you of the usual practices, health, and your programs. Monday will be the Burning Bowl.* Have your lists ready.

*The Burning Bowl is a ritual given to me by Claudette to be practiced and performed on New Year's Eve, though you can do it at any time. In the evening, you ask all your guardians to be present—angels, spirit guides, Masters, teachers, etc. Then you set up the Four Elements—a dish of water, a candle (fire), a plant (earth), and, of course, air. Beforehand, you make up two lists: one of the things you want to release and the other of things you wish to manifest in the coming year. You meditate and then set your intention by taking the first list, placing it in a receptacle, preferably outdoors, and lighting it, watching the smoke rise and disappear. You then set your intention on your desires by placing the second list in the receptacle, lighting it, and seeing the smoke climb, seeing those things come into your existence. You thank all your emissaries, and then you feast. The feast is an important part of the Burning Bowl ceremony and has been done at the end of ceremonies for millennia. When starting, you want to be grounded and in a peaceful frame of mind. There may be different variations on this.

2019

January 1, 2019

Hi, Harold. Not a great way to start the new year feeling ill, but I will make the best of it. I am looking forward to accomplishing some things this year and getting serious with my projects, health, and happiness.

Hi, Michael. Welcome to a new year. There are many wonderful experiences for you this year. Your illness is just a reminder that you have to look after yourself. And yes, it is time to get on to those projects. We would like to see plenty of writing, painting, and advancement in your spiritual awakening. It is all there for you. You simply have to reach out and grab it. You can do it.

January 2, 2019

I feel I am getting more out of my meditations. What do you think?

Yes, you are. You are sensing and going with that sense. Good. That is you progressing. You have so much help, and you are beginning to feel that help. Very good. It is all there for you. Breakthroughs are imminent.

(Note: A few days pass with little change; however, I am asked again to continue with my psychic art, which I have been neglecting.)

January 10, 2019

Hi, Harold. Okay, I will get back to my psychic art, but to be honest, I don't feel this is going anywhere.

You must persist. Look how far you have come with your abilities from a few years ago. This is the same. Stay with it, and you will see improvement. You will notice the difference. Patience, my friend, patience.

January 12, 2019

Hi, Harold. Is there anything you would like to say?

Just have a good art class. I know you enjoy that, and joy is important. It is what it is all about. The "joy" vibration makes your dreams come true. When you can stay with that "joy" vibration, you bring your desires to fruition, and you bring your soul into merging closely with your physical.

January 16, 2019

It is time to get back to your book project.

Yes, I agree. I need to get my enthusiasm for that going again. I seem to have stalled on that.

Once you get back into it, you will get your momentum moving. There is still a lot of work to be done.

I'm not feeling excited about it. I need to get that back. It seems like more of a chore.

We will help.

January 17, 2019

I assume my purpose is my art, writing, and improving my sensitivity to assist in bringing positive energy to the planet and those on it.

The art and the writing are parts of that. That is who you are in the physical. Bringing your frequency of vibration to a higher level is the spiritual part. Then merging the two together brings you to your highest good. Brings you in touch with your Higher Self. Brings you closer to that which you are. That is why we keep pressing you not to fall back from any of these. All these are what you should be putting your efforts into.

Okay, got it. Thank you for that.

As always, we are here for you.

January 19, 2019

I am very pleased to have Lord Melchizedek helping me. I'm looking forward to what's to come.

It is awesome. You have a very strong Master assisting you. Expect wonders to come. Excellent. We are excited for you. Now, have a good art class.

Yes, I am excited.

January 22, 2019

You are making your mother very happy by connecting with your brother* and his family. She is sad, though, that all the family isn't so joined together and is hoping that that will come about. She believes it will and that you will be a big part of making that happen. She is so proud of you and what you are accomplishing. She loves you so very much, as do so many others here.

Thank you all. I love you too and am grateful for all your love and help. I am hoping to bring the family closer together.

*My youngest brother is almost sixteen years younger than me, and I left home when he was growing up, as had my other brother and sister. My father had left when he was very young, so it was just my mother and him. My brother, sister, and I were around, but not in any real capacity. He didn't grow up with the bond that the three of us had. As time went by, I sensed that he had missed out on a lot. He didn't experience the family atmosphere that we had growing up. After my mother passed, it was evident that something needed to be done to bring him and his family closer. I've been trying to do that. We talk more, and I try to see him a couple of times a year, which is about the same as the rest of the family. My sister had grown closer to my younger brother in the last few years. They've renewed that relationship, but there is friction with my other brother, and I hope that can be worked out. I would love to have all the families together in one place at one time. I love them all. That would make my mother happy. (In fact, this did happen in 2021. Seeing my brothers come together and hug each other was more evidence of putting positive intentions out there to the Universe. I wasn't sure if that day would ever come. It shows that so much is possible when we get Higher Energy involved, and there is no doubt in my mind that Mom would be moving that along also.)

January 24, 2019

Nothing in particular right now. I'm glad you are almost done with the Estate. It's been a long process.

Yes, I will be very happy to be done with it.

It took some time, but it all worked out, just like many things that go on in the physical. Nothing lasts. Changes happen.

Right. Thank you.

January 25, 2019

Did that happen? You know what I mean, with the Hathors taking me and doing an adjustment, realignment on me?

Yes. You didn't dream that. Did you not feel yourself in their presence?

I did.

Again, stop doubting these actions when they happen. Keep opening yourself up to these possibilities. Trust them and yourself. There are reasons for all of this. There are so many that want you to succeed and are there to help you in that regard. Your appreciation is noted.

I thank them all very much.

January 29, 2019

I have a table coming to have a dedicated space for writing. It arrives tomorrow, but I won't be here. I hope you can safeguard it for me.

Yes. That was a good idea. I wonder where that came from (laughs). It will be here for you.

Thank you. I need to get more out of my day.

Yes, indeed. That is so.

January 31, 2019

Just a reminder of your psychic art. You must keep at that to improve. It is to be your communication with spirit. Stay with it.

Okay. I will try to do it more often. (I guess you are getting the idea of the constant insistence that I get on this. It will eventually hit home that I do need to pursue this. Little did I know at this time how important that would come to be and how much a part of my life it would become.)

February 07, 2019

Hi, Michael. Nothing in particular. Keep up with your plans. It's all about "Health and Happiness."

February 12, 2019

It was good to talk to John and Katie and get that confirmation (tingling). I feel better now with channeling. I will keep working on that. It will be interesting to see if I get some profound words coming through.

Yes. The kids were happy to talk with you and do that out loud. You are coming along with that, and, as was said to you, practice makes it come easier. To have someone like Lord Melchizedek helping you is awesome. This is very beneficial to you. Once it gets simple and becomes quite natural for you, then those words will come through, and, as was relayed to you, they won't be just for you but for others to benefit from the wisdom.

Wow. I look forward to that.

Good. It will come. It was foretold.

February 14, 2019

I will continue to work on channeling. I can feel something.

Yes. Continue to do so. You are getting there. Again, it is going to happen. One day you will look back and think, "That was so easy. Why was I worrying about it?" (I'm not sure if that day has arrived just yet, but it is getting closer, lol.)

February 22, 2019

There is much I could be passing on to you, but right now, it is more important for you to be reminded of the things you should be concentrating on. Once you have got to a place where all those things are being practiced routinely, then we can expand to other topics.

February 25, 2019

Don't get caught up in those little disturbances that bother you. It's just day-to-day stuff and will resolve itself. Keep on doing what is important to you. Stay positive and be Happy.

February 28, 2019

Yes. I think this would be good for you to go to this event* and see how others channel. Experience it.

*Steveston Village has many unique shops, one of which carries crystals, spiritual cards, books, etc. The store occasionally holds a "Message Night" at the back where one or two mediums give readings. On February 2nd, I saw a posting for this event and reserved a spot.

March 2, 2019

I'm looking forward to this evening and seeing what transpires.

Yes. Enjoy the experience. Try and feel the energy in the room. See if you can pick up anything. Let your senses expand. Relax and take it all in.

March 3, 2019

Interesting evening.* A few things came up that Claudette had also mentioned to me, most notably the cabin and how important nature was to me.

Yes, that is something that you should keep in your heart, for it is a part of you, who you are. It radiates from you. It keeps coming up for a reason. It is something for you to stay with. There was a lot of good energy there last night. Are you glad you went?

Yes. It was interesting to see how others do their mediumistic work.

Yes. It was valuable for you to see that. There may be more in the future.

*The medium at the event gave me a reading and mentioned the cabin and how important nature was to me. We had a cabin for a few years in the Interior of B.C. It was on a lake, surrounded by trees, and I loved it. We gave up our share when we bought the place in Birch Bay, which was closer and where we could spend more time. I didn't know it at the time, but that evening would play a pivotal role in my future. A chance meeting, sitting next to someone I had never met before, would change my life. More to come on that.

March 10, 2019

I had quite the dream this morning. All I remember are very vivid colors—light blues and purples.

You will start to experience that more often. You are traveling to places.

It was very enjoyable. I wanted to hold onto it.

Yes. Your awareness began ending as your left brain took over. You will get better at staying with it the more you experience it.

Excellent. I look forward to more of that.

Enjoy.

March 11 to March 23, 2019

Harold talks to me about the usual topics—stay positive, stay with the plan, get out and enjoy nature, diet, exercise, and create psychic art.

March 25, 2019

Yes. Trust the process. Believe in what you are experiencing. Believe in what comes through to you, be it psychic art or any of the experiences you may be feeling or sensing. It is all there for you, and it IS happening.

March 27, 2019

Happy birthday. You are having a nice day with many well wishes. It shows you how much love you have coming in from your family and friends.

Thank you. I felt the well wishes from everyone on the other side when I woke up this morning.

There were many here passing on their good wishes.

I felt that. It was much appreciated.

You are much appreciated, and that was shown to you.

Definitely. Thank you all.

Thank you, and treat every day as though it were your birthday. Those here are always showing their love to you.

Wonderful.

April 4, 2019

Glad to see you doing the taped version of the Merkabah again and not the Merkabah "Activate." Try to use the recording a little more, as I believe you get more out of it right now. The other is working, but still not quite as well as the recording.

April 10, 2019

Psychic art. What do you think?

This is your medium. It is important for you to work on this as much as possible. The more you do this, the more adept you will get. You should be trying this every day. You will see results.

We want you to enjoy this. Give it your Love and watch what happens.

April 11, 2019

Yes. Write down that dream you had. Glad you are following up with the Merkabah and the psychic art. Well done. I know you will be busy for the next few days with art class, and we know you enjoy the golf (PGA Masters), which ties up a lot of your time. That's okay. If it makes you happy, then it is all good. Enjoy.

(I love The Masters. I used to watch the Saturday play every year at a local bar with my good friend Dick. I miss that.)

April 15, 2019

Okay, my weekend of events is over, and I'm ready to get back to it. I had a very good experience with the Lemurians during my meditation. I am glad they keep stopping by.

Yes. They will continue to do that every so often. You are one of them, and they want you to hold on to that. You will be working with them some more.

Great. I look forward to that.

April 20, 2019

Yes. It's important to keep this line of communication open even if you think there is nothing much coming through. We don't want you slipping backward. There is always energy present for you, even if you don't realize it. You are spending a bit more time cleansing your chakras. This is good. Try to stay with that. It will help immensely. Look again to your Tai Chi or yoga. It will serve you well.

I may have to plan my time better.

There is enough time for all of it. And yes, you need to prioritize your time better. You can do this. You will succeed.

April 28, 2019

A lot has happened the last few days with trying to help my friend and then my doubts, but I'm ready to get back on track, and I have a Merkabah class today, so I hope that helps.

Okay, as far as your friend, you have done everything possible to help. You can only do so much. Now it is up to them. There is a lesson here for you: "You can't help everyone. Sometimes you just have to let it go." Some of their negativity was shifted to you, which is why you began feeling those doubts. Let that go now. Re-energize yourself. Tonight's class will help in that regard.

May 1, 2019

Yes. We are glad you have seen the doctor (I had some concerns with blood pressure). This will reassure you, and there will be some notes you can write down. You are getting information on healthily reducing your weight and ways to keep yourself strong. Follow up with this.

May 8, 2019

It is important to keep up with this connection even when it seems like there is nothing much coming through. It is the act of connecting itself which is important. It is that relationship between us and you. Please don't let that start slipping away. I know you don't think that anything is happening with our words sometimes, but there is more going on than you realize. So keep this line open.

Okay. I didn't realize how much time had passed since we last communicated.

May 9, 2019

Will there ever come the point where I will see my guides, Masters, Hathors, etc.?

That will happen in time. You are not there yet. Keep doing what you are doing, and it will come.

May 11, 2019

Master Quan Yin (or Kuan Yin).* What do you think? Was I channeling?

Yes. The words and thoughts are hers. Did you think they were yours? Your voice, but hers. You must let go of these doubts and be confident of what is taking place. It is so wonderful that you have all this help coming to you. This is Higher Vibration, and it will be easier when you raise your vibration. Relax. It is happening.

*Quan Yin is an Ascended Master of compassion and mercy. She is a Master of the Third Ray, which is unconditional love represented by pink. She protects the helpless, particularly women and children.

May 17, 2019

I am here almost like your conscience, to keep thoughts of what you need to be doing – your health and your duties, your art and your writing. If you start to fall away from that, then I will be there to remind you. You have a path that you chose. Let's see if we can't stay on that path.

May 22 to 28, 2019

Let it be. Everything is happening as it is supposed to. There is no rush. Relax, and let it all occur accordingly.

Do not neglect your writing. This is something you should be doing. You have words that need to be put to paper.

You are making headway. Stay the course.

Have a good class today. All will be well. No fear. All are with you to assist. Feed off the energy.

May 29, 2019

I feel I am getting inspiration from my guides for this new manuscript.

Yes. We are here to help you with it. Look for the inspiration. Write down your thoughts to be used in it. This will be our guidance. We would like to see something good come from it – a complement to your first book.

June 1, 2019

Try that thirty-day diet. It popped up for a reason. It would be very good for you if you can do it. You will notice a big difference.

June 4, 2019

I am here to help and to send little reminders to you. You can act on them or not. There is no judgment. We want to see you succeed. It is all good. We would like to see you get back to the psychic art, though.

Yes, though all the faces seem to be very similar.

Don't worry about that. It's the process we would like to see you keep working on.

Okay.

Good.

June 13, 2019

This is very good that you have this chance to tell about your book and do some signings.* This is an excellent start. Positive things will come of it. There will be more. Heed the advice you are getting. It will pay off.

*Claudette suggested doing a "Message Night" at Serendipity's Backyard, a metaphysical gift store in Steveston, and I could give an overview of my book and do a book signing at the end of the evening. The store was more than happy to have Claudette present and accommodated me doing a talk and signing. It was set up for July 27, 2019.

June 14, 2019

You are concerned with the price and cost of your books. Let that go. Do what you can, and then let everything else take care of the rest. It is all good, and it will all work out for you.

June 16, 2019

You know what needs doing. I know you have your golf (U.S. Open) today and having days where you just relax is not a bad thing. Everyone needs those. Tomorrow is a new day, and there is still a lot to do.

June 23, 2019

I don't like the long drive to the classes. I don't see myself making this trip again.

(Our Merkabah group was dwindling in numbers, and it was put forth that we could hold our monthly group meetings at a metaphysical shop, but it was a long drive away.)

And that's all right. You have an aversion to that ride. It's a long way for someone who doesn't drive that much anymore. Don't think about your age with regards to this. That has nothing to do with it. You have lived your life to this point and have the right to accept or decline what others may have in mind for you.

Good. Thank you, Harold. I needed to hear that. I am comfortable in my place and am willing to go to certain lengths.

You be you.

June 24, 2019

Well, that certainly worked out for me yesterday. I am sorry they are not well, but happy I didn't have to drive out there. The Universe was looking out for me.

(The class was canceled because the person holding the class became ill.)

Yes. Ask, and you shall receive. That is not a place I see you going to. It remains to be seen whether your group (Merkabah class) can continue. That may be it for a while. You have the choice of whether you want to take the mediumship classes or not.

Yes, though I don't really see myself as a medium. I communicate with you, and I have some sense of spirit, but it's not very strong. I am at a place where I can accept that. It would be nice, but it is what it is.

You might do well to let it go for a while and see if anything develops from that space.

Yes. I think so.

July 1, 2019

Hi, Harold. I feel I'm getting help from you and my guides with what to say at the upcoming Message Night, and I thank you for that.

Good. We are here to help you get that down to a good time and also make it interesting. We want you to succeed in this, and the more you rehearse it and go over it, the better it will get.

July 4, 2019

Hi, Harold. It looks like I've overcome my computer troubles for the most part. I can get back to normal now.

(My laptop crashed, and I had to take out the hard drive, buy a new laptop, and transfer my files over to it.)

Yes. Hopefully, you are over your frustrations. It may not be ideal, but it is good for now, and you recovered all your essential documents, etc. So, yes, time to get back to what needs looking after.

Good. I received more books for the signing, so that's done.

The more you sell, the more you can buy. The more you buy, the better your chances of expansion as the word of your book gets out there and becomes noticed. It's all a process. Bit by bit.

Great.

July 5, 2019

Stay with the psychic art even if you are not sure about it. It's there for you for a reason. It is something you need to keep doing. Trust the process. One day you will understand.

Okay, I will work on it.

July 8, 2019

That was an interesting meditation. I'm not sure what I felt, but it felt like I was somewhere else.

Yes. You were traveling. That is good. You want to feel more of that, and you will begin to get pictures of places you are going to. You had a brief glimpse of a figure. That also will pick up, and it will last longer. And, when that happens, you can ask who it is. Try to keep using the player recording (taped Merkabah) for activation. I think that works better for you.

Yes, I will do that.

July 10, 2019

You were wondering why you would give yourself this annoyance with your electronics. Part of it is that you need to realize how dependent you have become on them. You don't need to spend the amount of time you do on them at all. Realize this. Then, of course, you have your emotions getting upset with them when things go wrong. It is not necessary for you to do that. It is what it is. This was brought about by you for your understanding—dealing with adversity even though it is a small matter. Do you see?

Yes, Harold. As always, you are right. I need to catch myself and not let this rule me.

Exactly. You got it.

July 12, 2019

I will test out my talk today. I would appreciate any help from my guides. I want to give a good talk and make it interesting with a little humor thrown in. This is just a start. I will continue to work on it.

Good. We are there for you. Look for inspiration in the days ahead.

July 16, 2019

Mostly the usual things that you should be working on. Your book is going to get noticed, but you have to do your part. Momentum creates more momentum. You want the ball rolling and gathering speed.

That's good to hear. Yes, I will do what needs to be done. It is nice to hear from those who have read it and enjoyed it.

There are many who have liked what you have written, and there will be many more.

July 22, 2019

(Claudette invited me to attend a Message Night at the Universal Brotherhood Spiritualist Church, where she and another medium, Peter, would do readings.)

Very interesting Message Night. I'm glad my dad came through, and I knew Peter would come over to me when he did.* Also, the psychic art Claudette had done looked like what I had done a couple of days before. I felt validation and reinforcement for what I'm doing. I'm very glad I went.

*Peter was reading a woman sitting behind me, and I knew without a shadow of a doubt that he was coming to me next. He left her with her reading, turned to me, and said, "I want to come to you, sir." It was my dad coming through. Dad started by saying he thought his hair was better than mine, laughingly. And in fact, it was. He then said how proud he was of how far I had come and in all that I was doing. Peter said, "Your father was a good handyman, could do many things, but he says you would do them better than him. He also says you need to keep writing. He says, 'I wish I could walk a mile in his shoes.' (That always gives me the chills.) He passes on his love, and he will be watching your progress."

You are absolutely right. This was very important for you. You need to understand completely that it is not your imagination. You have abilities, and they need to be worked on. And there were a lot of people there telling you that they were excited by the book and that you need to keep writing. (I had lent a copy of my book to someone who had passed it around to others, and they were present at this affair.) *Now also, you have an outlet for your art.* (I was put in touch with someone else who gave me information on a gallery where I could display my art.) *So there is much that you can be doing. This will only get stronger and improve as you go on. There were a number of positives to take away from attending this night.*

Thank you, Harold. Yes, I get it now. This made it pretty obvious, especially with my father stating that also.

Spirit is guiding you, and this was almost like a hit to the head to get you to understand.

July 24, 2019

You are getting there bit by bit. Maybe just a recommendation is to spend a little more time each day on your projects. I know there are other things that crop up that need to be taken care of. But, where you can, invest some more time on them. This is not a criticism, just a suggestion. It will move everything along that much faster.

July 25, 2019

I will ask my guides to give me the confidence I need to do a good job with my book presentation if you would, please.

We can do that. We will be there with you. You will be fine. You know what you want to say.

July 26, 2019

Things are moving forward for you. Be on top of it. Be ready and available. You don't want any delays or setbacks, but be quick to jump right in when the opportunity arises. There will be some travel ahead. Keep being optimistic and look to all the good things that will be coming to you. If you put in the effort, there will be success.

July 27, 2019

(Message Night and book signing)

Don't be nervous. Be confident. They want to hear what you have to say. Enjoy the moment. It is all yours.

This is the announcement that was posted on Serendipity's Backyard front window and their website for the upcoming Message Night:

> Claudette Godin is a Spiritualist Medium since the mid 80s with the Spiritualist community, an accredited clairvoyant, healer and lecturer with the Spiritualist Church of Canada (SCC). She has had membership with a long list of healing and spiritualist organizations

in Canada, England, and the USA throughout this wonderful journey.

"I had the privilege of being part of a couple of documentaries on the afterlife and working as a medium and teacher nationally and internationally. I was a regular worker as a workshop facilitator, medium and healer at the Lily Dale Spiritualist Assembly, New York, for a 10-year period. Then I moved to B.C. and opened a holistic center, Wings of Dove, in Steveston Village that was in operation for nearly six years. Though I'm semi-retired, I'm very active in the Spiritualist community here and abroad. I am the Canadian representative for the International Spiritualist Federation in England, www.theisf.com. I had the pleasure of serving the ISF as a medium and workshop facilitator while taking educational courses to continue my mediumistic development in subjects that are not available for me in Canada. I love my work with spirit in all the varied aspects of mediumship, whether it is various modalities of healing, spiritual counseling/readings, or facilitating workshops and retreats. I offer mediumistic sessions for humans and animals, Intuitive Art/Spirit Portrait, Reiki, Sound Healing, CranioSacral, E/M restructuring, and Healing Matrixes as inspired by my Higher Guidance and Divine/Universal Life Force.

Lastly, I have been featured in Mike Ellis's book, *Guided Messages from the Other Side,* and it gives me great pleasure to support Mike and his book by doing a demo of spirit messages at Serendipity's Backyard during his book signing event on July 27, 2019."

> *Messages from Spirit – Claudette Godin*
>
> *Details*
> *Date: July 27, 2019*
> *Time: 7:00 pm - 9:00 pm*
> *Cost: $39*
> *Venue: Serendipity's Backyard*
> *12111 First Avenue*
> *Richmond, V7E 3M1 CA*
> *Organizers:*
> *Serendipity's Backyard*
> *Claudette Godin*
>
> *An Evening of Messages from Spirit with well known local psychic-medium Claudette Godin*
>
> *July 27th Saturday 7:00pm to 9:00pm, doors open at 6:30 pm must pre-register with the store to reserve your spot at 604-275-1683 as seats are limited and this event will sell out.*

July 28, 2019

Hi, Harold. I appreciated your help last night. It was a good evening. I forgot a couple of things I was going to touch on, but not too bad, and selling several books was good. I am happy with it.

Yes. It went very well. You realized you missed Verine coming through. I know you are sorry about that. Don't worry. There will be other opportunities to come. She is very proud of you and grateful for all that you have done and continue to do. We are happy for you. There are going to be many good days ahead. Expect more. It will show up. This was a good start, and you felt fairly comfortable. That is another of those things that the more you do, the more relaxed you will feel. Very good.

The evening took place in a comfortable-sized room that held approximately forty people at the rear of Serendipity's Backyard. Claudette and I sat at a table at the front of the room.

I started by giving a summation of my book, which lasted a little over five minutes. I mentioned that the book would be available at the end of the evening. I then introduced Claudette, who then did readings for the crowd.

As she approached the end of her readings, a female came through. Claudette said the woman had passed from many illnesses in October a few years before. A few people thought the reading might be for them, but no one seemed convinced. I was sitting behind Claudette, looking for someone in front of her to step up and accept the message, not even considering that it might have been for me. Spirit isn't concerned about where you are sitting or whether you are a part of the group there for a reading. It wasn't until after I got home that I realized it was Verine, my ex-wife who had passed in October, three years prior. I couldn't believe that I had missed the chance to connect with her.

Now, little did I know at the time how that night would change my life. Several people had purchased my book. This lovely woman, Stacey, came up and wanted to get her copy signed. I recognized her from the Message Night on March 2nd. I had sat next to her during that evening, and we had pleasantly chatted about ourselves. "Serendipity," fittingly, was the name of the boutique. The Universe was stepping in. And I don't believe in coincidences.

Claudette messaged me a couple of weeks later, asking if she could give my email address to Stacey, who wanted to talk to me about my book. I said I'd be happy to talk to her. I received an email from Stacey, and we set a time to meet over coffee. We had a lovely conversation for over two hours. Some days later, I received another email from Stacey saying she had another book she thought might interest me. We set another time to rendezvous. Once again, we spent a lovely couple of hours talking and decided to meet the following week near her place, where there was a picturesque place to walk. That led to the two of us meeting at least once a week for a month and then, more often, constantly messaging each other every day. It didn't take us long to realize that we were made for each other. This was the person who was foretold to me a couple of times in sessions from my first book, *Guided Messages from the Other Side*.

Me signing a book for Marlene, who purchased my book at Serendipity's Backyard.

July 29, 2019

Yesterday's workshop was very good. I am still amazed that I could do a reading and get some things right. But to receive the name "Al"* was truly awesome. That was an ah-ha moment for me, confirming I can do this, but with your help, of course.

We are there to help, but you are doing this. You have the abilities. They just need developing, and that's what the workshops can do for you. And practice what you are learning. Yes, you can do this. It will all come to you.

Yes. I need to practice what I'm learning.

Absolutely. No doubts. You can see that you can be confident that you can do all of this. Again, you need to do the homework.

*In this workshop, we were paired off and asked to do a reading for the other while they took notes. When it was my turn to do a reading, I sensed an older gentleman, either father or grandfather. Then the name "Al" popped into my head. The person I was reading said his grandfather had passed and that his name was Al, and the other things that I mentioned fit. I was astonished to hear that I got that right.

August 1, 2019

You are making progress with this new manuscript (this one). Keep at it. We would like to see this turn into something exceptional, and it will. Continue to plug away. We are there to help you. Look for inspiration. Look for bits to add, and we will help you flesh it out. The first book was to get you started, to see what you can do. This one will be much more. So there is a lot to be done.

August 3, 2019

It's nice to get some good feedback on the book and another chance at a book signing.

(Someone from our workshop asked Claudette to do a Message Night and me to do a book signing at their gift store.)

Yes. The book is being well received. This is good news because it means that people are interested in it, and it just needs to get out there. The more it gets into other people's hands, the more interest it will generate. All is moving forward—the book and paintings. Let's get them steamrolling and picking up speed.

Great. I will do what needs to be done.

Yes. There is work to do.

August 4, 2019

Banish all negative thoughts, especially those about money. Stay positive. The funds will be there for you to do the things that are to be done. Have faith. Know that this is so.

Okay, that is good to hear. I feel I could do more if that were so.

It is so.

August 6, 2019

I felt I communicated with a Hathor last night.

Yes, this is so, and you remember what he told you. Relax. Open yourself up. There will be more interaction.

Yes, very good. I look forward to that.

Excellent.

August 8, 2019

Hi, Harold. I am going to the gallery today to see how that works out.

It will be well received.

I'm considering working solely on my oil paintings. When I finish that, I will work solely on the book. I can do both when using

watercolor because the paint doesn't dry out like oil paint. What do you think?

Give it a try and see how it goes. You don't want to fall behind on your writing, though.

Yes, I understand. I still have some watercolors to do, so I will wait.

Okay.

August 10, 2019

I received a very nice email from someone named Stacey the other day. It seems my book resonated with her. And I just had a feeling in my throat chakra.

Your book will have similar effects on others that read your book. We want to see that wave of people getting the book and liking what they are reading.

Yes, you can still feel some tingling in your throat area. That is good. That's where voice comes through from spirit. You want to keep working on that.

August 12, 2019

Yes. Look into the Past Life Regression. It is something that you have been interested in, and there is a benefit to you doing this. Quit concerning yourself with money aspects. It is there for you.

Yes, I would like to do this. I will see if there is an opening.

Good.

August 13, 2019

Last night, I had a lucid dream about Jack.* It came through as me helping him cross over with help from angels and guides. But he has been gone for more than twenty years. Was this just his way of coming through to me? Again, it was vivid and has stayed with me.

This was his way of coming through to you, showing you the tragic way he died and how he felt when he passed. There was anger there, but there were those on the other side to help him. He had family and friends waiting to assist him. You were seeing that as he wanted you to see it, and he was helping you to understand that you can do this. It was another step in your development and understanding.

Okay, good. Thank you, Jack, my friend, for doing that for me.

He is happy to do so. It was his time.

*Jack was a colleague and friend. He left the brokerage business and started a dog sled business up north, taking people on sled excursions. He left one day by himself with a team and was never seen again. They did an extensive search and found nothing. They believe he decided to take a shortcut back over a frozen lake, and he and the team fell through the ice. It was springtime, and, though the lake was frozen, some soft spots might have given way with the weight of the sled and the dogs. He loved his dogs and would have tried to do everything to save them. He took a chance, and it cost him. He was quite the guy, a real outdoorsman.

August 15, 2019

Very sad news regarding A.* I wonder if I could have done more.

It is sad for you, but you did all that you could. Nothing was changing. They needed help but were having trouble in their mental facilities to do what was necessary. In the end, it was their decision. You know you could not make their choices for them. It was their life to live. Yes, it is sad, but, in the end, it is what it is. Send them "Love and Light." They will be reviewing this life.

*This was the friend I had tried to help earlier. I had just learned that they had passed.

August 17, 2019

Yes. Follow up on some of those thoughts that you have. These are inspirations moving you forward in your endeavors. The Book. Paintings. You need to help get the word out there. It is why you do these creations. It is for others to enjoy and get some benefit or happiness from.

August 19, 2019

There are some things I would like to do, but they cost money. I want to go to England next year, I want to do more with my painting, and I want to publish my book. I am putting money out there, but I don't want to put myself in debt. Thoughts?

Yes, there are costs to be had. Pick your spots. They don't need to be done all at once. Try to cut back on unnecessary desires. Money will be there for you. Know this. Relish this. It will be there for the important things that will move you forward. Your progression. Remove all doubts. No fear. Know that it is there for you.

Okay, I will try to remove my doubts.

August 21, 2019

I seem to be having a lot going on in my head these days. I'm not getting the most out of my meditations.

Yes. Part of that, though, is inspiration on certain things which is coming from spirit. You should take that into consideration. It is meant to be acted on if you so desire, of course. It is there to help you. Remember, take what you get and then stay with concentrating on your breathing and third eye. You will get it back.

Good advice, as always.

August 22, 2019

Yes, A made it across okay. They were welcomed and are receiving healing and light work to get them over their passing and their trauma.

Okay. I am so sorry I couldn't have done more for them.

You did what you could. Don't chastise yourself. This was their decision. They weren't able to move ahead. They were despondent, and it may have been that what they did was a cry for help, but it went further than they anticipated.

Okay, thank you.

August 23, 2019

I am excited about my Past Life Regression session on Tuesday. I hope I can go to a past life and experience it.

This should be a unique experience for you. We look forward to this and what takes place. You will have no problem going under. Don't concern yourself with that. Let yourself go. You know how much you want to do this.

August 25, 2019

You are prejudging your upcoming development class. Go. Relax and enjoy the process. Don't concern yourself with what you are getting as far as what others are achieving. It's there to help you. Open up to that help and receive what is coming to you.

August 26, 2019

Thank you for your help in class yesterday. I'm still not comfortable doing those practices. I feel like quitting, to be honest.

We are there to help you. You have to do what is being told to you—to let yourself go and give yourself over to spirit. There's too much going on in your head. It is to your benefit to persevere and stay with it. Each class that you take will make you better, and you have the assistance of the group energy. It would be much harder on your own.

September 3, 2019

Get your shoulder checked (rotator cuff). It is persistent, and it is better for you to know why. You may want to do light exercises and consider getting back to your Tai Chi. Set aside some time for that each day.

September 4, 2019

We want to mention diet and exercise. This is why you are feeling the way you do. You know what you need to do. Don't go overboard with the exercising.

September 6, 2019

There is a lot going on tomorrow. Relax through it all. Look forward to the Message Night (at the gift store). You know what you want to say. We are there with you. We would like to see you press forward now with your projects. Be open to receiving gifts from the Universe. It is there for you. Anticipate it and feel joy for what is coming to you. The time is ripe.

Thank you, Harold. That is very good to hear, and I am ready and grateful. It was good to hear that news from my doctor.

(I had a slight tear in my rotator cuff, and the doctor gave me some light exercises to do.)

September 9, 2019

Hi, Harold. Is there anything you would like to say today?

Painting. Writing. Psychic art.

Yes. Got it. What did you think of the Message Night?

It was a little long and a lot for Claudette. It was nice to have your nephew there. The more that you do this, the more comfortable you will get and the better your story. You wanted to rush it because of the number of people. Don't. A few extra minutes doesn't matter.

Quite a few people came to the Message Night, and I didn't want to take away from Claudette's time, so I rushed my part. One of my nephews showed up with his girlfriend, which was a nice surprise. It went very well overall.

September 11, 2019

You are not helping your blood pressure by constantly focusing on it. Let it be, and know that you can fix it by diet and exercise. Dwelling on it creates what you are concerned about. The doctor was okay. You know what you have to do.

September 12, 2019

Remember, you have the power to be, do, and have anything. Be positive. Let go of the negative. Keep your thoughts on your desires. Gratitude and Love. It is all there for you.

Thank you, Harold. Keep sending me that guidance, if you will.

September 13, 2019

Would it be useful for me to do a Past Life Regression again? And is there a past life that is significant for me?

(My first past life regression a couple of weeks previous didn't go the way I had hoped, but the process still held some interest for me.)

There is always some benefit to doing a past life regression. Is there a necessity for you to do one right now? No. I see you doing this at a later time. There is a significant past life that will be beneficial to you but now is not that time. You have been doing a lot of work on your own with your meditations, even though you do not realize it, and you benefitted a lot from your work with the Merkabah. There were Energies in those travels that helped you. Continue with the Merkabah. You won't get the benefit of the group, but you will still succeed. The Higher Energies are watching and are there for you.

Thank you. Good words.

September 15, 2019

Just the usual today, which you are already aware of. That voice you heard was spirit, and it did shock you. You weren't prepared for it, so it had that effect on you. This will begin to happen more often, which is what you asked for so that you can get comfortable with it. It has taken a while to get to this point, but again, it is the process that you needed to go through. More to come. We are, as always, happy for you.

Thank you, Harold. I hope I can adapt to it without pulling back.

(I heard a voice while meditating, and it startled me, and I lost the connection.)

You need to know and be absolutely positive that it is there not to scare you or do you harm but to come to you with love and assistance in your development.

September 19, 2019

Hi, Harold. It was a lovely day yesterday. She is very nice, and we have a lot in common.

(I'm referring to my walk with Stacey.)

Hi, Michael. Yes, she is a good match for you. We are glad for you. We are happy to see you continuing with this. There is more here and more to come.

Okay. I am going to my brother's this weekend. Any communication will be by internal voice or mind, and, as always, I appreciate you watching over me.

Of course, and we will resume the writing on your return. Enjoy the natural surroundings. Feel nature. Feel the vibration of the trees. It is rejuvenating for you.

I will. Thank you.

September 25, 2019

Okay, I am back from my few days off. I had a good time with my brother. I'm ready to get back to it. I'm having trouble going to the workshop on Sunday, though. I liked the Merkabah and the smaller group, but I'm not as comfortable with the new workshop group.

It is good to have you back communicating. Yes, a nice time with your family.

I can feel your discomfort. You know, though, that this is there for you, for your development. Can you take this one off and continue with the next one?

Yes. However, I think I need to see or feel or hear something to let me know that this is what I should be working towards. Should I be putting energy and time into this or other areas?

Well, that is a consideration for you. You have abilities, but they need to be worked on. They will get stronger. You have to decide if that is something that you want to pursue.

Yes, I know. And, I'm not sure now. I was before, but now, I don't know.

Well then, take some time to decide.

I will always meditate. I will always keep the communication open with you and my guides. If there is more, I must believe that it is what I should be doing.

That can show up.

Then that's when I will move ahead.

Okay.

September 26, 2019

You should think about getting your paintings in the gallery as soon as space is available. You need to get your work out there. There are benefits to you for doing that. This is an area you need to exploit.

September 27, 2019

That was a good meditation. I had a positive feeling about it. Also, I just received psychic art mentally, so I will get back to it.

Yes, that was a good meditation. Keep it up. Feel that 'Love' vibration. It is important. You felt it. And yes, we would like to see you doing more of the psychic art. Manage your time better.

Yes.

September 30, 2019

It's time to get on with it. I know you know what I am referring to, so I won't dwell on it. You know what you need to be doing (the usual).

Yes, I do, but thank you for being considerate with how you tell me.

You're welcome, but it needed to be said.

As always...

October 1, 2019

Hi, Harold. You are here to help me with what I need to be doing, I gather, rather than passing on information about spirit or other metaphysical matters.

That is right. You had guides who were there for that. My responsibility at this time is for you— to remind you what is good for you and to be there to support and keep on you for what you need to be doing to expand yourself and keep you on your path.

Okay. Yes, I see that. Thank you for being there and doing that for me.

You're welcome. It is my privilege to be a guide for you and see you succeed.

October 3, 2019

It is good to see you back doing what needs to be done. Stay with it. There is much to be gained from this, which is why we continue to stress this for you. It is for your benefit. You are helping yourself. This is what you want, even though you may not always see that. It is your path. Walk it.

October 4, 2019

We are glad you are forming this relationship. It is good for you and her. Relax into it and see where it leads

(Harold is referring to Stacey and me.)

October 6, 2019

No, not really. You know what I would be saying. It just went through your mind. Reminders. Reminders.

Yes. Got it.

(I'm not sure what this is referring to, possibly keeping up with my projects or diet. I got the mental words, and Harold is confirming what I got, whatever that may have been.)

October 12, 2019

Enjoy your class. And you are getting some good info again while you are writing your book.

Yes. I want to expand on some of that once I get through it. I hope you or a guide will help me with that.

Spirit will be there for that. We want this to be an excellent book as much as you do.

October 15, 2019

Yes. Time. You need to allocate your time for what you want to do. What is important to you?

I understand. I haven't been doing a very good job at that.

You understand.

October 16, 2019

This new relationship is good for you. It is good to communicate and have a close tie to someone else. You haven't had a lot of that for a while.

October 18, 2019

I sensed the presence of the Hathors. I felt there was confirmation of them being there. I thanked them for their presence and everything they had done for me in past Merkabah sessions. They were there to continue to help me in my development because they wanted me to help them, along with others, bring the planet through the transformation to a new era of harmony and peace—the next step towards that.

Very good. You did indeed. That is wonderful news, and we are glad to see this relationship continue. We are also happy that you picked up on the Universe sending events to you to move you on your way to showing and being more involved with the art world. Also very good. Opportunities are coming to you, and you need to recognize that and take advantage of them. You did. Good job.

October 19, 2019

Enjoy your class. Enjoy your day. Hold on to a raised vibration with joy. Stay in the "Now" moment. Be present.

October 20/21, 2019

Enjoy your time at the gallery. It is a good opportunity to see what others are doing and also what kind of price they are asking for their art. This will help you, and you will be able to display a couple of your paintings.

(The art gallery asks its members to volunteer for a few hours every month. They phoned and asked if I could help as someone had canceled. I agreed.)

This art gallery connection is helpful for you. New people who are creative, with similar interests.

October 24, 2019

We are happy you have found someone to share your time with. This is beneficial for both of you.

Yes. It seems to be going very well.

Excellent.

October 28, 2019

Yesterday's workshop was very interesting. Thank you for being there. I am sure you were sending information, but I wasn't receiving it, which is why I need to keep attending these workshops. Even though I am uncomfortable being unable to complete some of the exercises effectively, I realize I need them if I want to succeed, and I do. Also, I am so very glad I was there for that flash of light that was A.* That was awesome. I also provided information to the person I was working with, which validates that I have some abilities.

Very good. Don't worry if you don't feel like you are getting it. You are, and you are realizing that these workshops are important even if they make you feel uncomfortable. You can get over that. Think of the progress you are making. Do not concern yourself with what others are doing. Everyone is at a different level. You were told by one in the group that they like your energy. That is important for you to recognize that your energy helps the overall group energy. It will not be the same if you are not present. We are so glad that you got to experience A's communication. It was brilliant and good for you to experience that phenomenon along with the others in the class. You got some very good information in writing. Heed that advice. Look back and reread that sometime. It is confirmation.*

Thank you, Harold, and I felt Phillip was also there for me.

Yes. You are right. Phillip was present also and sends his regards and love.

*The workshop class did a meditation together. A few minutes into it, I saw a flash of light zoom across my inner vision. I remember thinking, "Was that an electrical occurrence in the building?" It was bright and appeared almost like a comet. I then continued with the meditation. At the conclusion, everyone talks about their experiences. Everyone confirmed they saw the flash of light, and one of the members confirmed it was A telling us they had passed safely. (This was the friend with personal problems I tried to help.) My being able to share this experience with others meant a lot to me. It confirmed that I had the ability to sense spirit, and of course, it meant a lot on a personal level. I was pleased that they had made the transition easily.

October 31, 2019

Did Craig pass safely?

(Craig was my wife's son from a previous marriage. My daughter-in-law, his ex-wife for many years, phoned to tell me that she had heard from the police that Craig had accidentally crashed his car into a pole and died. The police think he may have had a heart attack and died before hitting the pole. Craig suffered from substance abuse, which had taken a toll on his body. In my first book, I mentioned that those who pass after suffering addiction go into rehab on the other side—a form of cleansing.)

Yes, he made it through. He has a lot of work to do now that he is here, but first, he will connect with all of those who were waiting for him. There is much love, as always, for all of those who return, and the healing begins. Remember, there is no judgment, and the person returning is usually their own harshest critic. There are many here to help him. Sending your love also helps more than you know.

November 2, 2019

First, I will always say that it is important to keep this open line between us. One day there will come a time when you will start to hear spirit. But there is a reason for you to be doing the writing. You can see how a book comes from it, and there is more. The psychic art can also benefit by the use of your hand. So there are many reasons for communicating this way.

November 5, 2019

A is here. They pass on their best wishes to you and thank you for all you did for them. They are doing well and are happy now. There will be more to come.

Please tell them I am glad they are okay and give them my love.

They send their love to you.

November 6, 2019

That was a good meditation. Could you feel it? You can still feel the vibration. Good. Hold onto that feeling. Bring it back to you as often as you can and see if you can hold onto it longer and longer. You will get good results from doing this.

November 10, 2019

Psychic art. We would like to see you practice this more often.

Okay, I will try. I'm not seeing much change in this.

Well, you are not doing it enough, which is why we are suggesting that you do it more.

Okay.

November 13, 2019

Yes. That was your uncle Alf coming through, acknowledging his presence and thanks. He is happy you have made contact with his grandson and great-granddaughter,* that you have made a connection with your relatives in England, and he looks forward to the time when you get to meet them in person. He sends his love.

Thank you, Harold. I'm grateful for him coming through, and I return the love.

*I had recently been in contact with some cousins on my father's side of the family, residing in England, whom I had never met and didn't know anything about. They contacted me on Facebook, and we've been connecting ever since. My uncle Alf was my father's older brother, who I also had never met but knew a little about from my father. It is quite something when you see the family resemblance. I am looking forward to meeting them one day.

(Note: A few months later, his great-granddaughter came to Canada with her boyfriend and worked in Vancouver for a year and a half. Stacey and I have been out with them only a few times, though, as we had to abide by COVID restrictions.)

November 14, 2019

We are sending you some guidance with respect to this relationship that is in progress.

Thank you. That is welcomed.

Good. We feel this could be very good for you.

Again, thank you. I feel good about it also. Let's see what happens.

Yes.

November 16, 2019

That was a very good performance with your painting.* This process that you did will help you with your psychic art. You now have a better idea of shading and light. Your drawings will get more depth. Again, practice, practice. This is a good medium for you.

Thank you, Harold.

*I decided to do a self-portrait in oils.

November 17, 2019

Dream. Dream. Dream. Keep dreaming. Keep your dreams alive. See your dreams come true. It's all there for you. Feel the joy as your dreams manifest. You can have it all. Those desires that come into your thoughts can happen. That is why the opportunities present themselves. What can be, can be.

November 21, 2019

I see you are struggling again with whether to attend the upcoming workshop. This seems to be happening as the workshop approaches. You have doubts and you are also wondering if there is any real reason at this time in your life whether there is any benefit to continuing with this.

Let us say that there is. You want the experience of closer ties to spirit. To get that, you need to improve. That will occur quicker by attending the classes than if you were to try on your own, even though this causes you some discomfort, which by the way it shouldn't. Sometimes you have to endure some discomfort to get what you want. Sometimes you have to push through.

(I had always had an easy time getting good grades in school. The fact that all these years later, I'm in a class and, in my mind, I wasn't up to the standard of the others was disheartening. There was this sense of non-performance on my part. This wasn't the case, though. Everyone in the class was at different levels, but I felt like dropping out when I believed I wasn't succeeding or improving, not to mention that I didn't care for the drive. Harold stressed to me the importance of these classes for my development. I could move ahead on my own but, without the benefit of the added energy of the class, it could take longer.)

But why do I need the discomfort? Why can't I get there from a place of comfort?

You can, definitely. But as we stated, it is a longer path. Shorter path versus longer path. As always, it is your choice.

November 22, 2019

We are happy to see that you are going to the workshop on Sunday. Enjoy the experience. Nothing can go wrong. Fill yourself with the energies.

November 25, 2019

That was a very good workshop. I like the healing ones, and the traveling reminded me of our Merkabah travels, which were always great. Thank you for your presence. *

Yes, very good class. That is the kind of class you like. We see that. Healings are always good.

Yes.

You always get a lot from attending these classes. So, again, you see how important they are for you.

Yes. It was wonderful to have that visit with family, friends, and pets.

Excellent. I know that you are disheartened that you didn't sense John and Katie until near the end. Don't be upset. They were there, but there was so many present that it was a little overwhelming, and it drowned out their energy. They saw your happiness, and they know you love them. They were very happy to see your joy. They are with you often. You can always ask to feel them, sense them, and they will be there. There was great joy and love. It was a wonderful experience that you would have missed if you had not attended.

Yes, as always, you are right.

*These are my notes from that workshop:

> Guided meditation: I felt I was in a cocoon of strong energy vibration. Easy, deep breathing. Energy flowing.
>
> Guided healing meditation with our medium teacher: I felt an energy flow starting at the top of my head and moving downward. Very peaceful. I felt the energy of the Spirit Doctor, and I was in that energy field. I was detached after that (in a deep state of trance).
>
> In the next guided meditation, our medium teacher took us to our loved ones in spirit: I saw myself and my guide in the Golden Flower of Life Sphere. We were moving through space and portals and landed in a garden. I could sense flowers, trees, and animals. There was a beautiful waterfall filled with many colors. A white horse appeared. I did not sense an Ascended Master. We entered a Rose Garden, where my family, friends, and pets were present. I had an overwhelming feeling of "Love," and I didn't want to leave. Many smiling faces. We were there for a while and then had to leave. We returned to the Sphere and came back.

(I felt a little sad afterward because I hadn't sensed John and Katie at the reunion. They were there, but as Harold said, there was so much energy that theirs was subdued.)

December 2, 2019

Just to keep with the psychic art. Try to get a few in each week and see if you can connect with the energy coming through. Relax. Free your mind and be aware of anything that may develop. Make a note of it.

December 3, 2019

We are sending thoughts your way – call it inspiration with regards to your writing. Be attentive to this. Take notes. These are things you might want to consider for the book.

Okay, I will try to be open to that.

December 5, 2019

I had a very enjoyable time with Stacey. It is nice to have someone I can talk to about some of my experiences and you and my guides.

Yes. This is an excellent match for you. You can have open conversations, and she also can be candid; plus she can benefit from some of your experiences and knowledge. A win, win. We see a splendid future here.

That is good to hear. I am happy about that.

December 6, 2019

It helps to go back over my notes and journals while doing the book to refresh and remind me of some of those talks.

Absolutely. You are getting the benefit again of guidance from spirit. And today, you had an important message from Archangel Michael. Keep practicing what He told you.* Spirit is there for you, helping you along your path to where you aspire to be.

*He told me to relax my mind and give myself over to spirit, which I wasn't doing, not completely anyway. I was reminded that I was protected from any possible negativity, and I was reminded to go into that deep trance state but not so deep that I lost awareness of what might be taking place. I was to work on this in my meditations. I had the ability; I just didn't trust myself completely.

December 8, 2019

I felt a jolt in my meditation. Was that my soul returning from somewhere?

Yes. You went deep, and in that state, your soul was traveling. You were about to come back, and it returned suddenly too fast. That was the jolt. Normally there would be an easy return with you feeling nothing.

There was a connection with your Higher Self.

December 12, 2019

You are looking for the resources in order that you can obtain those things that you desire.

Yes, indeed. There are certain desires, like going to England and having the finances available to do the things I can see coming up in the future.

Okay. So keep working on your vibration. Keep those thoughts on your desires. Keep putting them out there to the Universe. The Universe is complying with your wishes. It is just a matter of having them manifest. It is there for you. Feel as though you already have them. Feel the joy of them. Feel the comfort of having them.

December 13, 2019

I had a good Merkabah meditation where I saw my Vortex and what it held for me. Also, I felt like the Pleiadians were showing me the "Grid."*

Yes. Very good. Believe what you experience, that it is there, and it is true. You know this now. It is all up to you.

Thank you, Harold. Maybe we can start to do longer communications about other things that I can expound on for the book.

Yes, we can do that. It is all a matter of you being there, giving the time, and your willingness.

*This refers to a Merkabah group meditation taking place on December 22, 2019. There will be more on this later.

December 19, 2019

You are giving some very good advice.* See how you can help others from your interaction with spirit. Also, now you can see the benefit you are getting from going over your past notes. There are things mentioned that you have forgotten. Now you are revisiting them and noticing how you can improve.

Yes, I see that now.

You can see the value of having our words put down in the written form. Spoken words would have been quickly forgotten. Continue with trying to hear spirit. Keep the communication lines open to that.

Okay. I'm going to work on that.

*I'm not sure what this refers to, but I believe someone in our group was having a tough time with A's passing, and I had given them my thoughts on the matter.

December 21, 2019

How can I hear spirit? How do I practice that?

You need to open yourself up. You are going about it the right way through your meditations. Today you went too deep. You are asking for help. Good. Relax and listen. You quiet the mind and listen. It will happen.

December 22, 2019

I hope spirit will help me to get into the state I need to experience what is taking place this afternoon.

(The Merkabah group was getting together at the request of the Pleiadians to assist in cleansing the Electromagnetic Grid around Mother Earth.)

Yes. Spirit is with you and will assist you. Relax. Enjoy the experience and be in a place of gratitude and love. You are doing a great service. Be aware of that and feel pride in what you are accomplishing.

December 23, 2019

That was exceptional—what a wonderful experience to be a part of.* However, I wish I had experienced everything the others did. I feel I missed a bit. Nevertheless, I am grateful for what I did sense.

Yes. It was very well done by all of you. And don't fret that you didn't have the same experience. Everyone had what was for them. You had enough for you at that time. There will be future endeavors, and you will receive more and more as your abilities increase. Keep working on that knowing that you, too, can get to that place where the others are. Don't lose hope. Have faith. Love and Light. You will get there. You weren't chosen to fail. You have a purpose. Isn't that good to know?

Yes, of course, you are right.

To the reader:

Do you believe man has walked on the moon? Why? Most of us accept that as fact. But some don't. They say it is all an illusion perpetrated by big corporations or the government. I have had several spiritual experiences, and some will disbelieve and reject me and my convictions. Why? Because they don't believe it is possible, or I may be delusional. These experiences are as real to me as those who believe man has walked on the moon. But just because I have had them and others haven't doesn't mean they didn't happen. We have to expand our thinking. Broaden our vision and consider that there may be other realms and dimensions of existence. If you believe we have a soul and spirit energy with no form that is not tied to space or time, is it possible to accept that we can come into contact and communicate with other intelligent energies/higher beings?

My world opened up the more I became involved with spiritualism (the belief that our spirit survives our physical demise). As I started taking classes and studying more with very gifted mediums, I was coming to slowly understand the magnitude of what existed outside our normal realm. There were angels, Ascended Masters, spirit guides, worlds, and dimensions beyond anything I could have imagined. Communicating with these enlightened beings showed me how intent they are to help us and our planet. They want us to succeed and raise our vibration, and it all revolves around "Love." Once you have felt this pure "Love" vibration, you are hooked.

These Highly Evolved Beings say that a huge awakening is taking place. More and more people are now opening themselves up to the possibility of more out there. There are increased sightings of objects in the atmosphere that can't or aren't being explained. I believe that in the coming decades, the truth will show itself. Contact is going to be made. We have been told that we are very close to where we will accept this. New generations are incarnating that already have this built-in acceptance or willingness to acknowledge this possibility.

I had reservations about putting this in the book, but my guides advised me always to be true to myself; I must have the courage of my convictions. If I didn't include this part, I would have always regretted it.

*December 22. 2:22 pm PST 2019. This is the exact moment we were previously told to start by the Pleiadians. After a Merkabah meditation, our group was taken to the Grid surrounding the planet. We were met by the Pleiadians and other Highly Evolved Beings at a central part of the Grid. The Hathors and the Galactic Federation (Crystal people, Bird people, Lemurians, Light Reptilians, and more) were present. The Pleiadians put us into teams. My team was sent to work on the northern part of the Grid. Anne L. and M (the other members of our group) were east and west, respectively, and Claudette was south. The Grid is made up of Golden tubes, and these tubes had dark, ugly splotches of negative energy placed there by the shadow Reptilians.** Our task was to cleanse the tubes. My team consisted of me, a Pleiadian, a light Reptilian, and others. We then sent White Light Energy into the tubes and did a tonal (vocalizing) cleansing of the tubes. This lasted approximately half an hour. We had been given buckets of Golden Energy. We were to pour this Golden Energy into the tubes and seal them once they were filled. We then met back at the Center. We were told that we would be asked to partake in similar undertakings in the future. Before we incarnated to the planet, each of us had been chosen by Source to do this type of healing. We were told that we needed to visit the Galactic Federation often to send our experiences to them. We were also told to be mindful of our physical health, and if we were ever in a dark place, either physically or mentally, to ask for their help, and they would be there for us.

They said this next decade would be very important. There will be a few setbacks, but overall it will blossom, and new positive energies are coming.

We gave them our gratitude and said we looked forward to future experiences. They sent us "Love and Light."

I wish we could have taped the last fifteen minutes when Claudette channeled their words. I know I missed some of what they told us.

This is what I wrote to Stacey upon arriving home from the session:

> Okay, I'm home but feeling pretty drained. Also, I have a slight headache. Lots of energy. Amazing. Did you see the sky this evening? It was such a beautiful golden color before turning pink. I almost feel like we had something to do with that.

** The Arcturians are protecting our planet from the dark Reptilians who are infusing our Grid with negative energy.

(In 2021, the Merkabah group, who haven't met in some time, will partake in another cleansing. The Ancient Ones are telling us that there are holes in the Grid around Mother Earth, and negative energies are attacking these from above and below, creating chaos and instability on the planet. We are to meet in early August to cleanse and stabilize a Grid once again. We had been told that we might be asked to do this from time to time. And so it is.)

December 24, 2019

I feel like I connected with A.

Yes, you did, and they gave you the words to help you. You were concerned that you could have done more for them. They resolved that for you. They are happy to be here. They have a very strong energy. They will also be helping you with your sensitivity development.

I was very glad to have that connection, and I am grateful to them and their help.

December 26, 2019

Yes, family is important. There is that close bond between all of you. All of you share similar vibrations. There is this closeness on this plane, but you also have that in the spirit plane. You can feel that, can't you?

Yes, I can. There is a lot of love there.

Good. I hope you are considering your duties. I know this is a festive season, but you also have other things to be doing.

Yes, I am going to get back to it.

Okay. Just reminding you.

December 29, 2019

I am trying to work a bit on clairaudience and clairvoyance. How am I doing?

Okay. Keep it at the forefront of your thoughts. Continue to do what you have been doing. Don't force it. Let it come. Relax. There is no timeframe. It will happen when you are ready and the time is right.

December 30, 2019

I'm still feeling off with this cold, but I want to make sure we are connecting again. (There's more to come on this 'cold', which started December 27.)

Very good. You will begin to feel better soon. You don't often get sick. Just a reminder to take care of yourself.

December 31, 2019

I'm feeling a little better and going to work on the book. Last day of 2019. I hope 2020 is a good year.

I am glad to hear you say you are going to work on the book. 2020 is going to be a very good year for you. One of the best. There are so many good things waiting for you.* We are excited for you. There are many here that are rooting for you.

That's good to hear, Harold. Thank you and all my angels, guides, family, friends, and associates.

*2020 was an extremely important year for me, though it started on a rough note. I was ill like never before, and then there was this new relationship with Stacey that would change my life in the most amazing ways. My spiritual abilities were finally improving. There would be new people coming into my life and the sad loss of others. My painting was getting better, and there was a noticeable difference in my psychic art. Even though we would have this new virus, COVID affecting everyone globally, I was in a very good place. You could say this was a pivotal year for me.

2020

January 6, 2020

This has been a nasty cold, and I'm not over it yet.

Yes. You are getting there. We spoke yesterday about it.

Yes.

Just take it easy. It has to run its course.

Okay. Not the way I envisioned the New Year starting.

No. That's okay. It has nothing to do with the year ahead. You are normally very careful about keeping germs away. This time they slipped past. You are not invincible.

January 9, 2020

This cold has really thrown a monkey wrench into everything—two weeks of upset with my regular routine.

Yes. You are working through it. Hopefully, by next week you will be able to get back on track. Painting and such have been put on hold. We understand. Sometimes these issues in the physical are wake-up calls. Sometimes reminders of how quickly things can change.

Yes. I would like to be done with it and not go through that again.

Stay positive. Anything that comes into your experience was brought by you. Why this? Reflect on that.

Okay.

January 10, 2020

I want to go to the Message Night tonight. I hope you can help me get through the evening without this cough.

We can do that. Relax. Keep your throat loose with drops. Let's see who may come through and what interesting and meaningful words are given.

That would be great. I am so looking forward to that and seeing Stacey; I miss her.

Yes.

January 11, 2020

That was an excellent Message Night. I'm so happy I could attend. Thank you for helping me with not coughing.* It was so nice to spend some time with Stacey. I missed her. It was a wonderful experience to have Mom and Dad come through together with such love and for Mom to say how much she liked Stacey. That was very good.

Now, Stacey is much more sensitive (in a psychic sense) than I am, and I say that with love. She definitely feels more than I.

Hi, Michael. It was a good night. We are glad you had that opportunity to connect with your parents, and there is so much love there. Others could feel it, especially Stacey. It was almost overwhelming for her, and she is very sensitive (to spirit). The two of you make a strong couple and complement each other. This is a very good relationship, confirmed by your mother. It is going to be an excellent year for you. You have your parents pushing you forward. Good things await. We are very excited for you.

That is gratifying to hear. I am also excited to see it unfold. I am going to try to connect with Mom soon.

She is ready for that.

*Now is the time to talk about this cough I had which goes back to December 27. I felt off in an unusual way. I very seldom get sick. This cough was like something I had never had. I coughed non-stop for days. It got so that the only way I could get any kind of sleep was to try and sleep sitting upright on my couch, which I did for two weeks. If I lay down on the bed, it was brutal. It finally got to the point where I thought I must have pneumonia. I visited both the Emergency ward and my doctor with incomplete conclusions.

Finally, I began to recover from this illness. From the beginning to a complete finish, it lasted six weeks. This was not something I ever wanted to go through again, and I certainly was careful not to pass it on to Stacey. It was only sometime later that we started hearing about this virus that was to change our world.

Thank God it wasn't worse for me. As bad as it was, it could have been much worse, as we would all find out. I was lucky, had great genes, or someone was watching over me. Whatever it was, I am grateful.

So, not a great start to 2020, but it would turn into a fantastic year for me. I had met this incredible woman who would change my life beyond my wildest dreams. We share so much. We are a complete match for each other in every way—our creative endeavors, thoughts, desires, and interests. I could go on and on, but it is time to get on with where I left off.

January 14, 2020

I am trying to work on my third eye some more. It seems like a long process. I am attempting to focus more attention on it.

Good. Well, keep at it. It is coming along. It does seem to be taking its time. Continue to send your vibration, your intention out there. Feel it build. Feel it raise. Let it expand and expand. It's all about raising your vibration. You can do it. We've told you this many times. Believe it. Don't get down because it hasn't happened yet. You know it is there for you.

January 15, 2020

Was my clearing of old emotions and letting go of past negativity during meditation helpful today?

It was. You should continue with that every so often. You are doing well with letting go and working on your third eye. Stay with that. There is an improvement.

January 17, 2020

Well, that was an incredible session with Trish yesterday.* I could feel the vibrations at the end, and a lot of good came out of it, a lot of clearing for me and others. It will be interesting to see what effects this has.

Wow. That was quite the experience. There was an immense clearing out of old emotions. You may not notice anything right now, but this was very good for you and, as you said, good for others as well, even those who have passed. You can even feel it now as we speak.

Yes. Energy. Very good. I am tired today.

That is part of it. It can be draining. Rest. You had many from spirit applauding you yesterday. They were very happy for what occurred.

*Trish is a personal coach, but she is much more than that. She spent many years as a licensed Physiotherapist. She has several different post-graduate certificates from her years in her physiotherapy career, and now, along with all that knowledge, she has added other things like working with people's trapped emotions, facilitating past life regressions, and clearing unwanted energies. She is combining Science and Spirituality in a perfectly harmonic approach. Trish has now added several Holistic healing skills and techniques to her repertoire. One of particular interest to us is the technique known as the 'Emotion Code' I am simplifying it here, but it is lower vibrational emotional baggage that we take on throughout our soul's journey that gets trapped in our subconscious and stored in our tissues. And it's not just our own emotions, but our parents and ancestors can also play a part in these emotional releases. Holding on to these can manifest in all sorts of ways, usually in the form of physical discomfort and pain. Trish is a healer who is very sensitive and has had years of experience and expertise working with the human body; therefore, she can find and release these trapped emotions by having the patient breathe in positive reinforcements and breathe out the heavier concerns causing the problem. As I said, this is an overly simplified explanation. There is much more to it. For further interest, *Emotion Code*, written by Dr. Bradley Nelson, goes deeply into all the nuances. I have now had many clearing sessions with Trish, and Stacey and I are blown away every time by what takes place.

If you are interested, you can contact Trish at www.healingwithtrish.com.

Note: I was having regular back pain in the small of my back. It was constant and seemed to worsen. The doctors said I had degenerative arthritis in a couple of my lower lumbar vertebrae, and there wasn't much they could do. I went to see Trish. She did a little physical work on me, and through all the work done with releasing these trapped emotions, I began to notice a big difference. As of this writing (July 2021), I have been pain-free now for several months to the point that I don't think about it anymore. Thank you, Trish. You are a wonder.

January 19, 2020

Okay, back to the painting tomorrow and hopefully a routine. A couple of small things on the horizon but nothing major. The weather and all have been a hindrance.

Good to hear. There have been some things that came up that got you out of your rhythm. Your cold/cough is slowly getting better. That's a help.

Yes. I will be glad when I'm back strong and healthy.

You are almost there.

January 24, 2020

There is a lot of information coming through for Stacey and me.*

Yes, and it is good information for both of you. The two of you have a fantastic future together. Take the advice that is coming through. It is coming from spirit…Source Energy. It is all there for you. Be aware of situations when they occur to help you move forward with your progression into this new environment. You will be shown the way. As was stated, "Don't over-think it," which you tend to do. Look to your heart. Follow those feelings. They will guide you true. There are wonderful days ahead for the two of you.

*This is coming from Stacey's Emotion Code session, her connection with spirit, and information I had received during meditation. The advice was that we were meant to be together and not over-think it but get on with it. Our subsequent conversations would lead to us moving in together into her place. I had been on my own for quite a few years and had a nice apartment in a senior center I was comfortable in, so this was a big step. Normally, I would have dwelled on this for some time, but because of all the messages we had received, we decided not to hesitate and move ahead with this. It turned out to be the best thing I have ever done. The synchronicity of this timing turned out to be another sign from the Universe, with unforeseen COVID lockdowns happening mere weeks later. And, much to the delight of my spirit guides, I have learned to listen to these signs when they show up.

January 26, 2020

This move is just what you need. It will help you in many of the things that you should be remedying. More time for the things that matter. Consistent exercise. A better diet and getting more done. Less TV watching. All the things that will compliment you. The Universe is sending this to you to assist you. Don't disappoint.

Okay. I understand.

January 29, 2020

You are going to have a lot going on in the coming months and year overall. There is going to be a lot to do. You will have help from us through inspired thoughts on how to get things done. This is all good for you and Stacey. You are going to be a strong couple, helping each other and helping others. This is where you are meant to be. Stacey knows this. There is so much that is to come from this bonding of the two of you. It has already started. Keep that energy flowing.

January 30, 2020

You are getting a lot of ideas. Don't let it overwhelm you. Go with what feels right at the moment. Remember what was said, "Trust your heart." Stay with the heart, not the head.

February 4, 2020

I'm interested in your thoughts on the pendulum. Does spirit work through the pendulum, or is my energy doing it?*

Right now, it is your vibration making it swing. There will come a time when you have been using it for a while where spirit will get involved. It is another tool that is available to you and is accurate, as you saw when trying it on your chakras.

You will get a lot of information from the book you bought.** We sent you that positive vibe to make that purchase as we knew it would help you.

*I've started asking simple questions and then using the pendulum to get "yes" or "no" answers. It will flow in a certain direction, i.e., clockwise for "yes," counter-clockwise for "no," or vice versa for each response. Start with a question you know the answer to and see what direction is "yes" or "no." It's quite amazing how well it works.

**The Soul Truth by Sheila and Marcus Gillette.... *The Teachings of Theo.*

Good book. A lot of excellent information.

February 12, 2020

Thank you for helping me find my knife—a true inspiration—and assisting me out of that situation with the inverter.

I had lost my favorite pocket knife, so I decided to ask the pendulum where it was and narrowed the answer down to "couch." I searched Stacey's couch but could not find it, even though the pendulum said I would. The next time I was at my place, the notion popped into my head during my meditation to check my couch, even though I was sure it wasn't there. Hah, it was under one of the cushions. The pendulum was right. I had wrongly assumed it was Stacey's couch. You must be very specific when you ask the pendulum questions.

I have an inverter that I use when my back acts up. I usually only invert about three-quarters of the way. I decided to do a complete invert on this day, meaning hanging from my feet completely free. I have occasionally done this before with no problems, but it has been a while. It locked into place, and I couldn't get myself back upright. I had tried almost everything other than tipping the whole thing over and probably doing severe damage to myself. The thought had crossed my mind that "Is this it? Is this how I go out?" I started to panic a bit when I gave an extra-strong tug and got it out of the lock position. Funny now, but not so much then.

Yes. That was a strong push from spirit to check there, and we did help you with your situation. We don't want you exiting yet (chuckle).

I'll be more careful in the future.

Okay. Get back to your basics when you can. We know you have other things to work on, but you can still slip in your painting and writing here and there.

Yes, I've been getting your thoughts on that.

February 17, 2020

I feel like I am getting a lot of things thrown at me physically: my back, this lingering cough, and pain in the back of my legs. Is this something I must experience to move on?

Yes, you are getting a lot coming to you. There is the reminder of diet, but there is more to it. Remember, you will go through some bad stuff to get to the good. By contrast, showing you what you don't want, you then see what it is that you do want. You are to shoot the positive thoughts (about where you want to be) out to the Universe. In your case right now, you need to be putting out the positive concept of well-being physically to go along with the spiritual, and you can add to that mental well-being. Contrast leads to desires fulfilled. That is how you need to look at it. There will always be some contrast for you to expand—to experience. You can get through this. Remember, it is all about your vibration.

Yes, got it.

February 20, 2020

What Stacey picked up on was quite amazing, and having Pearl* there was understandable, but you being there was something else. That was quite the vision she had for me.

Yes, it was. I wanted her to feel my energy to add to Pearl's so that she could receive that message. You have an amazing time coming up; quite extraordinary. This was a small window into that.

I know you have a lot going on, but take your time. Get it done and be ready for what is coming. Wow.

That is very exciting. Thank you, Harold, and thank you, Pearl.

*Stacey is sensitive to spirit and recently contacted Pearl, one of her guides. During a meditation, Pearl showed her a clear vision of me shooting upwards, in a spiritual sense.

February 21, 2020

We are sending you a number of inspirational thoughts to assist you with your transition, your move. We want to see this work for you in the easiest manner. We want this to go smoothly for you. So take heed of what is coming through to you. It will help.

February 22, 2020

I feel I am picking up your hints on how to go about some points for moving.

(I would move in with Stacey, but because of COVID, it would take a few months of moving clothes and smaller items in several trips. I was moving from a senior center, and there was a great fear of COVID transmission. I had to pick my times.)

You are. They will help you. Get as much done as you can. But take it bit by bit. Have a good art class today and a good mediumship class tomorrow. We realize that you continue to have doubts about that. You still feel there is no improvement, but it is there.

February 23, 2020

What do you think of my decision not to attend class? I'm reading my older notes where my guides tell me I should be hearing spirit at any time, which was three years ago. Time and space may mean nothing to you, but it is different here. Not much is changing. I should be concentrating on other things.

I understand your dilemma. You aren't noticing anything different because the changes are subtle. But they are happening. You have made a decision. This is something that can always be changed. Keep up with your meditations. Change will continue, although at a slower pace. No worries. See what Claudette has to say in response.

February 27, 2020

I know you have a lot going on, but try to keep this communication flowing. It is still very important not to lose this connection. It continues to be the means of communication for us. Keep the line open.

Okay.

February 29, 2020

That was certainly interesting the other night, especially the confused looks on the mediums' faces when they came to me and the high energy they mentioned.*

It is confirmation for you that you are getting there. That validates the work you have been doing on yourself. It is proceeding, and there is still much for you to do and much more for you to experience. Doesn't it make you feel good to know that? And, doesn't it make you want to continue with your progress?

Yes, it certainly does.

*Stacey and I participated in a Message Night given by three mediums with seven other people. The mediums had already read five people before me, and I just knew I would be next. While one medium was giving a reading to someone else, I saw the other two mediums look at the tarot cards laid in front of them and then at each other with confused faces, then at me. I said to Stacey, "I'm next. Look at them. They look baffled." Sure enough, I was next. They said they weren't sure what to make of the cards, having never encountered those symbols in that grouping before. They said that what they could tell me was that there was tremendous energy around me. They continued to look rather bewildered. The last medium said she saw a Joy guide with me named Sampson. He had long flowing hair and a silk scarf around his neck with a jubilant smiling face. It was an interesting evening. Stacey also had a very good reading, with the mediums stating she had empathic abilities and how the two of us were a powerful couple, complementing each other. Fascinating.

March 2, 2020

It is amazing the way everything is coming together.

All according to plan, with much more in the works. You have no idea of what is waiting for you and Stacey. We see a wonderful time ahead for you both.

Excellent.

March 4, 2020

Yes. These physical ailments that you are experiencing. It is a reminder that you need to get in balance with your Source. You will get through this. Continue to meditate and see yourself free of these ailments. Send them love. Release them.

March 6, 2020

Hi, Harold. Is there anything you would like to say today?

Only that you are getting it. You are finding that feeling that will create your desires, your dreams. It is all coming about. Wonderful. Good for you. Perseverance. Practice continuing to keep your goals in sight and never giving up, bringing about the fruition of your dreams. Continue to dream. Continue to create. That is what it is all about.

March 14, 2020

I had an excellent session with Trish the other day.

That was an excellent time with Trish indeed. You saw all the good that came out of that for you and especially your siblings. Very good job. It was also encouraging for you to feel your mother's presence and to hear from Verine, Lisa, and Craig.* Wasn't that special for you?

Yes, for sure.

You can see now your importance, your worth. You need to build on that feeling of Love for yourself and all that you are. There is no ego there. **Yes, I get it.**

Good.

*Lisa and Craig are Verine's children from her first marriage. Sadly, all have passed. They came through in our session, expressing their appreciation for me and all I was doing. It was very heartwarming.

March 19, 2020

Would you like to give me something for my Facebook page about COVID?

Yes. Yet you already have an inkling of why this is happening. It is the dark before the light. You are entering a new era, and this is something that you as a planet must experience. It is bringing together all of the populace. Something that affects the population as a whole. From this will come a closer bonding of all, an ushering in of a new time for you. But you had already considered this possibility on a soul level. There will be better times to come with a kinder understanding ushering in this new day.

March 25, 2020

You are doing very well together with all that is going on. (I have now basically moved in with Stacey and was slowly bringing my stuff over to her place while being cautious about the virus.) Get into a rhythm and back to doing your creative activities. The two of you complement each other. There is a lot of time now for you to do this.

March 31, 2020

I had an interesting meditation today. First, Mom came forward with encouraging words, and then John and Katie got amused with some of my antics. Then I had the meeting with Stacey on the spirit plane while she was still sleeping, and I'm curious whether she remembered me in a dream. (She didn't.)

(I'm an early riser and like to get my meditation in before she gets up.)

Yes. Good connections. You were deep but still aware. That is the place you want to be, and that is where you will see and/or hear spirit. You were forging a contact with Stacey, but whether she will remember that or not is like any other dream. It has to be a conscious effort to remember, or it must be so vivid as to make an impression. Good. Let's keep working on those things.

April 3, 2020

I had another interesting Emotion Code session and a nice visit from A the other morning.

Yes, but first, you know what I want to say, so I won't go into it (keeping up the communication). Very good Emotion Code for everyone involved, and yes, that was nice for you to hear from A. These Emotion Code sessions are clearing up and clearing out a lot of old debris, freeing you and Stacey up. Everything you do with regard to this is beneficial. Keep up with your other endeavors and keep this line of communication open. (Oops.)

April 7, 2020

I am getting a lot of positive responses for the quote you gave me a few days ago regarding COVID.

Excellent. It is appreciated by them. Words they need to hear, plus it gets your book title out there. There could be a benefit to come from that. The right person might pick it up and do something with it. We will wait and see. Keep working on getting the word out there. Your book isn't done yet, and finishing the new one will help with that.

April 9, 2020

This is a tough time for many people, but you and Stacey are faring well. You are doing all the right things, and you will both come out of this stronger than ever. Do all the little stuff and keep busy with your hobbies. Keep in contact with your loved ones. Everything is going to be okay. Stay vigilant.

April 13, 2020

We already had our little chat (mentally) this morning, and I will do better with this after missing so many days.

Yes. Good. We must keep this going. There is much to be discussed, and this is still the most desirable way for you now. There is a reason why it is being done in this manner, and it is in your interest. We want to see you succeed, and this is a part of that.

Okay. I will do better.

April 17, 2020

I had another interesting Emotion Code session yesterday. I find it intriguing and amazing.

There are many wonderful advantages coming from these sessions. The letting go of much intrusive and negative energies that can be affecting you, plus there is the additional benefit of releasing all of that from others, including those in spirit who are being freed from past negativity (the releasing from Akashic Records*). Very good. All of it strengthens you and Stacey.

> *The Akashic Records are a dimension of consciousness that contains a vibrational record of every soul and its journey. They are an experiential body of knowledge that contains everything that every soul has ever thought, said, and done throughout its existence, as well as all its future possibilities. –How to Read the Akashic Records by Linda Howe

April 18, 2020

A riveting meditation, seeing that vibrant red color across my vision.

That was your root chakra showing up. It is an important chakra, and this was a reminder to keep it clean. Work on that chakra. See the Divine Light cleansing that chakra. You want a vibrant red. Stay with that one for now. Ideally, you want all your chakras perfectly cleansed and aligned. Get that root one nicely cleansed first.

April 20, 2020

Just to reiterate what I said a few days ago. Try to get back to your duties or passions; however you look at it. This is more important than you are realizing, which is why we keep harping on it.

April 28, 2020

I had the feeling that the Lords of Light joined me for my meditation today.

Yes. You called, and They were there. And, They told you why They were there to help you with raising your vibration and your sensitivity, along with the many others who were also present. You have powerful energies available to you who are willing and wanting to assist you. Be very grateful for Their support.

Yes. I am.

I know you are.

April 29, 2020

Okay, so this morning, during my Merkabah meditation, I felt that the Hathors were present and were giving me a healing.

Very good. That is right. They were there for you, and they will continue in the future to help you.

I appreciate that. There is a reason I am having this back problem.

(The last year, I have been having some issues with my back on and off, but the last few weeks, it has been particularly bothersome.)

I just wish I could figure it out.

There is a reason, and you will get there, but that is a part of your journey. It would be easy for us to tell you, but there are things that you must figure out on your own. We can't hand you everything. Meditate on it. It will come to you.

Okay.

April 30, 2020

I believe I got an answer during my meditation regarding my back problem. Subconsciously, I am stressing over not being able to get out of my other place or being capable of moving my belongings from the storage locker due to COVID concerns, even though I don't feel that it is bothering me.

This is a deep stress that you are not aware of. Sometimes these can creep in, and you are unaware of it happening. Work on going deep within and cutting the ties, releasing them. You can get rid of it, and you will see improvement in your situation.

May 4, 2020

I thought I would try writing in this new notebook, possibly attempting to connect with a Higher Energy Being. I feel now that it might be my Joy guide, Sampson.

Yes. That is there for you. Do a short meditation. Ask and write. You need only ask. He is excited to have this opportunity.

May 7, 2020

Hi, Harold. I'm just following up on our earlier thoughts. I understand that I need to keep up with writing, but I also need to keep working on the mental process.

Yes, that is correct. Both serve you in their own way and need to be continued.

May 12, 2020

Just that we are encouraged to see you back painting, writing, and not to forget your psychic art. I know you have other things going on, getting settled with your new arrangements and dealing with this virus, but it is important to continue with your own endeavors. Some things will improve; nevertheless, be careful and protect yourselves.

(Some time has passed. I am continuing to move clothes and items into Stacey's place and not connecting as much with Harold.)

May 20, 2020

You already know my thoughts to you (keep the communication going). I understand there is much happening with this new environment, but it only takes a few minutes to connect with me, which you have. It is easy for that to slip by. Try to manage it into your routine. It is important.

May 21, 2020

That was a very good meditation just now. I felt the Hathors were present to help me with my back problems.

That is so. They were there for you. There will be a good rapport between the two of you which will continue. This will be an excellent connection that will progress in time—a great benefit to you. We know you are grateful for this and look forward to the continued association.

Wonderful to hear.

May 24, 2020

Try to catch those negative thoughts that creep in and turn them around or erase them altogether. Try to keep that positive aura around you. You will be surprised at what a difference it will make.

May 25, 2020

Book. Book. Book. There is still a lot to be done. Put aside some time every day for this. We would like to see more progress happening, and there are benefits to reading some of those past writings.

May 28, 2020

Keep trying to hear me. We will continue to work on that sound connection. Relax. Let yourself go. Expect, but don't strive for it. Be open to it. We will get there.

May 29, 2020

We are liking what is taking place with the Emotion Code session. There is a lot of clearing and cleansing taking place. This is having a profound effect on so many energies on so many different levels. There is a remarkable value coming from this. We are happy for all concerned and know that there are wonderful releasings yet to come bringing more benefits to all. Very good.

Thank you, Harold. I can see how that can happen. I'm very glad to be able to partake in this.

June 3, 2020

I think the best way for me to keep this going is to bring my notebook with me when I meditate so that it is right there when I finish.

Good. We sent that idea to you because you were easily getting sidetracked.

I thought so. Okay. Hopefully, this will work better.

Yes.

June 4, 2020

There is an immense benefit to you going through your past notes—in remembering practices that you should be doing or continuing. Aside from putting them into a book, it is good for you to relook at these communications.

June 5, 2020

It is merely getting back to that routine that will assist you in these writings, and we will remind you by interrupting your present thoughts that we are here waiting.

June 9, 2020

Amazing about the Fairies.

(A gifted close friend had seen Fairies in their garden and informed us that two of them were for Stacey and me. Mine is named Cody and would come by our place occasionally and is there to help me. Rose would be there for Stacey.)

Yes. That is very interesting, and you have another ally to assist you when you feel you need some clearing. Excellent, and he will show himself to you at some point.

I am excited and looking forward to that. I have looked for them in the past.

I know, and because of that, they are ready to reveal themselves. What you imagine can manifest, as you see in this case.

June 11, 2020

It was good to do the recorded Merkabah again. And I am looking forward to my session with Trish.

You should try and do the recorded Merkabah at least once a week, if not more. You are connecting with the "Advanced" (Merkabah), but you get more from the other.

You will have another good session with Trish, and you will remove some more unwanted emotions. All these removals help to clear you and move you forward.

June 17, 2020

We are sending you inspirational thoughts with regard to your book. Be mindful of what is coming your way. Keep notes of these ideas. They will help you down the road when putting it all together.

June 18, 2020

Okay, a lot to discuss right now. First, I asked to go with Cody to the Fairy Kingdom during meditation. I had the sense that I was there. Next, near the end of the meditation, I got the name Robert, and

I sensed he would be my new guide. Can you talk about all of this, please?

Yes, you did have a brief visit with Cody to the Fairy Kingdom—Rose (the Fairy associated with Stacey) and Rachel were there along with many other Fairies. You are welcome there any time.

Now you definitely got the name Robert. He is to be your guide. He is there to help you with further development. You will have new guides that will step in every couple of years for the purpose of advancing you with your life plan. Phillip and I are always here for you, as is Arthur, who was there previously. We will be monitoring your progress. Try to implement what we have shown you and discussed with you over that period. We have enjoyed our time with you. We love you and want you to succeed. You have a new partner, and Robert is going to be working with you in this new time with all that is taking place in your life.

Harold, I so appreciate all you have done for me—all the words of wisdom and encouragement and all the help you have given me to get me to where I am. Thank you so much. I love you.

Michael, it has been my pleasure, and I look forward to great things in your future, with many wonderful days ahead. I am always there for you. Blessings and Peace and Love.

Thank you.

Robert, are you there?

I am, Michael, and I am looking forward to us moving ahead with more development and continuing the fine work and association you had with your previous guides. Good times to come.

Thank you, Robert. I am also anticipating this new partnership. Thanks. I will be in touch tomorrow.

Good. Have a wonderful day. Peace.

The changing of guides is always a sad moment. You have been participating daily with this guide, who has shared so much with you. Who has given advice, kept you on your path when you started to wander, nudged you to do better or try harder, encouraged you to look after yourself in a more health-conscious way, and prescribed antidotes when you encountered obstacles in your day to day goings-on. He or she, if that be the case, is a confidant. They know you. They're aware of everything that has happened with you and how you fared – good and bad. Once you have made this connection with your guide, they are there at the ready, no matter what you are doing or where you may be. There's a sense of comfort in that. So, a changing of the guide creates this sorrow, even though you know in your heart that the new guide will be just as loving and caring as the one that is leaving and, of course, they are not gone. Any of your guides are available; you merely have to ask. I felt the same way when Harold took over from Phillip and probably will again when a new guide steps forward to replace Robert, although I expect to have Robert for some time yet. And remember, your guides were a big part of the preplanning for your adventure into this new dimension.

June 19, 2020

Hi, Robert. Is there anything you would like to say?

Hi, Michael. Thank you. It is nice to be here with you. All of us are happy to see you back with the psychic art. That is one of the things I will be helping you with. It would be great if you could spend a few minutes with that every couple of days and go about it very much as you did today. That was a good start today, and don't be concerned about whether what you got is accurate or not. It is all about the process. The constant practice will bring about the proper results. Right now, we want to see you get into the rhythm. All else will follow. Good start today.

Okay, Robert. Thank you. Let's see how it goes.

Good, Michael. It will be fine; just watch how it progresses. You will be surprised.

June 20, 2020

Yes. We like the visualization you are having with regard to your desires. We want to see this come to pass for you. It is very close. Keep visualizing. Keep that "want" out there to the Universe. It has been granted and is waiting to manifest. Let it happen. See it. Believe it. It is there for you.

Thank you, Robert. That is good to hear.

Yes. Let it be.

June 21, 2020

I had some very interesting dreams last night. I don't usually recall them unless I make a concerted effort, but these were quite vivid.

Yes, and these had to do with the planetary influences that were being experienced. You were doing some shedding of your own. Even though you didn't think you were being affected by this, you were. When you have these very vivid dreams, it is you being made aware that something more is taking place than your ordinary run-of-the-mill dreams. There is something going on; in this case, you shedding old emotions that have been stored up deep in your subconscious. This is good. You're a little freer.

June 22, 2020

(Laughing) Because you started to say "Hi, Harold" (which I did). You went very deep with your meditation today, but that's okay. It is not a waste. Things were taking place for you while you were in that deep state. You could sense something going on even if you couldn't know what that was.

June 23, 2020

You have been attempting to hear spirit for quite a while now, and it has happened a couple of times. You are getting words forming in your head, but you are looking for more than that. The words will develop better, with more than just a word here and there. You will get sentences, and from that, you will get a voice. Continue to try connecting to us and attempt to get more than just a few words. Work on this during your time that you set aside for your meditations. It doesn't need to be long, just a few minutes, and see what you elicit. You should begin to capture more and more. This is an excellent practice for you and will provide results. Good job with the psychic art. Keep it up.

Thank you, Robert. I will work on that.

June 25, 2020

We've already had a good communication during my meditation. You told me to continue to do this, and it will become straightforward and matter of fact.

Indeed, we did, and I told you not to doubt all that you are perceiving. This will become second nature to you and will lead to more sensitivity.

June 26, 2020

Thank you for what you said regarding Cody and for working on that strong connection with him.

Good. Feel his presence, and you will eventually be able to see him. It may start out as a movement in your peripheral vision.

June 29, 2020

Yes. Change. Catastrophes like the pandemic you are going through right now will bring about a change for the better. It is a wake-up call to humanity that the current order needs to improve. Situations are taking place where the populace has had enough of the way things have been and are now making their voice heard to bring about changes to raise vibrations—conversations are arising for the betterment of all. This new decade begins with turmoil but will end with a greater understanding and collectiveness. And so it is.

(I had asked Robert for something for my Facebook page.)

June 30, 2020

Hi, Robert. Is there anything you would like to say? And thank you again for that quote yesterday.

Habits can be hard to break. You sometimes have to make that concerted effort. But, as you continue, you break the old and begin new ones. I was happy to give you those words and will have more if you wish.

Be aware of your thoughts and the inspiration coming your way.

July 1, 2020

I was very deep in my meditation today but came out of it suddenly.

You were deep. Your soul was traveling, though you were not aware of that because you were so deep. That sudden emergence was your soul returning rather abruptly, too fast, instead of a slower return. No harm done.

Was there a place I was traveling to?

No specific destination. More of a roaming.

July 3, 2020

Further to our mental discussion—your psychic art gives these spirits (energies) a chance to come forward and talk. Once you have become more advanced with this process, they will be able to speak to loved ones through you. You will be their medium. So, of course, there are so many here who are willing to help you become better in order that their voices may be heard. You will be doing them a service. That is why it is important for you to perfect this process.

Oh, I clearly see why this is significant and why I need to do it more often.

Good. You get it.

July 6, 2020

Good job with the psychic art. You must see that you are doing better. You notice the improvement. You are going about it the right way. More and more, you will improve. More and more, you will feel spirit and get their impressions. You will get more insight into them. We are excited to see where this goes for you.

I do feel as though I am improving. Thank you, Robert.

July 09, 2020.

That was an amazing session with Trish yesterday and with Stacey also present. She is so helpful in reminding me of dates and episodes.

First off, Stacey is very sensitive to your energy. She easily picks up things from you, and she is and will continue to be a big supporter and assister to you going forward. Now, that <u>was</u> an exceptional session for you. So many good things coming out of that. You released a lot of old emotions in this session, as well as releasing them from others in your family, even to the point of your great grandparents. Fantastic. So many good energies supporting you. Verine, Mom and Dad, and Lisa (Verine's daughter who is in spirit) all were really showing their love for you. Beautiful. That alone should make you feel wonderful.

Yes. I knew that Mom, Dad, and Verine would do that, but I was surprised when Lisa showed up and came through with such thoughtfulness and appreciation. That was very nice.

You made an impression on her, which was fully realized when she passed. She was bringing that forward now. It was quite moving for you as you felt that emotion. Excellent morning.

Yes, it was.

July 10, 2020

Well, that was some amazing insight and pronouncement from Trish. Your thoughts, please?

Yes, Trish has sensed and been given that insight for you. All your meditations and prayers, all of your readings and practices, have been adding up and moving you forward. You have been raising your vibration. It was told to you a few months ago that there would be this shift upwards, and that is now happening. You see the vast improvement in your psychic art. Trish is telling you that the people will come into your life to help shift you. Claudette is still a dear friend but no longer that teacher to you. You felt that change occurring some months ago. You have new people in your life, and they are there to help you, but you are your own person now moving forward with all that you have learned and practiced, and, of course, you have the continuous help from spirit—all your guides, teachers, and Masters are still here working with you.

July 11, 2020

You have guides that are there to help you with your writing and your art. If you are feeling stumped, we are there to assist through inspired thought or to move you along with a helping hand. You can always ask for assistance.

July 12, 2020

I got the inspired thought that I should set aside a day and spend that day solely working on the book.

Yes. Do you not think that would be a valuable way of getting more done? You can still continue to do your normal writing, but this way, it speeds things along.

That's a good idea. I will do that.

Let's see how that works. There should be good progress.

July 13, 2020

The physical ailments you are experiencing are all being brought on by you, and it all has to do with getting this move done. Once that has been accomplished, you will notice a vast improvement. Try and keep positive thoughts that this is all going to work out just fine. Stacey has been a big help to you. There are good days ahead. Don't worry.

July 16, 2020

There are many synchronicities showing up lately. Old thoughts and old times are cropping up. I'm finding things from the past.

Yes. More clearing. These are bubbling up from your subconscious. Sometimes they come through as dreams. Other times they will manifest, as they have been doing lately, as old memories—that past part of your life that is like another you. They all helped to shape you, but you are no longer that person. It's as if you are a new individual. A better version of yourself. A progressed you. A transformational you. You have gone from the caterpillar to the butterfly. So continue to fly higher. Continue to raise your vibration. There is no limit.

July 17, 2020

Stay with it (psychic art). It's coming around more and more. Try to do it every other day and see where you are with it in six months. You will be amazed.

Good session again yesterday with Trish. You and Stacey are both benefitting from these releases. Shedding. Shedding. Freeing yourselves from those old, old blemishes. It is very good.

July 18, 2020

Take things in stride. It is in your nature to go after things that are on your to-do list, but you don't have to get them all done at once. Take them one by one, and you can prioritize them. They will get finished. You want to jump in and see them all finished right away. It doesn't have to be that way. Don't be impatient, which is a part of your nature. Patience. Relax. It will all get done.

July 19, 2020

(Morning meditation)

Immediately I had the sense that CH (the grandkids' other grandfather who had passed in recent months) was contacting me. He wanted everyone to know that he had an easy transition and was thrilled that he could communicate with me so that I could pass on to the family his happiness. He is very happy and is still in the process of meeting his family and friends, but he wanted to make a quick connection with me as he knew I could do this.

He wants everyone to remember him the way he was and not the person in the care facility, who could be grumpy with staff and have memory problems (Alzheimer's). It was his time to go. I sensed he had a big smile and was happy to be where he was. If anyone in the family notices a picture off-kilter or something has moved, that is him saying he stopped by for a visit. Acknowledge him. He gave me a big thumbs-up.

July 20, 2020

I got your transmission about the start of the book. I like it, but I'm going to need your help remembering it. And I like the idea of having a recorder handy when these thoughts come through. Thank you for that.

Of course. We are always here to help, and that is a good way for you to have a record of your thoughts and so forth. You are getting more information right now from your meditations than anything else. Oh, and good job with your response to CH's daughter.* It was well done, and it is on them what they do with that. You have fulfilled your responsibility.

*I had doubts about passing on the message from CH because the family was unaware of my capabilities regarding connecting to spirit, and I wasn't sure how they would take it. I didn't want to create any strange feelings. But by connecting to me and requesting my assistance in passing on his message to the family, I then had a responsibility to do just that. I particularly didn't want CH on my case for not carrying out that obligation. He confirmed his gratitude once I had passed on his message.

July 21, 2020

(Morning meditation)

I sensed the presence of the Hathors. They told me they were there to assist me with my development, as they had done previously. They asked me to breathe deeply and relax—they wanted me in a deeper state. They were going to download something for me. I was in this state for some time. I also got a few images of possible scenarios for finishing the book. Once they finished, I thanked them and ended my meditation. I then continued with a psychic art portrait.

Hi, Robert. That was very good.

Yes. The Hathors did say to you that your progression is a benefit to all, and they want you to succeed in this, which is why they are assisting you. Very good. Plus, we like where the psychic art is going. Keep at it. You are doing well. Also very good.

July 23, 2020

Have another really good session with Trish today. It will be special. Immerse yourself into it and feel the vibrations. We will talk more tomorrow. It is good to see you back with the taped Merkabah.

July 24, 2020

Yes. With the psychic art—go with the impressions that you are receiving. Free your mind and put down what comes through. That is how it works. That is what you are doing. Trust that. That is the mediumship working. Keep doing it. It will get stronger and easier.

July 27, 2020

There is a lot going on. There is Charlie's transition (a family member's pet dog that passed today) which, although very sad, will be fine. It will go very well, and he will be greeted by Toby and Buster. He will be so happy.

July 31, 2020

Yes. Psychic art. Don't lapse on this. You now have the freedom to do the things you want – painting, lots of writing, psychic art, walks, biking, kayaking. Enjoy nature. Enjoy each other. Visit other areas for these activities. Relish in it all. Take it all in. Love what you do. Love it all. It is all there for you now.

August 1, 2020

Just to reconfirm to you that you need to trust the process. Go with what you are getting. You are doing it. Don't doubt. It is coming to you and through you, and you are putting that down on paper. Don't be concerned with the drawing. Let it flow. The depictions are accurate enough. It is all a part of the process, and these will get better as you go along. Right now, keep with what you are doing and be confident in what you are producing. It is good. Better than what you think.

August 4, 2020

What happened today with the psychic art was that you presumed it was a male, then suddenly it goes ahead, and you have a female coming through on the page. You let it go where it needs to go. You are the vessel that spirit works through. Let your hand go and make the marks that are needed. Keep your mind free from any predilections.

August 5, 2020

Keep visualizing what it is you are desiring. You know this. You have to stay with it. When the vibration is a match, when the time is right, it will happen. You are so close. It is inevitable. It is Law. It is ready to manifest. See it. Feel it. You have this.

That is good to hear. I am ready.

Yes, you are.

August 7, 2020

It was wonderful to have Lord Metatron there for me today in meditation.

Yes. As He stated, it benefits you, but also the Whole. When you succeed, the Whole benefits. All want you to move forward, and He was there to help you in that regard. We want you to understand how important you are, as are all, to have this Ascended Master* present Himself to you and bestow power for you to move forward.

I am grateful.

*Major Archangel/Ascended Master/Divine Voice of the Father.

August 8, 2020

Stop worrying over the little things. Actually, stop worrying. There is nothing to be concerned about. All will play out. All will be fine. It is not worth the expended energy worrying over things that are going to be okay. So let it go. Stay positive, knowing it all is good. There are better things to be thinking about.

August 12, 2020

You are becoming a believer. And when I say that, I mean that, yes, you already believed, but now you are starting to see results of your sensitivity coming to fruition. Those little serendipitous things showing up. You are believing, truly now, what you are seeing and experiencing. When that faith brings results, it will become more predominant, easier, and faster. See what I mean? You know this, but now you really know this because the proof is there for you to see. Good. It's about time.

Yes, thank you, Robert.

And you have been given a lot of help from here.

Yes. And I appreciate all of it.

Amen.

August 13, 2020

Act on the information that comes your way. Inspiration "in spirit." It is there to help you. We are here to move you along and are sending information to you to assist in that. See what you are receiving and go with it.

August 14, 2020

I had a clear impression of A coming through. It was nice to connect with and hear from them.

Yes. They are doing very well. They were happy to make the connection, and they spoke of their appreciation to you for your help. They are right where they need to be, filled with all the love that they could ever hope for. This is what this person needed. They are also there for you in any way that they can be, in gratitude for the help you gave them.

That's very nice. Thank you. I send them love.

August 15, 2020

Look to your dreams. Try to hold them and remember them. Don't worry about analyzing them. You can see, remember, and release if you want. Some you may want to keep. That is good, and you will know those that you want to hold onto. There is more to this at a later time. Remember, action on those inspirational thoughts.

August 19, 2020

I had a very good session with Trish yesterday and an excellent Merkabah this morning. I felt I went deeper and got the impression of seeing slightly with my Third Eye.

Yes, another good release session. There is a lot of shedding going on for the two of you.

(Because of COVID, Stacey and I are doing our sessions with Trish using Zoom. It is amazing how powerful these online sessions can be. It is so true that energy has no limits!)

You also had the sense of your grandfather as there was some releasing from him. He made a point of connecting with you, and you felt that. Excellent.

You did indeed go deeper this morning, and we would recommend doing the taped version more often as you seem to go deeper with that. Hold onto that feeling, and then see if you can duplicate it with your regular meditation.

Yes. I like that.

August 20, 2020

Continue to feel yourself in that place of "Love" when meditating, going deeper and deeper. Good meditations. See if you can sense a presence. Don't look for it. Let it come. Try and feel that spirit energy. Work on that for a while.

August 21, 2020

In the psychic art yesterday, I got the name "Phillip" and felt it was my guide from before. Is that correct?

That is correct. You have been improving, and he decided to come through and show himself. Very good. You have another face now of one of your guides. The art is coming along. Now start to connect with that energy. Spend a little time on that. Try and get more information.

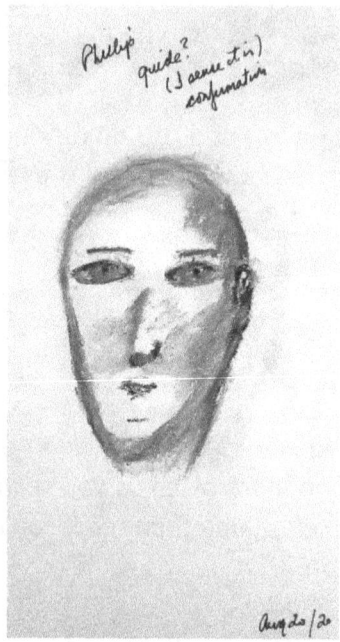

(I've been doing these portraits with oil pastels. I find I can blend them easier. This was what I got that day. I sit with my eyes closed and try and see if I get any impressions or words. I write whatever comes into my head. Usually, it is just a couple of words. Note: In the future, I will find myself changing to pencils. The drawings will get more detail, and I will begin to get more information.)

August 23, 2020

Things are moving along with your manuscript. You are getting thoughts. Write them down. That is inspiration (in spirit) sending ideas your way. This will help when it comes to putting it all together. You are moving along nicely. Again, try to put in a full day once a week on this. Start going over it and consider where you might expand, what may need to come out, and where pictures might go. Begin to notice possible chapters or breakpoints. Write down your thoughts on an Introduction. Keep this handy so that you can refer back to it.

Okay. Very good. Thank you, Robert.

I am your guide to help you move this project forward to fruition.

August 24, 2020

You have a lot of good days ahead. Enjoy all of it. Every bit. Relish it and appreciate it all. That will build on itself, producing more. The better it gets, the better it gets. We see a lot of movement on the book. You are getting there, but there is still much to do. It will be well received.

August 26, 2020

Enjoy your day. Getting outside and seeing and being in Nature is important to you. It is good for the soul, and it refreshes and renews you. It is an excellent balance for the other things you are doing. Psychic art and writing day tomorrow. Is it becoming clearer why those pages went missing?*

Yes, I guess so, but I thought what I had written was pretty good. I'm not sure if I can reproduce it.

You will, and it will all flow much better. This was a wake-up call that you can do a greater job on this and not merely write from the journals.

Okay, I see.

*I had written twenty pages of dialogue for the book and was proud of what I had done. However, the next time I sat down to write, it was gone. I'm typically careful always to save my work, so how it all disappeared was a mystery. I was disappointed because I couldn't remember the exact words I had used and had to start again. When I finished, I realized what I had written was better than the original, hence, Robert's question.

August 28, 2020

This is a good time for you. Everything is aligning in your favor. It is a magical time. Enjoy and appreciate the abundance that is coming your way. Wow. Happy days. Feel the Love that is there for you. Be in harmony with all that is coming. Be in the flow. Again, wow. Fortune is smiling on you.

Well, Robert, I can't imagine hearing anything more welcoming than that. Good health is always very important, so to have that is great. Then to have much more is a bonus and is appreciated. I am grateful for all that I have and where I am. Thank you.

Good. That is what we like to hear, and that is the way to accept your gifts. Great.

August 29, 2020

Did you just get a glimpse of where this communication would be going in the future?

Yes. Easy mental communication with more insightful comments and a record kept of those comments with the possibility of more writing—a continuation of progress.

That is correct. Good. So you see, it is an ongoing scenario. This is your work. This will be your Legacy. You are doing what you set out to do when you came to this physical existence.

Wow. Okay. That is interesting.

Now you know why we keep pushing you forward with this.

Yes.

All right. You know where you stand.

This is where I decided to stop transcribing my journal entries.

I continue with my everyday meditations and my daily discourse with Robert, who is still with me as I write this. He maintains his guidance and advice. He keeps me on track and looks out for my well-being.

My psychic art has improved dramatically and continues to get better. There is a distinct difference between when I started to now. I am getting a sense now of the spirit that is coming through.

My sensitivity to spirit is stronger, and I believe much of that has to do with finally having faith in my abilities and trusting what I am getting. The confidence is there. All of my guides would be sighing and saying, "Finally." I held onto that doubt for so long, even when my guides told me to trust myself. I think my stubbornness played a part in this, which I believe was carried over from my dad, and he would agree with that.

The following chapter is a small sample of the psychic art I chose to demonstrate my progression. I hope you can see the improvement. Even I was surprised to see my progress from pretty crude drawings, where I didn't see any reason to be doing this, to my guides constantly on me to continue and not give up, to finally, where I was truly surprised by what I was producing. Wow! Who knew? Well, my guides did. There's a message here for those in contact with guides or who want to be: Don't ignore their guidance; they know what they are doing. Their guidance is for our betterment, to make us the best version of ourselves we can be.

I look forward to these spirit drawings. I get excited about who will show up, and some of them have been quite amazing.

Psychic art

In one of my many conversations with Claudette, she suggested that I try doing psychic art. I had never considered doing something like that. She had brought in a portrait she had done for one of our mediumship classes. Claudette stated that she was terrible when it came to portraiture; she had trouble even drawing stick figures. Yet, here she showed us this amazing portrait of a person, in spirit, that she said had come through to her. It turned out to be a portrait of my mother at an earlier age. It wasn't an exact likeness, but close, and when added to the information she had gleaned from the person, I knew my mother had come through, and the rest of the class agreed it was meant for me. Claudette said my mother came through with tremendous love.

Because I drew landscapes, psychic art was initially something that I thought might be interesting, but then I let it slip away. Claudette brought it up again and said I needed to give this a try. I usually have a few sketch pads lying around, so I decided to try one morning after my meditation. I found that the best thing at the start was to use oil pastels because I could blend them with my finger. I was told to relax and just draw, and when I finished, I was to see whether any information came through.

Here are a few of my early attempts. These are crude, but I had never done faces before, and the general impressions are there with some information. I wrote down whatever came into my head.

When I showed this one to Claudette, she thought it was one of my guides.

Claudette said this one was a Multidimensional Light Being from the Federation.

This one blows me away. I sensed her in a past life as a nurse who died from an illness in the Crimean War. This was just one of many lives this spirit had lived.

I have filled up two and a half good-sized sketchbooks with all manner of faces—slim ones, chubby ones, from all walks of life. Some I get a brief glimpse of a story, and others nothing. There are men, women, and different races. You've noticed how often my guides would be on me about continuing with this work. I wasn't always into it and probably would have given up if it wasn't for their relentless insistence.

Here are some later portraits where there had been some improvement.

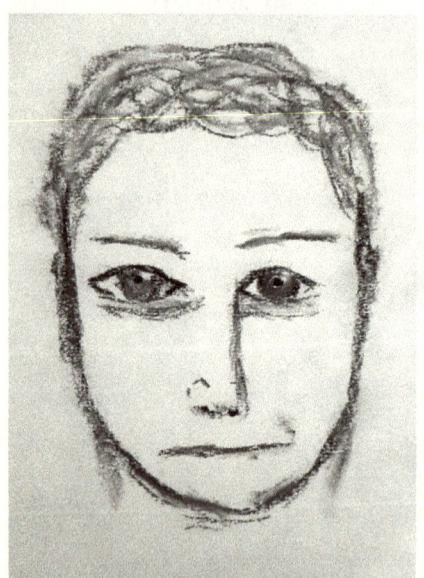

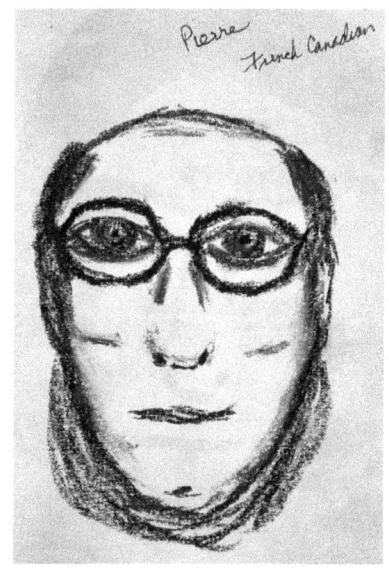

Pierre
French Canadian

Neal ashamed
mistreatment
Family – bad
connection

Roscoe cereer, one of the workers putting up and taking down the tents during the wagon. travelling around the country.

lived in the south (Florida) when not travelling.
Feb 17/21

Here are several more from the last couple of months. I've now switched to pencil sketching.

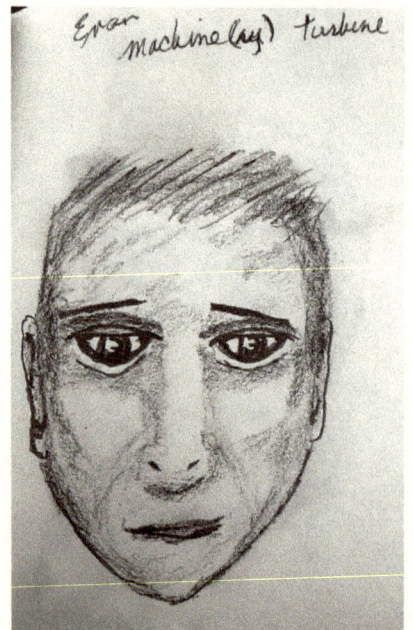

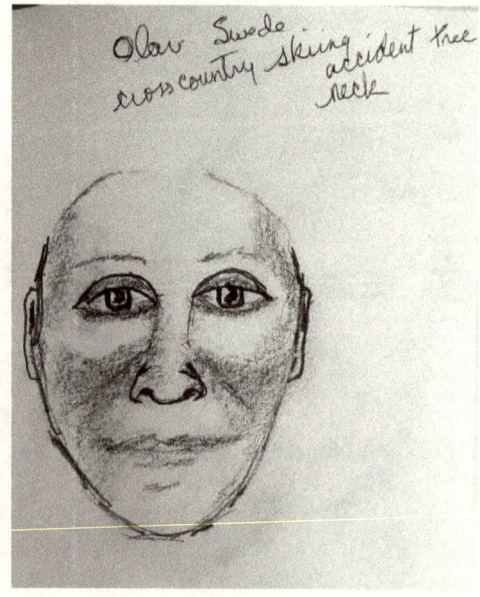

These last two are my latest as of this writing, and I must say, I even surprised myself with them. When I mentioned this to my guide, Robert, this was his reply:

Yes, you did a good job, or should I say "spirit" working through you. Those were excellent portraits and good connections.

Robert reminded me that spirit is using my hand, and the improvement is merely spirit getting better at connecting with me and utilizing my increasing ability to manifest these portraits, hence the improvement.

This is the way they have chosen to come through to me. I always thank them and give them my blessings because they are helping me with my process. Those on the other side want to make contact. They have messages for their loved ones, whether unresolved issues or merely to pass along their love. So it was driven home to me how important it is for me to improve to assist in this course of action.

Finally, I must mention these next two and their significance.

On January 20, 2021, after my meditation, I did this portrait. I sat with it for a few minutes, and this is what I sensed coming through. I felt sadness and the words "lost child," "boy," "young," "illness," "David," "coughing," and "pneumonia."

I have always been an early riser, which works out great because I have time in the morning for my meditation and psychic art without any disturbances. Whenever I do a psychic art portrait, I leave it for Stacey to have a look at when she gets up. This time, she looked at the picture and said, "Wait a minute," as she ran upstairs. The following are her notes.

> Wednesday, January 20, 2021
>
> Mike does a psychic art portrait of Muriel with a description of a little boy named David who died young from coughing/pneumonia. The woman is sad.

My maternal grandmother is Muriel, but the description of the dying young boy is the story of my paternal grandmother (who I never knew). Mike feels it may have been Muriel introducing Ethel.

That afternoon, I am exercising and get interrupted by spirit to go to the three boxes of Mom's stuff in my room. I quickly find a small framed photo of a woman I haven't seen before. I take the photo out of the frame and see that "Hopper," my paternal grandmother's maiden name, is written on the back. The picture was taken around age twenty, whereas Mike's portrait looks around age thirty. Trish later confirms that his drawing was indeed of my paternal grandmother, Ethel Hopper. Important to note: the child she lost was named Derek (as opposed to the similar name David) but clearly the same boy.

Friday, January 22, 2021

Appointment with T (a medium).

She validates Mike's psychic portrait of my grandmothers (which I showed her on my phone) and chats to Mike about it.*

*T is another well-respected medium. She told me I was gifted with the ability to communicate with spirit and that the portrait she had seen was extremely well done in that discipline, considering my experience.

Here's a side-by-side of the portrait and the photo.

I know you may be saying, "Well, it's something like it." Psychic art isn't always an exact replica, though it can be, and I am still working my way through it. It's all about the connection between spirit and the receiver or medium. I'm getting better at it but feel I've got a ways to go yet. The best psychic art mediums have been doing it for many years. There's no doubt that the impression I got was pretty accurate. David and Derek are a little off, and my guide has told me that I should spend more time trying to glean information and not let it go so soon. If I had taken longer, maybe the name would have become clearer.

> Friday, March 26, 2021
>
> Mike showed me this morning's psychic art, and it is my maternal grandmother Muriel (in early adulthood). She wants to give thanks for all the lineage work being done.

Here's that follow-up portrait. I wasn't thinking at all about the first one when this second one came through until I got the words "coming through again," "validation," and "thanks." I felt these words were for me making this connection for Stacey and for the effort Stacey was putting forth looking into her ancestral roots.

I'll let you be the judge.

By sticking with my psychic art, I discovered that this was to be my mediumship. Here I was setting out to improve my mediumship in the way I thought I was meant to while getting advice and instruction on trying this art (which seemed farfetched). How unpredictable was that? lol

If you're interested in seeing more psychic art from very talented mediums, check out Coral Poge. You can find some of her demonstrations on YouTube. Meanwhile, I will continue to work on improving my abilities in this sphere of mediumship, both in art and communication.

Wind up

Before I go any further, and as I continue with finishing this book, I must mention that I recently learned that Claudette had taken ill. Her good friend Lesley was keeping me apprised of her condition. The prognosis was not good. She had been given a short time frame and had entered palliative care. She passed very quickly on December 10, 2020. This was a terrible blow to me and so many who knew Claudette.

Claudette was an awesome person with tremendous powers and abilities. She had told me many times that her great passion was teaching mediumship. She had so many students, many with amazing and varied gifts of their own. She welcomed them all and was truly interested in helping them flourish and strengthen their talents. She knew people from all over the world in the Spiritualist community, many of them well known in their own right, and was the representative for Canada with the International Spiritualist Federation. She had countless stories, and I was privileged to hear many of them, along with various adventures and experiences. She's gone home, and I know she is happy to be reunited with family and more friends.

I'm going to miss your friendship and our twice-monthly Skype sessions.

Love and Light to you, Claudette.

There you have it—my continuing journey from meeting Claudette in 2006 and the five sessions I had with her over eleven years, which led me to write *Guided Messages from the Other Side*.

From these sessions with Claudette, my interest grew. I followed her advice, bought a notebook, and started writing whatever came to mind. That is when I began to put down the words that changed everything.

It was July 06, 2016, ten years after my very first meeting with Claudette.

A spirit guide.

Love is the answer.

Love is the be-all.

Don't be afraid.

I am here to help you.

It is all good.

Spirit was making itself known to me and stating that They were my guide. For the longest time, I had trouble deciding whether this was spirit coming through or merely my imagination. It truly hit me when I would read back what I had written and know in my heart it wasn't something I would have ever said. It took a while, but it began to sink in. I was communicating with spirit through writing, and this spirit was my guide. Amazing. This was happening.

My enthusiasm to explore this further was boundless, and this became my routine. There was wonderful wisdom coming through, offering advice and guidance, laying the groundwork for what was to come. A marvelous bond developed between us.

When next I spoke to Claudette, she was happy but not surprised to hear about my experiences. She recommended that I take her mediumship classes, saying they would greatly benefit me and move me along quicker, plus I would get to observe others in the class (some who were considerably gifted) and what they were experiencing, along with the advantage of the group energy.

My curiosity led me to attend the new Merkabah group and experience the encounters that followed. This was a new world for me, full of incredible journeys, meeting Ascended Masters, Archangels, Higher Beings, and more to help us improve ourselves and, thereby, the planet. And, always present, my guides.

My guides are a big part of my life now. I talk to them every day, at least I try to. It's a rare day for me to miss that communication. I have benefitted so much from their guidance. All of them were helping me improve my knowledge when it came to spiritual matters. They were showing me ways to get better with my meditations so I could get more out of them. They were helping me to connect with spirit by advising me on the best means of accomplishing that. My guides were there to push me along when my doubts, which were many and often, got in the way. They admonished me very gently when I fell behind on those things I was supposed to be involved in. And they were relentless in bringing up the psychic art because they knew that this was important, even though I didn't understand just how relevant it was. It was something that I was meant to do in this incarnation, and they were there to help me to succeed in that regard. There was untold aid when it came to health matters, offering advice on fitness, and well-being, and when it was in my interest to see a doctor, even if it was only for peace of mind.

Whenever I took workshop classes, the guides were there to support me and were ready the next day to discuss my experiences and how I fared. They were always available to bolster my misgivings and strengthen my purpose and always with unconditional love.

Through these writings, I have had three guides—Phillip, Harold, and Robert (who is still with me, though I sense he may be moving on to make way for a new guide once this gets published). Each of them was there for a purpose. Phillip started with me to get me comfortable with the whole idea. Harold was there to move me forward, raise my vibration, and expand my consciousness. Robert came in to continue with that and help me progress with the psychic art and complete this manuscript. All of them were helping me daily. But there are many others in the background looking out for me—doctor guides, joy guides (which include my children), and art guides. There's probably a guide available to help you if you can name it.

I have come a long way. When years earlier Claudette mentioned that I had abilities, I could not have imagined sitting here writing about my amazing experiences or communicating with those in the spirit world, with those Highly Evolved Beings in other dimensions. It took a few years to get over my doubt and the feeling of dejection when I thought I wasn't progressing. Now, I am more secure in knowing that this is something I can do, and I look forward to improving and elevating myself to a higher level of evolution, doing that with excitement for what still lays ahead, the constant exploration of learning.

I hope in some way this may help anyone interested in connecting with their guides and learning from my experiences. Take comfort in believing you can do this. You don't need any special gifts. Meditate because I believe this is the way forward, and try and get yourself into that "Love" vibration—it makes a world of difference. Don't rush the process, which was one of my faults. As all my guides would say, "Relax. Let it happen. Let it flow." Most of all, don't give up if it doesn't happen right away. Stay with it. I know you can do this. If I can, you can. Use a notebook to write whatever comes to you, and see if it feels like communication with something other than your own thoughts. You have angels and guardians who are there looking out for you. Acknowledge them, and ask for their protection, knowing that you will always be protected when reaching out to spirit. Surround yourself with Divine Light.

The world is moving into a new era, though it may not seem so. There is a new awareness happening among the population, a higher consciousness. More and more lightworkers have incarnated to bring about this change. We are moving into a newer, loving reality. This can be hard to comprehend when we constantly hear of tragedies daily, but forces out there are at work to make sure this transformation takes hold. I have gleaned from different sources, from emails and websites, that there will be a noticeable difference and a much more positive perception from the population at the end of this decade. This has already started. Often you must go through the bad to get to the good. And, as the song says, "Love is the answer."

Thank you for going through these many months of conversations with me. I know there were many times when the guides were going over the same stuff, and I hope that wasn't too repetitive. I wanted to show their commitment to making sure that I kept at it and fulfilled my responsibility. They are there to make sure I'm doing my best to be the finest version of me that I can be.

I'd love to hear how you are doing and whether you found this helpful. I'm open to positive and negative comments. They will assist me in doing better with the next book if there is to be one. You can contact me at mikesart506@gmail.com.

Love and Light,

Mike

CPSIA information can be obtained
at www.ICGtesting.com
Printed in the USA
BVHW070727100822
644118BV00004B/6